7 HABITS

—— *of* ——

HIGHLY
FULFILLED
PEOPLE

JOURNEY FROM SUCCESS TO SIGNIFICANCE

SATINDER DHIMAN, PhD, EdD

Manjul Publishing House

First published in India by

Manjul Publishing House Pvt. Ltd.
Corporate Office
2ⁿᵈ Floor, Usha Preet Complex,
42 Malviya Nagar, Bhopal, INDIA-462 003
Email: manjul@manjulindia.com Website: www.manjulindia.com

Sales and Marketing Office
7/32, Ground Floor, Ansari Road, Daryaganj, New Delhi-110 002
Email: sales@manjulindia.com

This edition originally published in 2012 by Personhood Press,
PO BOX 370, Fawnskin, CA 92333, USA

Interior design:1106 Design

This edition first published in 2014

ISBN   978-81-8322-414-7

Printed & bound in India by Replika Press Private Limited.

Dedication

Tavadiyam vastu Govinda tubhyameva samarpaye:
O Lord! I offer unto You what is really Yours!

TABLE OF CONTENTS

Seven Habits of Highly Fulfilled People

Stories, Poems, and Exercises

LIVING PROFOUNDLY SIGNIFICANT LIVES!

Consider for a moment our present circumstances. Especially, for those of us living in a developed country, let's take stock. Food: we have more than we need. Water: plentiful, clean, and ubiquitous. Health care: ambulances, emergency rooms, and hospitals abound. Communications: internet, Iphones and Skype. Education, the arts and sciences—ingenuous institutions of all kinds flourish. For those of us fortunate to live in a modern 21st century country, we are endowed beyond imagination—living amidst marvels and prosperity that is shocking to behold.

And yet, when we take stock, we also confront the vast devastation and suffering that spreads out across our globe: on any typical day, the planet loses 40 to 100 species; and 24,000 children die due to poverty and 100 million people live without a home. And looking back from whence we came, we find that over 180 million people died in all the wars, massacres, and oppressions of the 20th century—far more than in any century in history.

And now, as the 21st century dawns, we find ourselves wildly endowed and facing profound crises—an invitation to take some portion of responsibility, no doubt. Yet, despite our circumstances, a peculiar dilemma seems to have grabbed our collective attention. Despite our endowment and despite our vast distress, we seem hi-jacked and dis-tracted—chasing a relentless often numbing promise: *the possibility of fashioning a seamlessly convenient world.*

Consumerism's nonstop entertainment; technology's ingenious toys; databases of endless information; modern medicine's devices and psychiatry's medications—as we brilliantly shape our future, we find ourselves chasing a promise—often unspoken, but shiny. Intriguing, yet shapeless: *maybe this new century will solve the problem of being alive!*

Now, pursuing an inspiring vision is not a problem, of course. As human beings, we have always chased our dreams and fulfilled our wildest aspirations. But, today our creative passions are being roused in a disturbingly bizarre direction—not in pursuit of fresh frontiers, but in search of distraction from reality; not in the service of wisdom and compassion, but in an anxious often pointless urge to shield our vulnerability. When we pause and consider our circumstances, we find that we are often mesmerized by materialism's false promise; searching for something—anything—to get us comfortably through the next moment—grasping for what's about to occur, rather than searching for what is fundamental.

In the midst of this frenetic 21st century race to "solve life" rather than face it, we find that many of us are well aware of our distressing dilemma. The relentless speed cannot deny our yearning to pause—a quiet weight in our hearts haunts us—reminds us to slow down and reconnect with something we have lost touch with. It's as if the faster we move, the more we long to linger. The more we communicate with tweets, email, blogs and posts, the less we have to say; the more we try to solve life, the more we long to live it.

And it is here, as this yearning merges with our daily life, that we may remember that we are connected with thousands of years of human history—that in our pursuit of what is new, shiny and intriguing, we can also reclaim our noble birthright, reaching back to our ancestors to take delight in their wisdom—to recognize what is profound and fundamental as we bring our new century to life.

And so in the midst of our marvels and crises, as we ponder our pointless pursuit of seamless convenience, a modern contemplative life gently unfolds: business men practicing Buddhist meditation; military officers following the way of Tai Chi; teachers bringing yoga into their classrooms; physicians healing with the "Prana-breath." Whether it's the wisdom of the Upanishads or the practicality of Aristotle's *Eudaimonia,* or the gentleness of Quaker silent prayer or the austere clarity of Zen, more and more of us are seeking the natural quiet brilliance of our humanity. And we are doing so in the very midst of our 21st century pace—fully attuned with the marvels and misfortunes; the hopes and fears; the yearnings and disappointments. Living such a contemplative life while engaging such fantastic demands—as a lawyer, doctor, scientist or chef—takes tremendous courage and gentleness.

And here in these pages, we are invited to explore such courage and gentleness—to reach back to our ancestors—to listen to them once again and to accept their gifts. Here, in this wise text, we are guided through a spiritual journey of stories and insights where our yearning for stillness can open wide to the wisdom of Vedic philosophy, the meditative disciplines of Buddhist psychology and the natural presence of yoga. And, as the title suggests, we can live these gifts of gratitude, generosity and kindness to become *"profoundly fulfilled people as we journey from success to significance."*

So, enjoy the wisdom of this text: let it invite, tantalize, shape and provoke. And, as we take stock of our 21st century circumstances, we might slow down and take a deep breath and just give in to our yearning for stillness and ease. And if we listen carefully to the voices settled within these pages, we may hear the lion's roar of our ancestors reminding us to step beyond our pursuit of pointless convenience and to wake up to the *"divine silence of our soul."*

Michael Carroll
Awake at Work
The Mindful Leader
Fearless at Work (Shambhala 2012)

In other living creatures, ignorance of self is nature; in man, it is vice.

~ Boethius

Setting the Stage!
A Rich Merchant and His Four Wives

There was a rich merchant who had four wives. He loved the fourth wife the most and adorned her with elegant clothes and provided her with the best food. He took great care of her and gave her nothing but the best.

He also loved the third wife dearly. He was very proud of her and always wanted to show her off to his friends. However, the merchant was always in great fear that she might run away with some other men.

He loved his second wife as well. She was a very considerate person, always patient and in fact was the merchant's advisor. Whenever the merchant faced some problems, he always turned to his second wife, and she would always help him out through difficult times.

Now, the merchant's first wife was a very loyal partner and had made great contributions in maintaining his wealth and business as well as taking care of the household. However, the merchant did not love the first wife and although she loved him deeply, he hardly took notice of her.

One day, the merchant fell ill. Before long, he knew that he was going to die soon. He thought of his luxurious life and told himself, "Now I have four wives with me. But when I die, I'll be alone. How lonely I'll be!"

Thus, he asked the fourth wife, "I loved you most, endowed you with the finest clothing and showered great care over you. Now that I'm dying, will you follow me and keep me company?" "No way!" replied the fourth wife and walked away without another word.

The answer cut as a sharp knife right into the merchant's heart. The sad merchant then asked the third wife, "I have loved you so much for all my life. Now that I'm dying, will you follow me and keep me company?" "No!" replied the third wife. "Life is so good over here! I'm going to remarry when you die!" The merchant's heart sank and turned cold.

(continued on next page)

(continued from previous page)

He then asked the second wife, "I always turned to you for help, and you've always helped me out. Now I need your help again. When I die, will you follow me and keep me company?" "I'm sorry, I can't help you out this time!" replied the second wife. "At the very most, I can only send you to your grave." The answer came as a clap of thunder, and the merchant was devastated.

Then a voice called out: "I'll live with you. I'll follow you no matter where you go." The merchant looked up and there was his first wife. She was so skinny, almost as if she suffered from malnutrition and lack of attention. Greatly grieved, the merchant said, "I should have taken much better care of you while I could!"

Actually, we all have four wives in our lives!

a. The fourth wife is our body. No matter how much time and effort we lavish in making it look good, it will leave us when we die.

b. Our third wife? Our possessions, status, and wealth. When we die, they all go to others.

c. The second wife is our family and friends. No matter how close they are to us when we're alive, the farthest they can stay by us is up to the grave.

d. The first wife is in fact our real self, our soul, often neglected in our pursuit of material wealth and sensual pleasure.[1]

Let's remember that our self is actually the only thing that accompanies us wherever we go. Perhaps it is a good idea to cultivate and nurture it. This book is a humble attempt to offer some pointers in the direction of cultivating our true self.

"Only those concerned with the problem of life and death should enter here. Those not completely concerned with this problem have no reason to pass this gate."

~ Inscription inside the main gate of Eiheiji (temple of Great Peace) founded by Dogen Zenji, in 1244

Dogen was once asked by another monk what had he gained by going to a monastery.

Dogen responded, "Since I lacked nothing, so I gained nothing."

"Then why did you go there?" asked the monk.

Dogen replied, "How could I have known that I lacked nothing if I had not gone there?"

CHAPTER ONE

THE JOURNEY OF SELF-DISCOVERY

Most of our lives are lived in empty agitation.
~ SRI AUROBINDO

Everything has been figured out, except how to live.
~ JEAN-PAUL SARTRE

If you have known how to compose your life, you have accomplished more than a person who knows how to compose a book.
~ MONTAIGNE

Happiness is your nature. It is not wrong to desire it. What is wrong is seeking it outside when it is inside.
~ SRI RAMANA MAHARSHI

Your vision will become clear only when you look into your heart. Who looks outside, dreams. Who looks inside, awakens.
~ CARL JUNG

Each man had only one genuine vocation—to find the way to himself....His task was to discover his own destiny—not an arbitrary one—and to live it out wholly and resolutely within himself. Everything else was only a would-be existence, an attempt at evasion, a flight back to the ideals of the masses, conformity and fear of one's own inwardness.
~ HERMANN HESSE

This Is Not a "How-to" Book!

This is not a "how-to" book. No universal recipes for success or happiness are intended or implied. Rather, this book seeks to help the reader find fulfillment by taking an existential approach to the "slings and arrows" of ordinary day-to-day life. Instead of merely suggesting what to do about fulfillment, it takes us to the very heart of "existential vacuum," to use Viktor Frankl's phrase, and asks us to re-examine our most cherished beliefs, expectations, and assumptions about life in general and human life in particular. "An unexamined life," said Plato, "is not worth living."

This book assumes that its readers have a willingness

1. to undertake an impartial survey of their assumptions and expectations about life;
2. to recognize and appreciate the most obvious, the most natural, and the simplest in life;
3. to view fulfillment in the larger context of the transformative art of living wisely; and
4. to seek fulfillment through self-knowledge.

A good place to start the journey of self-discovery is to realize that we often have false ideas about ourselves and our expectations about life. Montaigne, a 16th century French author, wrote: "My life has been full of tragedies, most of which never happened." Not much has changed during the intervening 400 years! We still often live most of our lives in what may be called voluntarily self-engendered anguish. While much physical pain is unavoidable, most psychological suffering seems to be optional. This book makes the felicitous assumption that right self-knowledge can ameliorate most of our optional suffering and pave the way to lasting fulfillment. Therefore it makes the plea that one needs to know oneself.

> ### The Power of Knowledge
>
> A certain billboard pictured a dog and a cat looking at each other. The ferocious dog was trying to pounce at the cat, yet the cat seemed unperturbed and even amused, sitting quietly in front of the dog.
> The caption simply read: The Power of Knowledge!
> The dog was on a leash. The cat was aware of this fact. This knowledge gave the cat the freedom to enjoy the moment with great peace of mind.
> Such is the power of knowledge.
> If the knowledge of our surroundings confers such security, imagine what level of security self-knowledge may engender.[1]

Self-Knowledge Is the Supreme Key to Fulfillment

All wisdom traditions of the world have upheld the importance of self-knowledge as a prelude to every pursuit of happiness and fulfillment. It is considered the alpha and omega of all searching, the ultimate end and purpose of human existence. Since happiness or fulfillment is sought for the sake of the self, it stands to reason that the journey should begin with knowing the self. This book takes it as axiomatic that self-knowledge is the key to lasting happiness and fulfillment. Therefore, in this book, every submission to attain fulfillment is presented through the prism of self-knowledge.

Observation and reflection make it evident that without self-knowledge we keep searching for happiness in the wrong places, without realizing that it may inhere in understanding our essential nature. Once we truly understand the nature and limitations of our pursuits, we begin to see the tyranny of searching for fulfillment in the external haunts of happiness. As Indian sage Ramana Maharshi succinctly put it, "Nearly all mankind is more or less unhappy because nearly all do not know the true self. Real happiness abides in self-knowledge alone. All else is fleeting. To know one's self is to be blissful always."[2]

The Utter Necessity of Self-Knowledge

By common knowledge, self-love is the highest form of love or the ultimate good. In the final analysis, everything that we do or seek is to satisfy or to fulfill the self. Since all love of objects requires knowledge of the object of love, the necessity for self-knowledge becomes paramount in every pursuit of happiness and fulfillment. One wisdom tradition explains the utter necessity of self-knowledge through a framework of means and ends. All forms of love can be divided into following three broad categories:

+ Love of Ends.
+ Love of Means.
+ Love of Oneself.[3]

Love of ends refers to various pursuits of goals that we hold dear to ourselves. These pursuits can be directed at attaining wealth and security; physical, intellectual, and aesthetic pleasures; values; and spiritual freedom. All love directed toward these ends can be classified as the love of ends or goals. It is quite obvious that in order to attain any ends, we need to pursue appropriate means. This brings us to the second form of love, the love of means. We love the means because they help us attain the ends that we want to acquire. In other words, means are not loved for their own sake; they are loved for the sake of the ends that they promise to accomplish.

Now the question arises, do we love ends for ends' sake? This brings us to the third form of love, self-love. A little reflection will make it clear that we do not really love ends or goals for the sake of ends or goals; rather, we love them for our own sake. For example, we do not desire wealth for wealth's sake; we desire it because we believe it will contribute to our sense of security and well-being. Means and ends are dear because they contribute to self-love. Thus, means and ends are not loved for their own sake; they are loved for sake of the self. This is a very important point to bear in mind throughout our journey to fulfillment.

Of these three forms of love, love of means is the mildest, love of ends is of mediocre strength, and self-love has the highest intensity. In other words, if love of means is dear, love of ends is dearer, and the love of self is the dearest. If self-love is the highest form of love, and if all love of objects necessitates the knowledge of the object of love, self-knowledge becomes a *sine qua non* to all overt or covert pursuits of happiness and fulfillment. To quote Sri Ramana Maharshi again, "Every living being longs always to be happy, untainted by sorrow; and everyone has the greatest love for himself, which is solely due to the fact that happiness is his real nature. Hence, in order to realize that inherent and untainted happiness, which indeed he daily experiences when the mind is subdued in deep sleep, it is essential that he should know himself."[4]

This book will present seven gifts as habits of mind geared toward attaining lasting fulfillment. Throughout the book, wherever possible, a conscious connection will be made between the gift under discussion and the knowledge of self. It is no exaggeration to say that self-knowledge is the atmosphere in which the pursuit of seven habits of highly fulfilled people will take place. For, as the following story illustrates, without self-knowledge one can overlook one's essential reality, even when completely immersed in it.

Story Time: What the Hell Is Water?

There were these two young fishes swimming along, and they happen to meet an older fish swimming the other way, who nods at them and says, "Morning, guys, how's the water?" And the two young fish swim on for a bit, and then eventually one of them looks over at the other and says, "What the hell is water?"[5]

A famous Urdu poet, Mohammad Iqbal, ruminates about the paradox of searching for the self when we are the self:

> *O Iqbaal, I am searching all around for myself;*
> *Albeit I myself am the seeker (traveller) as well as the sought (destination)!*[6]

The great Persian poet, Hafiz, casually hands over the keys to the kingdom thusly:

> *There is no barrier between the lover and the beloved;*
> *Hafiz, you are yourself the veil over your real self;*
> *Rise from within it!*[7]

Sant Kabir Das, another Sufi poet, takes the matter a step further: "The fish is thirsty in the water; when I hear this, it makes me laugh!"[8] This is an excellent example of missing out on reality due to self-ignorance. The following story shines further light on the importance of self-knowledge before starting any journey of self-discovery.

Who Is Lost?

A tale is told of a tourist who went to an exotic travel gift shop to buy some maps for the city he wanted to visit. He saw an item on display that looked like a compass. The compass had a lid, the inside of which contained a mirror. A little surprised over the combination of compass and mirror in one product, the tourist asked the owner about the rationale behind such a product.

The owner explained, "The compass helps to find out where one is lost, while the mirror helps to determine who is lost!"[9]

The World Is Made up of Stories!

A word of explanation is in order regarding this book's frequent use of proverbs, quotations, and teaching stories. Cervantes has defined a proverb as "a short sentence based on long experience." According to a Persian saying, "Epigrams succeed where epics fail." Hence, proverbs and quotations are used copiously throughout the book for their sheer brilliance and economy. "Great men," said Carlyle, "taken up in any way are profitable company." This book frequently seeks the sage advice of great souls to enlighten the path of fulfillment. I have spared no effort to find the most memorable utterances of past and present to illuminate the topics under consideration.

Of his *Essays,* Montaigne says, "It might well be said of me that here I have only made up a bunch of other people's flowers, and provided nothing of my own but the string to bind them together." Likewise, this book may also be seen as a book of strings, holding the beads of the wisdom of fulfillment together.

Muriel Rukeyser said, "The universe is made up of stories, not atoms." This book is made up of stories from varied sources, such as Indian gurus, Buddhist monks, Zen and Sufi masters, Hasidic rabbis, and Christian desert fathers. I know of no better way to underscore a theme than by using illustrative analogies, teaching stories, and illuminating anecdotes. As the following pages will show, this book frequently utilizes teaching stories to underscore and clarify certain concepts. Stories have been used universally to crystallize an abstract idea since time immemorial. Teaching stories have frequently been used in the wisdom traditions of the past for their entertainment and moral development values.

Most teaching stories contain an element of humor that ensures their longevity. The humor is also used as a cloak to conceal the more profound meaning underlying a story. The humor (in which Freud found something "liberating," "sublime," and "elevating"), in fact, is used as a skillful device for precipitating deeper understanding and as an expression of new levels of insight. Ludwig Wittgenstein, a preeminent 20th-century philosopher, is reported to have said that he could teach a philosophy class by telling jokes. According to Idries Shah, "The blow administered by the joke makes possible a transitory condition in which other things can be perceived."[10] As Plato has also pointed out, "Serious things cannot be understood without laughable things." But to stop only at the humor level is to miss the real meaning of the story. Robert Anton Wilson explains, "If you don't laugh, you've missed the point. If you only laugh, you've missed your chance for illumination."[11]

Multiple Dimensions of Teaching Stories

Psychologically speaking, stories possess the following key dimensions:[12]

1. ***Intuitive quality.*** The moment the speaker says, "Let me tell you a story," the listener shifts gears (figuratively speaking) and a different faculty of comprehension is brought into play. In scientific terms, a better harmony between the left/right hemispheres of our brain is established. We are able to see the nonlinear and subtler layers of meaning in a totally new way.

2. ***Participative quality.*** A story is a sort of invitation that prods the listener to participate in its proceedings by identifying him- or herself as one of its characters. Reading or listening to a story is really a collaborative experience in which the author/speaker and readers/listeners co-create the meaning as the story unfolds. Therefore, stories are essentially participatory in nature. And it is a matter of common knowledge that participation enhances the quality of learning.

3. ***Multiplicity-of-impact quality.*** A good story carries a constellation of impacts within its fold and thereby creates multiple impressions on the listener's mind. This enables listeners to view things from numerous perspectives, which, in turn, facilitates holistic thinking and learning.

4. ***Tip-of-the-iceberg phenomenon.*** At the surface level, a story presents its message in a simple, straightforward manner. However, this meaning represents just the tip of the iceberg, so to speak. At a deeper level, there are several underlying messages in a story. The listener/reader receives the nourishment

for which he or she is ready. As with the skins of an onion, one will peel off one depth after another, revealing the inmost layers. Thus, a story offers something to all levels of experience. This is the reality behind the concept that we cannot really exhaust the entire meaning of a story. This is probably the reason that all great teachers choose to speak in parables.

5. *Element-of-shock quality.* A good story also contains an element of shock—an unexpected incongruity to wake the reader from the slumber of habitual thought patterns. By an unexpected turn or twist, a good story is able to tease a greater attention span out of the reader or listener, besides preparing a way to a deeper understanding of the intended message. To quote Harvey Cox, "A parable is a story that draws the listener's attention to the normal events of ordinary life, but then introduces an unexpected twist, a surprise inversion that undercuts the audience's normal expectations and pushes them into looking at life in a new way."[13]

The parables of Jesus provide a classic example of the element of shock. For example, the extra-welcome reception of the younger son in the parable of the Prodigal Son, the extraordinary help offered by the Samaritan in the parable of the Good Samaritan, and the payment of the same wages by the vineyard owner in the parable of Vineyard Laborers are sterling examples of the principle of unexpected shock in operation. One can only imagine the feelings of the listeners of these parables—the feeling as if the rug has been pulled out from under them unexpectedly—after having been drawn into the very fold of the story!

6. *All-at-once quality.* Finally, stories have a special quality that can be described as "all-at-once." At the end of a story, the message becomes crystalized all at once without further need of a stepwise, linear process. There is no gap between the delivery of the message and figuring out the

meaning behind the message. When the story ends, its moral holistically captures the essential meaning of the story—all at once.

Shah, who has written more than twenty books on various aspects of teaching stories and is a master storyteller himself, likens a story to a ripened peach whose

  ✦ color and odor entail its entertainment value;
  ✦ nutrition entails its moral value; and
  ✦ kernel entails its psychological/symbolic value[14]

The following tale may serve as a good illustration of various dimensions of stories:

Lost Keys

On one occasion, a neighbor found Mulla Nasrudin down on his knees looking for something.

"What have you lost, Mulla?"

"My keys," said Nasrudin.

After a few minutes of searching, the neighbor said, "Where did you drop them?"

"Inside my home," said Mulla.

"Then why, for heaven's sake, are you looking here?"

"Because there is more light here!" said Mulla.[15]

The entertainment value of the story is quite obvious. One moral of the story is, do not look for things in the wrong places. Now let's dig further into the tale for its deeper dimensions of symbolic meaning in a few of the underlying dimensions. Mulla Nasrudin demonstrates that

+ there are *keys* (solutions to the problems);
+ keys are not conveniently located (that is, they are not placed next to the door);
+ keys are usually kept *inside* (the relevance to organizational management is obvious—solutions to an organization's problems lie inside the organization);
+ seeking is the key; and
+ knowing how and where to seek is to find.

Peter F. Drucker, widely acknowledged as the father of modern management, has pointed out that most organizations are very good at solving the wrong problems. This story, in a very subtle way, indicates just that. This methodology, used where appropriate, sharpens learners' conceptual skills and helps to develop a habit of mind so critical in life and leadership: the ability to look beyond the surface.

Vedanta and Buddhist Psychology

This book primarily draws upon two timeless streams of thought, *Vedanta* and Buddhist psychology. This choice is solely guided by my relative familiarity with these two systems. However, as the discerning reader will notice, the teachings from other wisdom traditions are also presented through illustrative stories and anecdotes. Three chapters specifically deal with the philosophy of *Vedanta* and Buddhist psychology. Chapter eight presents the gift of selfless service and builds on the teachings of the Bhagavad Gita, known as the Hindu Bible, which is a philosophical poem *par excellence*. The main theme of chapter eight is *Karma Yoga,* the path of selfless action. Chapter ten presents the gift of presence primarily in light of a Buddhist meditative practice called mindfulness. This chapter also narrates my recent experience with a meditative practice called *Vipassana* during a 10-day meditation retreat. These chapters are presented as self-contained, complete modules and assume no prior knowledge of Indian philosophy or Buddhist psychology on the reader's part. Finally, the last chapter brings these two streams together by harmonizing their teachings in a holistic manner.

Concluding Remarks

In fine, the ideas presented in this book are in the nature of keys—they only work when put to use; that is, their truth is not to be abstractly understood, but to be existentially realized. Without being put into practice, parables merely feed the intellect and may become, in the words of D.T. Suzuki, "mere bubbles."

No originality is claimed or implied in these pages. Will Durant, a Pulitzer Prize-winning historian and philosopher widely acknowledged as one of the greatest humanizers of knowledge in the 20th century, once said, "Nothing is new except arrangement." I lay no other claim, even for the arrangement of ideas in this book, except that they are guided by common sense, personal observation, and experience. The prefatory remarks by Bertrand Russell in his classic guide to happiness, *The Conquest of Happiness,* accurately describe my assessment of the nature of the information shared in this book:

> No profound philosophy or deep erudition will be found in the following pages. I have aimed only at putting together some thoughts which are inspired by what I hope is common sense. All that I claim for the recipes offered to the reader is that they are such as are confirmed by my own experience and observation, and that they have increased my own happiness whenever I have acted in accordance with them.[16]

CHAPTER TWO

THE PURSUIT OF HAPPINESS AND FULFILLMENT

Happiness is the meaning and the purpose of life, the whole aim and end of human existence.

~ ARISTOTLE

Nothing can bring you happiness but yourself.

~ RALPH WALDO EMERSON

A big cat saw a little cat chasing its tail and asked, "Why are you chasing your tail so?" Said the kitten, "I have learned that the best thing for a cat is happiness, and that happiness is my tail. Therefore, I am chasing it: and when I catch it, I shall have happiness." Said the old cat, "My son, I, too, have paid attention to the problems of the universe. I, too, have judged that happiness is in my tail. But, I have noticed that whenever I chase it, it keeps running away from me, and when I go about my business, it just seems to come after me wherever I go." [1]

Happiness is a butterfly, which when pursued, is always just beyond your grasp, but which, if you will sit down quietly, may alight upon you.

~ NATHANIEL HAWTHORNE

*Psychological stress is the gap between what we expect and
what we get. There is no cosmic law that says that we should
get what we expect. The sooner we come to terms with this
existential truth, the quicker we enter the abode of harmony and
fulfillment. Happiness is getting what we want. Fulfillment is
cherishing what we get.*

The Perennial Pursuit of Humankind

Happiness, by universal acclaim, has been the perennial pursuit of
humankind. In recent times, the pursuit of happiness has become a
favorite pastime of psychologists, psychotherapists, neuroscientists,
sociologists, policy makers, economists, and self-help gurus. There is no
dearth of happiness recipes, "from Buddha to Tony Robbins," as Martin
Seligman, the co-founder of positive psychology, pleasantly puts it.

An impartial survey of the human condition and a little reflection
confirm that pursuing happiness in worldly goods like wealth, power,
and success, has no end to it and ultimately leads only to frustration and
weariness of spirit. After all, no lasting happiness can be found pursuing
things that are inherently unstable, transient, and uncertain. Moreover,
no matter how much we have of these goods, there is always more that
we long to have. Speaking of the insatiability of human appetites and
our constant discontent, Machiavelli, though not a dependable guide in
this terrain, rightly points out, "We are so constituted that our appetite
for things will always exceed our ability to get them."[2] The business of
life, said Schopenhauer, does not cover its expenses.

Twenty-six centuries ago, Greeks recognized happiness to be the
"ultimate good" and defined it as the exercise of human faculties along
the lines of excellence. The chief purpose of education, said Plato, is to
teach young people to find pleasure in the right things. Aristotle, Plato's
star disciple, believed that, above all, men and women seek happiness.
For him, happiness was the ultimate, the highest, the supreme good
since it is sought for its own sake. We desire everything else—wealth,
fame, success—in order to be happy. For the Greeks, happiness was the
supreme good, firmly rooted in virtue.

More than a century before Aristotle, Confucius, a Chinese sage, also spoke of the good life in terms of a virtuous life, comprised of "learning extensively, having a firm and sincere aim; inquiring with earnestness, and reflecting with self-application."[3]

Confucius' whole teaching centers around the concept of goodness *(jen)* which denotes a feeling of compassion—a caring concern for the well-being of others. According to Confucius, "the superior person is firm in a good way, not merely firm." In his characteristic way, Confucius ruminates,

> At fifteen, I had my mind bent on learning. At thirty, I stood firm. At forty, I had no doubts. At fifty, I knew the decrees of Heaven. At sixty, my ear was an obedient organ for the reception of truth. At seventy, I could follow what my heart desired, without transgressing what was right.[4]

Aristotle's Recipe for Happiness

Aristotle defines a happy life in terms of a good life: To say that somebody is happy is the very same thing as saying that one is living a life worth living. Aristotle uses the Greek concept of *eudaimonia* to fully express his views on what he considers to be a life well lived. His definition of *eudaimonia* can be roughly stated as the exercise of human faculties along the lines of excellence, in a life affording them full expression. According to Aristotle, good life is identical with *eudaimonia,* which is defined as living and faring well and is denoted by the "activity of the soul exhibiting the highest and most complete excellence in a complete life…. The key terms are 'action,' 'excellence,' and 'reason.'"[5]

Excellence, according to Aristotle, is not an innate gift; it is achieved through repeated practice until it becomes a habit, a settled disposition, for we are what we repeatedly do. In a posthumously published manuscript titled *Heroes of History,* Durant captures the essence of Aristotle's view of happiness succinctly: "The goal of conduct is happiness, but the secret of happiness is virtue, and the best virtue is intelligence—a careful consideration of the reality, the goals and the means; usually, 'virtue' is a golden mean between the extremes."[6]

It must be noted that happiness is not mere pleasure, although a happy person feels pleasure. Experience and observation dictate that sensuous gratification is not an abiding route to happiness. Human apparatus is doomed, so to speak, *ab initio,* by the operation of what is called the law of diminishing marginal utility; that is, as we consume more and more units of a specific commodity, the utility of the successive units diminishes. This applies equally to all our experiences directed at consuming pleasures. Durant clarifies:

> Surely sense pleasure is not the way: that road is a circle: as Socrates phrased the coarser Epicurean idea, we scratch that we may itch, and itch that we may scratch…. No, happiness must be a pleasure of mind, and we may trust it only when it comes from the pursuit or the capture of truth.[7]

Therefore, for Aristotle, happiness is the "virtuous activity of the soul in accordance with reason." Aristotle further clarifies that, to be happy, we should seek what is good for us in the long run for we cannot become happy by living for the pleasures of the moment. Aristotle includes among the main constituents of happiness such things as health and wealth, knowledge and friendship, good fortune, and a good moral character. For him, a life lived in accordance with excellence in moral and intellectual virtue constitutes the essence of a happy life: "He is happy who lives in accordance with complete virtue and is sufficiently equipped with external goods, not for some chance period but throughout a complete life….A good life is one that has been lived by making morally virtuous choices or decisions."[8]

As Epictetus puts it, happy is the man who, in the course of a lifetime, has satisfied all his desires, provided he desires nothing amiss.

Positive Psychology and the Pursuit of Happiness

During the last decade, positive psychology has heralded a new research field called happiness research. Although the pursuit of happiness is as old as human civilization, "only recently has scientific evidence emerged to suggest a possible path to lasting happiness that is effective for majority of people."[9] In response to a self-posed question, is happiness a worthwhile goal, Jaime Kurtz and Sonja Lyubomirsky cite previous research that suggests that, across all the domains of life, happy people are energetic, creative, and productive in the workplace; cooperative; and motivated to help others. They have more friends, more satisfying social interactions, and stronger immune systems. They cope more effectively with stress, and, most strikingly, even live longer. Positive psychology, a recently conceived branch of psychology, aims to understand and promote lasting well-being or authentic happiness.

Positive psychology is built on three pillars: positive emotion, positive strengths, and positive institutions. It has its roots in the works of humanistic psychologists such as Abraham Maslow, Carl Rogers, and Eric Fromm, who focused on personal fulfillment and well-being. In fact, Maslow was the first psychologist to use this term in his 1954 classic, *Motivation and Personality*. The contribution of positive psychology is that it has provided scientific evidence consistent with what philosophers and humanistic psychologists intuitively believed. Positive psychology focuses on character, flourishing, and fulfillment. It aims to explore how to live a happy and fulfilling life, how to define and develop human strengths, and how to build character and resilience.

Seligman, one of the founders of positive psychology, believes that authentic happiness has three interrelated constituents—pleasure, strengths, and meaning:

1. The pleasant life, in which we successfully pursue positive emotions about the present, past, and future.

2. The good life, in which we use our signature strengths to obtain abundant gratification in the main realms of our life.

3. The meaningful life, in which we use our signature strengths and virtues in the service of something much larger than we are—and the larger that something is, the more meaning our lives have.[10]

To live all three lives, concludes Seligman, is to lead a full life.[11]

The Sustainable Happiness Model

Can people be lastingly happy? Until recently, psychologists used to explain our limits to achieving lasting happiness by invoking the genetic set point theory and the concept of hedonic adaptation: First, happiness is partially determined by genetics, and second, people tend to adapt or become accustomed to most positive life experiences. The genetic set point theory is based on decades of research done with identical twins and fraternal twins that suggests that each of us is born with a particular happiness set point that originates in our biological mother or father or both, a baseline or potential for happiness to which we are bound to return, even after major setbacks or triumphs.[12]

The theory of hedonic adaptation (or hedonic treadmill) is used to explain the tendency for the emotional impact of both positive and negative events to diminish over time. In an article published in *Scientific American*, Marina Krakovsky explains,

> The classic example of such "hedonic adaptation" comes from a 1970s study of lottery winners, who a year after their windfall ended up no happier than non-winners. Hedonic adaptation helps to explain why even changes in major life circumstances—such as income, marriage, physical health and where we live—do so little to boost our overall happiness. Not only that, but studies of twins and adoptees have shown that about 50 percent of each person's happiness is determined from birth. This "genetic set point" alone makes the happiness glass look half empty, because any upward swing in happiness seems doomed to fall back to near your baseline.[13]

Obviously, trying to raise our set point by altering genes is currently impossible, although some have challenged the pervasiveness of the set point theory.[14] And life circumstances—gender, ethnicity, marital status, education level, health, income, physical appearance, and settings—only account for a mere 10% of our happiness. Clearly, the key to lasting happiness lies elsewhere. Empirical research by Lyubomirsky and her colleagues has shown that we can increase our happiness as much as 40% by intentionally engaging in activities such as expressing gratitude, doing random acts of kindness, and creating a sense of optimism.[15]

Distinguishing between life's circumstances and intentional activities, Lyubomirsky et al. further explain that "circumstances happen to people, and activities are ways people act on their circumstances."[16] After all, if we cannot change the course of the winds (genetic set point), we can always adjust our sails (circumstances and intentional activity). These researchers clarify that these mindful actions—intentional activities—can make people happy only if they keep doing them. Intentional activity is, therefore, a matter of self-effort, and in order to derive full benefit out of intentional activities, the authors suggest that we need to invest efforts first in initiating the intentional activities, and then in maintaining them. These authors further maintain that the intentional activities, to be sustainable and meaningful, should be well timed, varied, and fitted to the person doing them. These activities require commitment and persistence.

Mihaly Csikszentmihalyi, who co-founded positive psychology with Seligman, believes that happiness is not an arbitrary gift but a hard-won reward of well-cultivated inner control:

> Happiness, in fact, is a condition that must be prepared for, cultivated, and defended privately by each person. People who learn to control inner experience will be able to determine the quality of their lives, which is as close as any of us can come to being happy.[17]

However, some fear that the recent enthusiasm about the science of happiness may have gotten ahead of the art of happiness. Writers like Frankl have cautioned that the very pursuit of happiness, paradoxically, may render it eminently unattainable. This chapter's opening story about the kitten chasing its tail splendidly demonstrates this point. According to this view, happiness is not a house that one can build with one's hands; it is the by-product of one's selfless dedication to a cause larger than oneself. "If you want to live a happy life," said Albert Einstein, "tie it to a goal, not to people or things."

There Is No Direct Road to Fulfillment

The road to happiness, at best, is circuitous and indirect. In the preface to the 1984 edition of his now classic work, *Man's Search for Meaning*, Frankl states that it seemed to be both strange and remarkable that the book he had intended to publish anonymously did in fact become a success. He repeatedly admonished his students about the circuitous path to happiness and success:

> Do not aim at success—the more you aim at it and make it a target, the more you are going to miss it. For success, like happiness, cannot be pursued; it must ensue, and it only does so as the unintended side effect of one's dedication to a cause greater than oneself.... Happiness must happen, and the same holds for success: you have to let it happen by not caring about it. I want you to listen to what your conscience commands you to do and go on to carry it out to the best of your knowledge. Then you will live to see that in the long run—in the long run, I say!—success will follow you precisely because you had forgotten to think of it.[18]

Frankl's work serves as a clarion call to rise above life's circumstances and bear suffering with courage and dignity. The life examples of Mother Teresa, Mahatma Gandhi, Rosa Parks, Martin Luther King Jr., and Nelson Mandela are testimonies to this discovery of meaning, to rise above life's conditions and make life worthwhile against all odds through dedication to a selfless cause.

Russell, a modern philosopher and an early explorer of this field, in his down-to-earth compendium of happiness called *The Conquest of Happiness,* notes,

I do not deny that the feeling of success makes it easier to enjoy life.... Nor do I deny that money, up to a certain point, is very capable of increasing happiness. What I do maintain is that success can only be one ingredient in happiness, and is too dearly purchased if all the other ingredients have been sacrificed to obtain it.[19]

In an Aristotelian vein, Russell adds that "the happiness that is genuinely satisfying is accompanied by the fullest exercise of our faculties, and the fullest realization of the world in which we live."[20] According to Russell, the secret of happiness is this: let your interests be as wide as possible, and let your reactions to the things and persons that interest you be as far as possible friendly rather than hostile.[21]

In his recent book titled *Stumbling on Happiness*, Dan Gilbert opines that we are grossly inaccurate at predicting what will make us happy and how happiness happens. Gilbert's main thesis is that through a sort of psychological illusion we imagine the future inaccurately, particularly in regard to what will make us happy. The solution Gilbert presents to accurately estimate our happiness is to learn from people with similar backgrounds and experiences. The variance in subjectivity of happiness, says Gilbert, is a lot lower than the distortion caused by our own imagination.[22]

In recapitulating the discussion so far, one is struck by the similarities between recent happiness research and Buddhist psychology. Using two different modes of exploration—empirical research and insight meditation, respectively—positive psychology and Buddhist traditions have arrived at essentially the same conclusion: the road to lasting happiness is paved by a selfless, caring concern for others. It is cultivated by harnessing our intrinsic goodness, by developing the spiritual qualities of mind and heart—qualities of kindness and compassion, gratitude and altruism.

The next section explores at length the Buddhist approach to personal fulfillment and well-being.

Buddhist Psychology and the Pursuit of Fulfillment

It is paradoxical that a religion that starts with the basic truth of existential suffering has contributed the most to our understanding of the elusive pursuit of happiness. Adherents of Buddhism (or *Buddha Dharma*, as Buddhists prefer to call it) like to point out that Buddhism is not a religion in the traditional sense with a creator God who punishes and rewards, but rather a do-it-yourself art and science of mind that is built upon the very experiences of our life here and now.[23] There are no articles of faith in Buddhism and no commandments to follow beyond the apperception of things as they truly are, the law of cause and effect, and the understanding that we are the creatures of our thoughts, the products of our mind.

The First Noble Truth taught by the Buddha states that life involves suffering. This has led some to conclude that Buddhism must be a life-denying and pessimistic approach to life. But Buddha taught Four Noble Truths about life, not just one. After analyzing the causes of suffering in the Second Noble Truth, Buddha goes on to state that it is possible to end this suffering (Third Noble Truth) and prescribes a path called The Noble Eightfold Path to the cessation of suffering (Fourth Noble Truth). Walpola Rahula clarifies:

> The Buddha does not deny happiness in life when he says there is suffering.... In his discourses, there is a list of happinesses, such as the happiness of family life and the happiness of the life of the recluse, the happiness of sense pleasures and the happiness of renunciation, the happiness of attachment and the happiness of detachment, physical happiness and mental happiness....The Buddha was realistic and objective. He says, with regard to life and enjoyment of sense-pleasures, that one should clearly understand three things: 1) attraction or enjoyment, 2) evil consequence or danger or unsatisfactoriness, and 3) freedom or liberation.... These three things are true with regard to all enjoyment in life.[24]

It has been noted that Buddhism does not deny that there are satisfactions in worldly life. The Buddhist insight into the real nature of reality helps us see the true nature of such forms of happiness clearly: "Pain is to be seen as pain, pleasure as pleasure. What is denied is that such happiness will be secure and lasting."[25] Rahula concludes,

> This does not at all make the life of a Buddhist melancholy or sorrowful, as some people wrongly imagine. On the contrary, a true Buddhist is the happiest of beings. He has no fears or anxieties. He is always calm and serene, and cannot be upset or dismayed by the changes or calamities, because he sees things as they are.[26]

Key Lessons of Buddhist Psychology

It is said that right after the Buddha became enlightened, he uttered the following, in the language of those days: *dukkham-dukkham* (suffering-suffering), *kshanikamm-kshanikamm* (momentary-momentary), *asvalakshanamm-asvalakshanamm* (non-self, non-self), and *shunyamm-shunyamm* (void-void).[27] Building on this, the key message of Buddhist psychology and its view of reality—the way things really are—can be captured in the following five simple axioms:

1. Our mind is the source of bondage as well as freedom.

2. All self-centered emotions lead to suffering.

3. Relative is impermanent.

4. Everything is dependent upon and related to everything else.

5. Practicing altruistic kindness is the most essential ingredient of genuine happiness and better mental health.

The Source of Bondage and Freedom

According to Buddhism, both happiness and unhappiness flow from our mind: if we train our mind in virtuous thoughts and act with wholesome intentions, happiness will follow, and if we act with unwholesome intentions, unhappiness will result. Buddhist practice places special importance on guarding our minds, watching our thoughts, as is clear from the opening verses of *Dhammapada*:

> *All that we are is the result of what we have thought:*
> *It is founded on our thoughts, it is made up of our thoughts.*
> *If a man speaks or acts with an evil thought, pain follows him,*
> *as the wheel follows the foot of the ox that draws the carriage....*
> *If a man speaks or acts with a pure thought,*
> *happiness follows him, like a shadow that never leaves him.*[28]

The heart of the Buddhist practice is about cultivating an inner calm and changing our mind-set. It is not so much about changing the circumstances or the world around us. Our experience and reflection make it evident that it is much more effective (and easier) to change ourselves than to insist on changing our circumstances.

Pave the Planet, or Learn to Wear Shoes?

Shantideva, an eighth-century Buddhist monk, provides perhaps the most concrete advice on the art of living:

> Where would I possibly find enough leather
> With which to cover the surface of the earth?
> Yet (wearing) leather just on the soles of my shoes
> Is equivalent to covering the earth with it.[29]

Self-Centered Misery

Buddhist psychology views desire or craving as the root cause of all human suffering. But, obviously, not all desire is bad. For example, desire to be happy, grow in goodness, or be more kind is not bad. Most distress in life comes from confusing wants with needs, so one needs to understand clearly the difference between needs and wants and try to simplify the desires. Our consumer-oriented society excels in manufacturing bogus pleasures and convincing us that we need them in order to be happy. This led Aldous Huxley to quip, "Ours is an age of systematic irrelevances." Simplifying our desires means understanding our desires so that we can monitor them rather than living in constant servitude to them. Explaining the difference between reasonable and unreasonable desires, Dalai Lama points out that "excessive desire leads to greed":

> One interesting thing about greed is that although the underlying motive is to seek satisfaction, the irony is that even after obtaining the object of your desire, you are still not satisfied. *The true antidote of greed is contentment* [emphasis added].[30]

When surrounded with infinite variety of things on sale, it is a good mental discipline to ask every now and then, do I really need them? This applies to other material acquisitions also, including wealth. Research confirms that beyond the provision of a basic level of material comfort, more wealth does not always contribute to greater happiness. I once saw a bumper sticker that said, "Why do you want everything? Where would you keep it?" Buddha would have agreed whole-heartedly with this message and probably would have laughed at the following as well:

+ Ever wonder what a Buddhist vacuum cleaner would look like? No attachments!
+ "O Master! is it proper for a monk to use email?" asked a young monk. "Sure…as long as there are no attachments!" replied the master.

Everything Changes

Shunryu Suzuki Roshi, a modern Zen Master, was once asked to sum up Buddhism in one sentence. His curt reply: "Everything changes." By understanding deeply that everything is subject to change and is dependent on everything else, we develop a new appreciation and respect for things, relationships, and our experiences. Actually, it is good that things change and that everything in the phenomenal world is impermanent. If things were not impermanent, we would be living in a fossilized world, doomed to the everlasting monotony of permanence! In such a static world, an acorn would remain an acorn, never growing into an oak tree; seasons would not change, and flowers would not blossom.

It is important to realize that impermanence is what makes change and transformation possible. "Thanks to impermanence," says Thich Nhat Hanh,

> we can change suffering into joy.... It is not impermanence that makes us suffer. What makes us suffer is wanting things to be permanent when they are not.... The teaching of impermanence helps us to appreciate fully what is there, without attachment or forgetfulness.[31]

Everything Is Interconnected with Everything Else

One of the most radical aspects of the Buddha's teaching is the concept of "non-self" or "not-self" nature of all phenomena. This concept signifies that what we call "I" or "mine" is really a combination of interdependent mental and physical conditions and causes that are constantly in flux, and that there is nothing inherently permanent and unchanging in the whole of phenomenal existence. Things do not have a separate, fixed self. Everything is dependent upon and reflective of everything else in this universe. Nhat Hanh, a Vietnamese Zen monk, has coined a beautiful term to describe this interrelationship of all and everything in the universe: he calls it *interbeing*. In his talks and seminars, Nhat Hanh usually underscores the principle of interbeing by inviting his audience to look deeply at a piece of paper:

> If you are a poet, you will see clearly that there is a cloud floating in this sheet of paper. Without a cloud, there will be no rain; without rain, the trees cannot grow; without trees we cannot make paper.... If we look into this sheet of paper even more deeply, we can see sunshine in it. If the sunshine is not there, the forest cannot grow.... And if we

continue to look, we can see the logger who cut the trees and brought it to the mill to transform into paper.... When we look in this way, we see that without all of these things, the sheet of paper cannot exist.... This sheet of paper is, because everything is.... As thin as this sheet of paper is, it contains everything in the universe in it.[32]

By seeing ourselves as we truly are—as a reflection of and interconnected with everything else in the universe—and by seeing things as they are—impermanent, transitory, and dependent on causes and conditions—we develop a realistic view of ourselves and things around us.

Cultivating Altruistic Kindness

According to Dalai Lama, "If you want others to be happy, be kind; if you want to be happy, be kind." The goal of Buddhist practice is to develop wisdom within and compassion without. It holds altruistic kindness to be the most essential ingredient of genuine happiness and better mental health. Matthiew Ricard states that

it is essential to understand at the most fundamental level that all living creatures share our desire to avoid suffering and experience well-being.... A series of studies conducted on hundreds of students found an undeniable correlation between altruism and happiness, determining that those who believe themselves to be the happiest are also the most altruistic.[33]

Buddhist practice recognizes the following Four Sublime States:[34]
1. Extension of unlimited, universal love and good-will to all living beings without any kind of discrimination.
2. Compassion for all living beings who are suffering, in trouble and affliction.
3. Sympathetic joy in others' success, welfare and happiness.
4. Equanimity in all vicissitudes of life.

In a verse that is also a favorite of Dalai Lama, Shantideva captures the essence of these four states and, perhaps, the ultimate in human compassion:

> For as long as space endures,
> As long as living beings remain,
> Until then may I too abide
> To dispel the misery of the world.[35]

A story is told of an elderly woman who used to attend every possible discourse of the Buddha she could. One day, she approached the Buddha and urged him to summarize his teachings in few lines for her recapitulation. Out of his inexhaustible compassion, the Buddha is reported to have uttered the following verse:

> Abstain from all unwholesome deeds,
> Cultivate the capital of wholesome deeds,
> Purify your own mind completely—
> This is the teaching of the Buddhas.[36]

Avoidable and Unavoidable Stress

The underlying premise of this book is that there are basically two types of causes of stress: unavoidable causes and avoidable causes. The unavoidable causes of stress include events like death of a loved one, terminal illness, and extreme political and economic insecurity. Outbreaks of war or any civil disturbance and loss of employment are some examples of political and economic insecurity. All of these events (especially death and terminal illness) call forth an unusual fund of human courage, faith, and hope. Each person has to garner these inner resources in a most unique way, and not much can be said by way of broad generalizations regarding these unavoidable causes. Frankl, a Viennese psychiatrist and a survivor of four concentration camps during World War II, calls such events "unavoidable suffering" and suggests that "if one cannot change a situation that causes his suffering, he can still choose his attitude."[37] Frankl further explains,

Man *can* preserve a vestige of spiritual freedom, of independence of mind, even in such terrible conditions of
psychic and physical stress. We who lived in concentration camps can remember the men who walked through
the huts comforting others, giving away their last piece of
bread. They may have been few in number, but they offer
sufficient proof that *everything can be taken from a man but
one thing: the last of the human freedoms—to choose one's
attitude in any given set of circumstances, to choose one's own
way* [emphasis added].[38]

One only has to read Frankl's masterpiece of hope and heroism,
Man's Search for Meaning, to be convinced of his tragic optimism.

The second category of stressors is mainly psychological in nature.
Under the avoidable type, the stress emanates primarily from mistaken
values, unwarranted expectations, and faulty assumptions about life
in general and human life in particular. In fact, stress stemming from
avoidable causes may be defined as a gap between what one expects and
what one gets. An impartial survey of human life will show that most
day-to-day stress is self-created due to what may be termed as wrong
habits of mind. The most universal cause of stress is a clash between
first-rate desires or expectations and second-rate efforts. This happens
when this basic fact of life is overlooked—that life is largely a fair equation in which inputs equal outputs. We basically get out of life what
we put into it.

A tale is told of a would-be seeker who went to a Sufi master for
study. After a few months of study, the student, anxious of progress,
asked the teacher, "How long will it take me to get something out of my
studies?" The Sufi answered, "As soon as you start putting something
into your study, instead of constantly trying to get something *out!*"[39]

Accordingly, the best antidote to the stress created by unreasonable expectations is to take inventory of our desires, assumptions, and
abilities and, based on that, make necessary psychological adjustments.
"Happiness," said Epictetus, "is a life in which one has everything he

or she desires, provided that he or she desires nothing amiss." Desiring "nothing amiss" means not putting "a grain of rice into a pot with the expectation of drawing forth a handful of food when it is cooked."[40]

In the category of avoidable stressors, there are basically two approaches:

1. Seeking fulfillment by changing our circumstances
2. Seeking fulfillment by changing ourselves

Both are valid approaches, depending upon what is doable in given set of circumstances. The first approach concentrates upon changing circumstances or increasing one's means: another job, a supposedly better relationship, a new car, a more expensive home, and so forth. A little experience and some reflection will dictate that the world is too vast for our undertaking and to the improvement of circumstances, there seems to be no end. Besides, we soon discover that no lasting peace of mind or security can be found in unstable anchors or in objects that are inherently impermanent in nature.

The second approach, on the other hand, relies upon understanding our desires, relying more on our inner psychological resources, natural harmony, and an attitude of gratitude and acceptance. Understanding desires and expectations is perhaps the most important first step one can take toward composing one's life. As Indian sage Satya Sai Baba pointed out, "Man's many desires are like many metal coins he carries about in his pocket. The more he has, the more they weigh him down."

Radical Psychological Transformation: An Experiment about Reality

Since changing the circumstances, for the most part, lies outside the control of an individual, it seems more prudent to change oneself until one is able to change the circumstances. Accordingly, fulfillment becomes more a matter of attitude than circumstances; more a matter of inner transformation than fixing outer conditions; more a matter of *being* than *having*; more a matter of *belonging* than *belongings*.

Mind-Transformation=Life-Transformation: An Experiment

The following simple experiment demonstrates the importance of inner psychological transformation in altering our perception of the world. It shows how by changing our mind-set, we can radically change our approach to life-experiences.

Take three small containers and place them on a table. Put cold water in the left container, regular tap water in the middle container, and hot water in the right container. Dip your left hand in the left container and your right hand in the right container. Now, simultaneously dip both of your hands in the middle container.

What did you find out? You will discover that to your left hand, the water in the middle container "feels" hot while it "feels" cold to your right hand. Yet you know very well that the water in the middle container is neither hot nor cold—it is just the tap water at the regular room temperature. The external conditions are identical: Same person, same container, and same water temperature—yet it "felt" simultaneously hot and cold to your left and right hands respectively.

By now, you probably have figured out the reason. How we will feel water temperature of the middle container depends upon which container we put our hand first. The moral: We do not see/experience things the way they are; we see/experience them the way we are.

The hot and cold sensations reside in our mind. They depend upon mind's reaction/interpretation to their contact. Similarly, the world is "contacted" by our mind. If we transform our mind appropriately, then our experience of life situations can be altered significantly.

(continued on next page)

> (continued from previous page)
>
> *We have a very little control over life conditions. We have much greater control over our reactions to life conditions. While we cannot always control life conditions, we can always manage our reactions to them. While we cannot change the course of the winds, we can certainly adjust our sails.*
>
> *We can alter the experiences of our life without altering the external world—just by altering our mindset.*
>
> *So, what should one really do?*
>
> *Pave the planet, or learn to wear shoes?*
>
> *The choice, as always, is ours!*[41]

English poet John Milton wrote, "The mind in its own place.../ Can make a Heaven of Hell, a Hell of Heaven." Helen Keller and Napoleon Bonaparte provide perfect illustrations of Milton's viewpoint. Helen Keller, who was blind and deaf, declared, "I find life so beautiful!" Napoleon had everything that human beings usually crave: glory, power, and riches. Yet he declared at St. Helena, "I have never known six happy days in my life." A tub was too large for Diogenes; the whole world was too small for Alexander the Great!

Legendary Encounters between Alexander the Great and Diogenes

The legend tells us that a tub was too big for Diogenes, whereas the whole world was too small for Alexander. Diogenes lived in a tub, scorning all possessions except the few necessities that could be carried in a purse. Having one time owned a drinking cup, he cast it aside as a superfluous, and hence worthless, encumbrance when he saw a dog drinking from a puddle.

On one occasion, Diogenes declared, "Alexander eats when his officers tell him that it is time to eat; I eat when I am hungry. I am the master of my life and Alexander is slave to his servants!"

Alexander, awesome on his white horse, appeared one day before Diogenes, who was sunning himself in front of his tub, and announced that he was Alexander, "the great king," to which Diogenes, the Cynic, replied that he was Diogenes, the dog. (The name Cynic happens to be the same as the Greek word for "doglike.") "Do you not fear me?" asked Alexander. To this Diogenes responded, "Are you good or evil?" "Good, of course!" said Alexander. And Diogenes asked, "How could anyone be so foolish to fear what is good?" The king was so struck by this that he offered the Cynic anything he wanted—to which Diogenes replied, "Please just stand out of my sunlight!"

Upon hearing this, Alexander the Great got off his horse and stood beside Diogenes, answerless and confused. Diogenes, acting as a good host, restarted the conversation by asking, "What are your plans, sir?" Alexander replied, "I first plan to conquer all Greece, then all Europe." "What will you do after you have conquered the whole of Europe?" asked Diogenes. Continued Alexander, "Then I will conquer the whole Middle East, and move on to conquering Asia." "What will you do after that?" pressed Diogenes. "Then I will conquer the whole world and rule the whole world." "And after that?" asked Diogenes. "After conquering the whole world, I will sit in peace and enjoy the splendor of my conquest," replied the emperor. Diogenes finally asked, "Why do not you sit in peace right now? Why this bloodshed, if at the end all you want to do is to sit and bask in your glory? Why don't you do that right now?" Alexander was so impressed with the force of this argument that he mused, "If I were not Alexander, and God had asked who else I would like to be, I would have said, make me Diogenes, the slave." Unimpressed by this, Diogenes retorted, "If God ever asked me what I would like to be, I would say, make me anybody but Alexander!"

The sun was setting on the horizon, the legend tells us, as Alexander and Diogenes walked on the beach; it was Diogenes who was leading, and Alexander following.[42]

We See the World the Way We Are!

The world that we perceive is an experience in our mind of our consciousness coming in contact with various objects. It is a construct of our mind. It rarely occurs to us that, in the strictest sense, there is no objective reality out there independent of our consciousness. We encounter the world exactly at the level of our being. What our mind does not know, our eyes cannot see. The following example explains this fact in a graphic manner.

Mindful Moments: Got Green Lights?!

It has been rightly observed that we do not see things the way they are but we see them the way we are. Thus, when we change the way we see the world, we actually change the world. The salutary effects of changing one's attitude on one's psychological well-being can be further illustrated by what may be termed as "traffic light phenomenon." Almost always, when we are in a hurry we come across more red traffic lights, whereas, if we are relaxed and unhurried, we get more green lights. Should we conclude that city administration adjusts the frequency of traffic lights according to our shifting moods?!

Perspective Is Everything: An Exercise

1. *Take a pen (or pencil) in your hand.*
2. *Stretch up your arm straight above your head and point the pen toward the ceiling or sky.*
3. *While pointing straight up, rotate the pen in a clockwise fashion.*
4. *Looking up, keep watching its clockwise rotation.*
5. *Now bend your elbow and bring the pen down slowly, carefully maintaining its clockwise rotation.*
6. *Bring the pen to a level below your chin so you're now looking down on it, then note the direction of its rotation.*

> *7. Is it still rotating clockwise?*
>
> *Looking down, you notice that the rotation is now counterclockwise, although you have not changed its direction. So why, when you look at it now, is the rotation opposite? Because you have changed your perspective! The rotation of the pen/pencil has not changed, but your perspective has.*
>
> *The moral of the exercise is very clear: By changing our perspective, we can change the configuration of reality. This exercise has a great message for leaders in all positions. When we view things at the leadership level—that is, looking down at the rotating pen—our vision, our goals, our policies may look a certain way to us (counterclockwise). And to those in the rank and file—that is, employees looking at the rotating pen from below—our vision, goals, et cetera may appear entirely opposite (clockwise).*

Suzuki Roshi, one of the first authentic Zen Masters to live in the West, explains the importance of changing ourselves: "...usually, without being aware of it...we try to order things outside us. But it is impossible to organize things if you yourself are not in order."[43] The message here seems to be that as we change our attitude toward life, life somehow changes its attitude toward us. Albert Camus said, "In the midst of winter, I finally learned that there was, in me, an invincible summer." We all have that "invincible summer" in us. The warmth of abiding faith and its consciousness can help us weather the winter storms!

Fundamental Problems of Life Cannot Be Solved!

An artful understanding of the challenges of life can go a long way in meeting them squarely. More often than not, correct understanding is the most expedient thing one can bring to bear upon an issue at hand. One might as well say that the fundamental problems of life cannot be solved but only understood. Jiddu Krishnamurti, a modern teacher, explains: "There is only the problem; there is no answer; for in understanding of the problem lies its dissolution."[44] Accordingly, it is more often a question of what *not* to do than doing something that helps to resolve an issue. Chinese wisdom calls it the "noble art of leaving things alone" or "not legging the snake."

The understanding of the problem may be seen as a higher perspective that, when reached, helps one to see the problem in its true light. Albert Einstein said, "We cannot solve a problem from the same level of consciousness that created it."

C.G. Jung, a psychologist who drank deeply at the unitive fountain of Eastern and Western wisdom, describes this process as "outgrowing" problems when they are primarily insoluble. *Outgrowing* essentially means raising the level of one's consciousness to enable one to experience challenges of life as "storms in a valley viewed calmly from a mountain top," to use Jung's analogy. In his commentary on an ancient Chinese book of life called *The Secret of the Golden Flower*, Jung observes,

> I have learned to see that the greatest and most important problems of life are fundamentally insoluble. They must be so because they express the necessary polarity inherent in every self-regulating system. They can never be solved but only outgrown.... This "outgrowing"...revealed itself on further experience to be the raising of the level consciousness. Some higher or wider interest arose on the person's horizon, and through this widening of view, the insoluble problem lost its urgency.[45]

An old Sufi saying expresses Jung's wisdom concisely: "When the house catches fire, the toothache flies out of the window."

Improve Yourself!

Krishnamurti suggests, "One must *start very near*—with oneself—to *go very far*." In the same vein, Huxley, one of the most often quoted writers of the 20th century, said, "There is only one corner of the universe you can be certain of improving, and that's your own self." One is reminded of a tale in which a socially conscious student went to a teacher with the question, "I want to make this society a better place to live. What should I do?" The teacher answered, "Just improve yourself!" "Your own self-realization," said Sri Ramana Maharshi, "is the greatest service you can render the world." Our own transformation is the greatest gift we can offer to the universe. Self-knowledge does not really result in seeing different things; it just helps to see things differently.

Once Zen teacher Maurine Stuart went to New York to see Soen Roshi, a famous Zen master.

"How did you get here?" asked the Roshi.

"I drove my car," replied Stuart.

"And how are you driving your life?" he asked.

"That is the question."[46]

Concluding Remarks

I do not want to give the impression that I have "figured it all out." I also have my share of difficulties. If this were not true, my attempt at writing this book would be but an empty intellectual exercise—what Gurdjieff calls "pouring from the empty into the void." In this regard, I feel a deep kinship of spirit with the German poet, Rainer Maria Rilke, who wrote to a young poet seeking his advice,

> Do not believe that he who seeks to comfort you lives untroubled among the simple and quiet words that sometimes do you good. His life has much difficulty and sadness.... Were it otherwise, he would never have been able to find those words.[47]

If the ideas presented in this book help even a single person to sort out his or her options more clearly, my efforts will be amply rewarded. In the final reckoning, everyone has to write his or her own life's recipe book for finding fulfillment. After all, nobody has more students than oneself. Nobody has more teachers than oneself. Rumi says it well: "You are the only disciple you have. All others eventually leave."

CHAPTER THREE

THE JOURNEY FROM SUCCESS TO SIGNIFICANCE

Fulfillment is not a place we go to; it is a place we all come from!

As human beings, we seem to be eternally caught in the vicious cycle of becoming. There is this desire for "being" and the struggle for "becoming." The world of becoming lies outside and is teemed with competition, comparison, aggression, and acquisition. It is a path without any final destination and a race with no visible finish line. The world of being lies within us and is paved with self-knowledge, contentment, contemplation, and understanding. It is already within our reach and ever attained. Struggle for becoming brings unstable anchors and invariably leads to unhappiness, anxiety, stress, and strife. Being is the road that verily leads to happiness, peace, serenity, and fulfillment. Choice is always ours!

"It takes us long to discover that the light we are seeking is in our own lantern,
That our rice has been cooked from the very beginning."
                                          ~ A ZEN SAYING

The Way of Heaven is like the drawing of a bow,
It brings down what is high and raises what is low.
                                          ~ LAO TZU

Success versus Significance: Making Habits of Gifts

This book is about discovering gifts of true significance in our daily life. It is not about the laws of success. It underscores the vital difference between success and significance, for one can be highly successful in the worldly sense and still feel completely empty inside. "What can it profit a man if he gains the whole world and loses his own soul?" asks the Bible. Sooner or later we come to realize that we are not going to take anything with us but we can certainly try our best to leave something behind.

This chapter presents seven simple gifts of consciousness devoted to the high art of leaving something behind. Just as a gifted artist must practice his or her craft to gain mastery, we garner lasting fulfillment in all aspects of our lives by developing our gifts habitually. It may at first strike us as counterintuitive to speak of gifts and habits in the same breath, but this is why we must consciously cultivate our gifts rather than passively wait for good accidents to happen. Reciprocally, we approach the seven habits of highly fulfilled people as *gifts* or *offerings* to the world—as our fair share of contribution to the well-being of humanity. Khalil Gibran has defined work as "love made visible." And this is what the seven habits are all about—giving expression to our love of living meaningfully and abundantly.

Dollars for Our Days

We are given a very limited span of life to live, a very short lease on life, if you will. But we are presented with myriad choices to spend our life; we have limited time, yet almost unlimited choices! Given these constraints/opportunities, a wise person wonders how best to utilize the limited time to redeem one's life. We want to know one best thing to aspire for in life. Consider the following exercise that underscores the urgency and calls for a serious reassessment of what matters most in life.

By universal acclaim, we all seem to pursue happiness, in some shape or form. However, an impartial survey of human condition makes evident the unfortunate conclusion that happiness is a rare commodity to come by. As English novelist Thomas Hardy observed, "Happiness is but a mere episode in the general drama of pain." Observing life as it is commonly lived, the Buddha came to a similar conclusion.

An Exercise in Urgency: Dollars for Our Lives!

What if someone were to give you 25,550 dollars?! What would you do with it? How would you go about spending this gift? What if you find out those 25,550 dollars is all you will get for the rest of your life? Will that be enough capital for your whole life?

Why did we choose this number, 25,550 dollars? Is there any special significance to this number?

A little math will explain the mystery: 25,550 = 365 × 70. It will now become evident that the number actually represents the days of our lives (365 days times 70 years of as an average human life span).

So that's all we have got, more or less, 25,550 days! One third of this time, spent in sleep, will be gone forever, and no one can do anything to recover it. Part of these 25,550 days is spent running around in diapers, learning how to count 25,550.

Accordingly, very little time is left to do what really matters in life.

Why so? Everyone wants to be happy, and yet when we look around we see more unhappiness, regardless of circumstance of birth and place. Perhaps we are looking for happiness in the wrong places or in a wrong manner or both. Perhaps we are too keen on chasing our own happiness around external haunts such as success, fame, power, or material goods. Perhaps we need to recalibrate our search for success and happiness.

This book is not about success as it is popularly understood. It is about living a life of real significance, a life infused with understanding, meaning, purpose, and fulfillment. Too often, amidst the unbridled pursuit of success we forget the real purpose of our life. It is important to understand the difference between success and significance at the very outset. Success is about getting; significance is about giving: we make a *living* by what we get; we make a *life* by what we give. Success is about doing; significance is about being: we are not human "doings"; we are human "beings." Success is external; significance is internal: Success aims to acquire external objects; significance aims to harness inner qualities. Success is temporary; significance is long-lasting: success comes and goes; significance stays and endures. Success is about having; significance is about knowing. Success is about changing oneself; significance is about understanding oneself. Success has to be freshly won and can be precariously lost; significance is our abiding nature and cannot be lost. Success is projected over "there," later in the future; significance is right here, right now in the present. We pursue success; significance ensues: success is acquired while significance is discovered and embodied.

If you are looking for the latest recipe for success—the surefire method to fulfill all your desires spontaneously and instantaneously or the so-called Seven Invariable Laws of Success—then you need to look elsewhere for you will not find them in these pages. As stated earlier, this book is about gifts of significance and not laws of success. In order to discover this significance for ourselves, we have to share these gifts with others. Since, truly speaking, there are no others, we essentially give these gifts to ourselves, the self and the others being inseparably, inextricably interrelated, interlinked, and interdependent.

Fulfillment: The Place We All Come from!

Interestingly, these gifts are already abundantly present within all of us. We just have to rediscover or take a note of what is there, recognize it, appreciate it, and find a way to cultivate it and generously share it with others. For the most part, it is not a matter of acquisition but of recognition of what is already there. Discovering, polishing, and sharing these gifts of abundance form the key message of this book. Paradoxically, in sharing these gifts with others, we ultimately bestow them on ourselves and unexpectedly discover a life infused with true significance and lasting fulfillment.

**Being, Doing, and Having:
Reversing the Prevailing Paradigm**

Having ⟹ Doing ⟹ Being

Being ⟹ Doing ⟹ Having

This approach can also be expressed as the art of being, knowing, and doing. Our current cosmetic culture tends to obsess itself excessively with *having* things and *doing* things, with little or no time left for *being*. In pursing the rat race of success, we tend to forget to live, to be. (This adage puts it well: "Even if one wins a rat race, one is still a rat!") As mentioned above, we also seem to be oblivious to the fact that, after all, we are human "beings" and not human "doings" or human "havings." Per Shakespeare, "To be or not to be, that is the question." So, in a way, the approach this book suggests goes against the prevailing paradigm in the modern affluent societies. It is almost a reversal of the current mode of "having-doing-being" by moving toward the "being-doing-having" mode. We start with the primal question, what would we want to be? We then proceed to the next logical step, what we need to do to be what we want to be; then, finally, we can wisely decide what we need to have to live a life infused with meaning and purpose. To be, to know, and to do—this is one good recipe to prepare the supreme meal of life!

Mindful Moments: Victorious!

The dictionary defines fulfillment as "a feeling of satisfaction at having achieved your desires." I firmly believe that any man's finest hour, the greatest fulfillment of all that he holds dear, is that moment when he has worked his heart out in a good cause and lies exhausted on the field of battle—victorious!
~Vince Lombardi

Financial Success Is Essential

And yet, a certain amount of financial success is perhaps necessary to provide for the basic fundamentals of life. Even Aristotle (384–322 bc), a student of Plato and the teacher of Alexander the Great, counted wealth to be among the essential ingredients of happiness along with health, friendship, and good luck. However, he regarded these as "external goods." "Time and money," said Lao Tzu, "to have enough is a blessing; to have more than enough interferes with our inner growth."

Pitfalls of the I-Making Business

The Buddha, the unfailing master metapsychologist, pointed out that life, as commonly lived, involves suffering. He declared that the root cause of all unhappiness and suffering *(dukkha)* is the selfish desire or craving *(tanha)*. Huxley, a life-time student of the perennial philosophy, called egoism "the fundamental human disability." "The most important technique to learn in life," according to Huxley, is "the art of obtaining freedom from the fundamental human disability of egoism."[1] Most wisdom traditions of the world are solely concerned with the art of obtaining freedom from this fundamental cognitive error of egoism.

In one of those endless meetings that many academicians like to busy themselves with, my mind tuned out, and I found myself scribbling down the following on a piece of paper:

> Our separate self, as we know it, just does not really exist. Life force uses the thought-process to construct a false sense of identity, a kind of separate self: it is life's way of preserving and propagating itself. This separate self—I or ego—has definite practical value: it helps us to function usefully in society. This "I-making" business is nature's way of preventing all of us from colliding with each other, so to speak. (Carl Sagan once said that "time is nature's way of preventing everything from happening all at the same time.")

But this comes at a very high price. Almost always, we over-compensate in this realm of I-making, and this inevitably breeds undue attachment—clinging and self-centeredness and host of other negative emotions, such as over-competitiveness, jealousy, hatred, aggression, anger, greed, and a million other forms of violence. These negative forms then get aggregated—writ large—at the macro level in the form of terrorism, crime, and war. Although society has tried rather unsuccessfully to domesticate this inveterate human tendency of I-making via mores, morals, and mess-*iahs*, an impartial survey of the human condition over the last 6,000 years shows us that we have failed miserably at weeding out this churlish trait.

There comes a time in our lives when we no can longer live just for ourselves. Our kith and kin need us—as do our true friends, our community, and people across the globe—to add meaning to their lives, to lend them a helping hand and give them hope in a world that is full of existential angst. I remembered seeing a sign at the entrance of a meditation hall: "Be more kind than necessary to people around you, for everyone is fighting some battle."

I am convinced that it is possible to live a life completely free of self-centeredness, aggression, and over-competitiveness. I find my life to be a work in progress in this direction, an ongoing journey of self-effacement. However, I must say that I have not always succeeded in this effort; as I grow older I seem to catch myself more frequently embarking on ego-trips. However, I also do not forget that I may be deluding myself. Such are the ways of the master magician—"our skin-encapsulated ego"—the socially induced hallucination of our separate self.

Many wiser souls, somewhat jaded with cynicism, however, have pointed out that there is no humility; only different shades of pride!

As I mused over these thoughts in that endless meeting, I recalled a story about a rabbi who was on his deathbed and had only few more minutes to live. His students were gathered around his bed to pay regards. Everyone was praising the master with statements like "He was very kind," "He was very wise," "He was very caring," *et cetera*. The rabbi was stealthily relishing listening to all this. In the end, the rabbi, gasping for the last breath, opened his eyes and said, "Don't forget to mention my humility!" Seekers beware! I was also reminded of a beautiful poem by Chuang Tzu, transliterated by Thomas Merton:

> *If a man is crossing a river and an empty boat collides with his own skiff,*
> *Even though he be a bad-tempered man he will not become very angry.*
> *But if he sees a man in the boat, he will shout at him to steer clear.*
> *If the shout is not heard, he will shout again, and yet again, and begin cursing.*
> *And all because there is somebody in the boat.*
> *Yet if the boat were empty, he would not be shouting, and not angry.*
> *If you can empty your own boat crossing the river of the world,*
> *No one will oppose you; no one will seek to harm you...*
> *...Such is the perfect man:*
> *His boat is empty.*[2]

The Journey toward Other-Centeredness

> *But to rid of the conceit "I am"—*
> *That is the greatest happiness of all.*[3]
> ~ BUDDHA

Our progress on the path to significance is directly proportional to the degree of freedom we have achieved from the compulsive shackles of self-centeredness. Dogen, a 13th-century Zen master, put it so well: "To study the Way is to study the self."[4] "To know one's self is to forget one's self."[5] Only in transcending our false self—the imposter ego—do we stand any chance of discovering our true self: "To forget the self is to be enlightened by all things of the universe."[6] Dogen, for good psychological reasons, starts with addressing this fundamental human tendency, the fatal flaw that prevents us from living in harmony with everything that is and constantly interferes with our experiencing fulfillment.

Mindful Moments: New GPS System

Have you replaced your GPS system lately? In order to navigate wisely through the rough terrains of our life, we need a strong life-positioning system, a dependable moral compass. While in the old GPS system greed, power, and selfishness reign supreme, the new GPS aspires to generosity, passion, and service. Using our life's passions gratefully and generously in the service of humanity is what fulfillment is all about.

Seven Habits of Highly Fulfilled People: An Overview

So, what are these gifts, or habits of mind, of highly fulfilled people? Let's take a brief look at them:

1. The Gift of Pure Motivation.
2. The Gift of Gratitude.
3. The Gift of Generosity.
4. The Gift of Harmlessness.
5. The Gift of Selfless Service.
6. The Gift of Total Acceptance.
7. The Gift of Presence.

Figure 1 presents the interrelationship between the seven gifts of fulfillment.

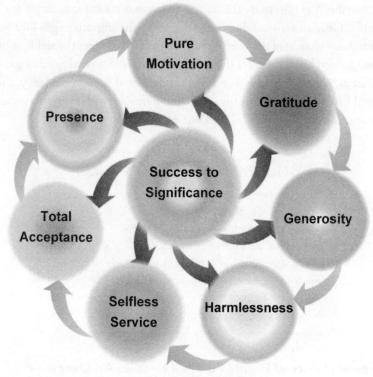

Figure 1: Seven Habits of Highly Fulfilled People

1. *Gift of Pure Motivation:* The journey for fulfillment begins with pure motivation. All conscious behavior has an expressed or unexpressed motive. We do things in order to accomplish certain goals. The gift of pure motivation requires that before every action we should mentally check our motivation for the action. Pure motivation signifies that, whatever we do, our every action should be motivated by our desire to help, to benefit others, without expecting anything in return. In other words, our intention to help others should be inspired by the pure motivation of just helping others. This gift builds on Immanuel Kant's Second Categorical Imperative: "Conduct is 'right' if it treats others as ends in themselves and not as

means to an end." If we are helping others in order to benefit ourselves—as means to our end—then it becomes a business "transaction," and our motivation ceases to be pure.

2. *Gift of Gratitude:* At the deepest existential level, the gift of gratitude is our resounding tribute to the universe for all its anonymous blessings. This is how we show our appreciation to existence for all its gifts, its bounties, and its blessings. These simple yet profound gifts include the gift of being alive; the marvel of our sensory apparatus; the miracle of the incoming and outgoing breath; the wonder of the blood circulating in our veins; the refreshing joy of a good night's sleep; the amazing gift of beauty of a sunset, a rainbow, and the majestic ocean with its ever-surging waves; the beguiling beauty of a Beethoven symphony or a Bach fugue or a Mozart concerto, and so forth. By appreciating these gifts through gratitude, we also open our hearts to receive more that is still to come our way.

3. *Gift of Generosity:* The gift of generosity flows directly from the gift of gratitude. Through this gift we share our bounties and blessings with others as a direct expression of our gratitude toward them as well as toward the universe. Churchill is reported to have said, "We make a living by what we get, but we make a life by what we give." Ever wonder why it is so fulfilling to share our gifts with others and to help others? Recent studies show practicing generosity is, in fact, good for us. When we act generously toward someone, it leads to deep, lasting fulfillment in an unexpected way. There is nothing mysterious about it. It is a common experience of everyone. But we have to check our motivation here—is it pure, or are we masking an ulterior motive with the guise of generosity?

4. *Gift of Harmlessness:* The gift of harmlessness represents the perfect embodiment of the Golden Rule and can serve as a sound foundation to any ethical and spiritual practice. The

gift of harmlessness is born out of our understanding of the previous two gifts, the gift of pure motivation and gift of gratitude. When all of our actions are inspired by pure motivation and we are mindful of our great gratitude for everything and for everyone, we gently come upon the gift of relating to all existence in a harmless way. At its very bare minimum, this gift means not causing any physical harm to anything that exists. The gift of harmlessness, however, goes much deeper than non-harming just in the physical sense. In its deeper meaning, it represents honoring and celebrating the preciousness of life and signifies non-harming by thought, word, and deed.

5. *Gift of Selfless Service:* The gift of selfless service is also a natural flowering of the previous gifts. When one truly understands the gifts of gratitude and generosity, one naturally devotes oneself to finding joy in selfless service. The present world is plagued by undue self-centeredness and rampant devotion to pursuing narrow selfish ends, frequently at the cost of others. Until we move away from this extreme preoccupation with our self, we will remain strangers to the deeper avenues of fulfillment. The urge to serve others is an innate need vitally tied to our happiness. As Albert Schweitzer expressed so eloquently, "I don't know what your destiny will be, but one thing I know: the only ones among you who will be really happy are those who have sought and found how to serve."

6. *Gift of Total Acceptance:* The gift of total acceptance means accepting ourselves as we are and accepting others as they are. As long as there is any aspiration to become something different from what we are, life remains a struggle. By relinquishing our constant need to be different from what we are, we step out of the cycle of becoming and enter into the peaceful abode of being that is always available to us in the present. Yet total acceptance means much more than resigning

ourselves to life's inevitabilities, which can leave us trapped in a cocoon of resentment and blame, with no possibility of any real peace and happiness; rather, total acceptance fosters composure, courage, and discernment—three virtues that accompany fulfillment and pave the road to self-knowledge.

7. *Gift of Presence:* The best gift we have to offer our fellow human beings is the gift of our presence, our attentive listening, our empathy, our kindness and compassion. This is possible only if we are truly present in all our engagements and interactions. Being present requires the cultivation of a special faculty called self-awareness. Intrinsically, our being is of the nature of pure awareness—of the nature of "wisdom-seeking wisdom." And this wisdom is always available to all of us right here and now, whenever and wherever we need it, if only we open ourselves to it unconditionally. The key here is to be alertly present in the present moment. This culminating gift facilitates the practice of all other gifts, as we mindfully remain alert from moment to moment. Highlighting the universal importance of mindfulness, Buddha observed, "Mindfulness, I declare, is helpful everywhere."

The Integral Nature of the Seven Gifts of Fulfillment

It is important to understand the integral nature of these seven gifts/habits in signifying our offerings to all and everything. When we cultivate one gift completely, the other six gifts come along by themselves. For example, cultivating pure motivation requires that we draw on our self-awareness—the gift of presence—to recognize life's interconnectedness, which motivates us to practice gratitude, generosity, harmlessness, and selfless service. When we are truly grateful, our motivation becomes pure, and we are more likely to share our gifts generously with others and to serve them selflessly. When our motivation becomes pure, we work selflessly for the common good of others without expecting anything in return. All this, however, presupposes a degree of self-knowledge and self-insight. By seeking perennially who we truly are and serving selflessly, we truly fulfill our existence.

Additionally, these gifts should be approached as seven offerings that highly fulfilled people share with others. The good news is that when we give these gifts to others, we end up receiving many more blessings in return. To quote Emerson, "It is one of the most beautiful compensations of life that no man can sincerely try to help another without helping himself." And as a Chinese saying goes, "A little perfume stays with the hand that gives flowers to others."

When we wake up in the morning, we have a choice: We can either go back to sleep and keep dreaming our dreams, or we can get up and go about making our cherished dreams a reality. It all depends on our orientation.

Gifts of Fulfillment and the Art of Leadership

As leaders, we should try to approach our work as an offering. As stated earlier in this chapter, Gibran, the great Lebanese poet, defined work as "love made visible." He explains:

> Work is love made visible. And if you cannot work with love but only with distaste, it is better that you should leave your work and sit at the gate of the temple and take alms of those who work with joy.[7]

By approaching our work as a gift of love, we make the art of leadership truly sacred.

The Bhagavad Gita states that a wise person only acts for the purpose of bringing communities of people together *(loksamgraha)* and is delightfully and constantly immersed in working toward the well-being of all beings *(sarva bhutah hitae ratah)*. What a wonderful lesson in the art and science of leadership. When we lead with a desire to bring people together and to ensure their well-being, we create a healthy work environment worthy of human habitation. In turn, we ensure harmony for others and fulfillment for ourselves.

> ## Mindful Moments: Business of Serving Others First!
>
> When we carefully look at the word "business," we notice that the "u" comes before the "i." We also notice that the "i" is silent. This is a gentle hint that not only our own motive should be secondary to serving others, but it should also not be too "loud." And if we do that, and if more and more businesses do that, surely, we will be more successful in the long run. Business is like the game of tennis: in order to win, one has to be good at service! This is what is meant by *doing well by doing good!*

It all boils down to how one approaches one's daily work, from big projects to small matters. Maybe extraordinary things are meant for extraordinary people. That may be! However, what we all can aspire to is to do ordinary things with extraordinary love and care. Even the smallest act or gesture deserves due importance and holds great significance. We thus approach our work as something sacred and try to live our entire life this way.

A leader's greatest gift is to help others connect to their inner greatness, to help others discover their authentic voice, and to help others be fulfilled. There comes a time when one starts focusing more on helping others achieve their goals rather than building one's own professional resume. Jack Welch, former CEO of GE, is reported to have said that "before you become a leader, your focus should be on developing yourself; after you become a leader, your focus should be on developing others."

After all, success is doing what one loves to do to the best of one's ability. It is about having just enough time and money to savor the beautiful gift called life. A person's success can be measured by how fulfilled he or she feels from moment to moment. One can be very successful in the worldly sense of the word and have all the wealth of the world and still feel impoverished, empty inside. It is an inner thing. Our experience will show that to seek wisdom and to serve others makes us truly happy. To seek fulfillment and inner joy by helping others is the key here. Nothing makes us happier than the feeling that we have been able to contribute to others' happiness.

Our leadership style is an expression of who we are. Leadership has been rightly defined as a journey into one's soul. So, one has to start very near—that is, to one's own self—to go very far in leading others. No wonder Confucius, the Chinese sage, believed that in order to become a great leader, we have to be a good person first. Building on what has been said earlier, business leaders would do well to focus more on self-development, self-awareness, and self-knowledge. When leaders go astray, it is almost always a case of failure of personal leadership or self-leadership.

Let's remember that the journey from success to significance (and from happiness to peace and harmony) is not only essential for personal mastery, it is also critical in developing and leading others.

Concluding Remarks

True happiness can never be pursued by a slavish devotion to one's selfish goals and wants. It is an inner thing that only comes when we have touched something deeper, something more profound within ourselves and within others. Abiding happiness can only ensue when we selflessly devote ourselves to a cause greater than ourselves, a cause that outlives us and outlasts us.

CHAPTER FOUR

LIVING OUR HIGHEST PURPOSE THROUGH THE GIFT OF PURE MOTIVATION

A story is told about a priest who was confronted by a soldier while he was walking down a road in pre-revolutionary Russia. The soldier, aiming his rifle at the priest, commanded, "Who are you? Where are you going?" Unfazed, the priest calmly replied, "How much do they pay you?" Somewhat surprised, the soldier responded, "Twenty-five kopecks a month." The priest paused, and in a deeply thoughtful manner said, "I have a proposal for you. I'll pay you fifty kopecks each month if you stop me here every day and challenge me to respond to those same two questions: Who are you? Where are you going?"[1]

~ A TRADITIONAL TALE

This is the true joy in life, the being used for a purpose recognized by yourself as a mighty one; the being thoroughly worn out before you are thrown on the scrap heap; the being a force of Nature instead of a feverish selfish little clod of ailments and grievances complaining that the world will not devote itself to making you happy.[2]

~ GEORGE BERNARD SHAW

Meaning, Fulfillment, and the Gift of Pure Motivation

This chapter is broadly divided into two sections. The first section addresses the perennial human quest for meaning, purpose, and fulfillment. It starts with the fundamental question "who am I?" as a prelude to discovering meaning and significance in life. After all, we cannot find our purpose in life without first knowing who we really are. More importantly, in order to arrive somewhere, one has to know precisely about one's current position. Analogically, in order to use a map, the first thing we need to know is where we are. The opening story underscores the importance of self-knowledge in our search for self-fulfillment. This section draws upon the ideas of Maslow, Frankl, and Csikszentmihalyi—the three paragons of human potential—to inform the search for meaning and fulfillment.

The second section deals with the first gift of highly fulfilled people—the gift of pure motivation. This gift teaches us that, before every action, we should check (mentally) our motivation for the action. Pure motivation signifies that whatever we do, our intention behind every action should be motivated by desire to help, to benefit others without expecting anything in return. If we are helping others in order to benefit ourselves—as means to our end, then it becomes a business "transaction" and our motivation ceases to be pure.

The Quest for Meaning and Fulfillment

We are born to be fulfilled. That's how nature intends us all to be. Each of us has a very unique role to play and a distinctive mission to accomplish. That is our silent pact with the universe. Unless we fulfill this purpose, this mission, we are not given to experience the deepest joy of fulfillment that life has to offer, no matter how successful, rich, or famous we may be. Fulfillment is an inner glow, an inner peace that is attained when we serve the universe joyfully, diligently, and selflessly. When we serve the universe and its creation selflessly, in return it shares its bounties with us abundantly. But we have to first realize our utter selflessness—our nothingness.

> ### Story Time: "I am Nothing!"
>
> At a court banquet, everyone was sitting according to their rank, waiting for the king to appear. A simply dressed man came in and took a seat higher than everyone else. The prime minister demanded that he identify himself.
> "Are you the adviser of a great king?"
> "No, I rank above a royal adviser."
> "Are you a prime minister?"
> "No, higher than a prime minister."
> "Are you a king in disguise?"
> "No, my rank is higher than a king."
> "Then you must be some saint."
> "No, I am above that."
> "Then you must be God," the prime minister said sarcastically. "There is nothing higher than God!" he shouted.
> The stranger replied calmly, "I am nothing!"[3]

The foregoing story splendidly illustrates that only those who have achieved a certain measure of humility are able to sit at an elevated position—symbolically speaking—where they can view the greater common good—the well-being of all beings—clearly. It is all about orientation and a viewpoint. Otherwise, the ulterior self-motive will always be lurking behind every act of overt kindness. And every step toward self-centeredness is a step away from self-fulfillment. All overt and covert acts of ostentatious kindness may provide us temporary self-satisfaction but they are unable to sooth our spirit with deep fulfillment in the long run. Only when our actions are infused with pure motivation are our feet securely planted on the path that leads to lasting inner peace, joy, and fulfillment.

The Quest for Self-Knowledge
The quest for self-knowledge and self-fulfillment is as old as civilization. In the Western philosophical tradition, Greeks were the first thinkers to

pursue these values in a systematic manner. Socrates' popular dictum "know thyself" is familiar to all of us, and Plato's well-known refrain that "an unexamined life is not worth living" is also a great place to begin our quest for self-knowledge. In the Eastern tradition, this quest dates back at least to the time of the Upanishads and the Bhagavad Gita and the writings of the Buddha and Lao Tzu. The Upanishads represent the earliest stirrings of human spirit to understand the self (the truth of our self) and its relation to the ultimate reality (the truth of the universe). The Bhagavad Gita contains the essence of *Vedas* (the Books of Knowledge) and teaches the paths of selfless action *(Karma Yoga)* and devotion as preparation to the sublime path of self-knowledge. In chapter eight, which discusses the gift of selfless service, we will explore the doctrine of *Karma Yoga* as a means to selfless service and as the alchemy of sagehood. The Buddha's teachings on mindfulness and Lao Tzu's exhortation for living in harmony with the *Tao* are examples of humanity's early attempts to live a life of self-awareness, meaningfulness, and mastery. The gift of presence will draw upon the practice of mindfulness.

In the late 19th and early 20th centuries, these questions preoccupied several psychologists and existential philosophers such as Nietzsche, Adler, Satre, and Camus. Likewise, several humanistic psychologists, such as Carl Jung (1875–1961), Carl Rogers (1902–1987), Abraham Maslow (1908–1970), Rollo May (1909–1994), Erich Fromm (1900–1980), Roberto Assagioli (1888–1974), Fritz Perls (1893–1970), and Viktor Frankl (1905–1997), have variously explored the question of self-actualization and personal meaning, fulfillment, and mastery. More recently, Seligman and Csikszentmihalyi pioneered positive psychology, which is the systematic study of the human strengths and virtues that make human life more fulfilling.

By critical acclaim, the two most fundamental questions we can ask are "Who am I?" and "What am I doing here?" These two questions are incorporated in the question "What is the purpose of my life?"

Why Bother to Know Our Self?

The reader may be wondering at this stage why one should even bother to know oneself or musing, "Don't I already know myself?" What is the practical utility of these questions after all? Broadly speaking, there are two types of people: those who know their purpose and those who do not yet know their purpose. Sooner or later, we all face life situations that challenge us to ask these questions and prod us to reflect on our true significance of life.

It is vital to address these questions at the outset since everything that truly matters in life depends on our response to these two fundamental questions. Without knowing oneself, it seems, one cannot figure out one's purpose in life—for how can we find out our purpose in life without first knowing who we really are? Thus, we may say that the very first purpose of life is to know oneself. Almost 2,600 years ago, Socrates framed it succinctly as "know thyself" (*gnothi seauton*). The intervening 26 centuries have not attenuated the gravity of this question. It is amazing, or shall we say a bit ironic, to ponder the fact that with our entire information deluge and material progress, we have not yet been able to satisfactorily address this fundamental point. Could it be that the real answer to the enigmatic question "Who am I?" lies within ourselves and not outside?!

Socrates, however, did not care to elaborate precisely on how to go about this search. One common pitfall here is to take Socrates' injunction to know thyself to mean to know oneself intellectually or emotionally. Those in the know have repeatedly pointed out that one has to know oneself at the experiential level—in the very depth of one's being, exactly as one really is, with diligence and without any masks whatsoever. And this requires some serious work on oneself that calls for self-insight, sincerity, courage, patience, and discernment. It seems that the faculty of self-awareness serves as both the cause and effect of self-knowledge. Self-knowledge is borne of self-reflection and blossoms as a certain unmistakable quality of self-awareness that accompanies and pervades everything one does—a sort of glow that illuminates all our activities. This condition is often referred to as the faculty of mindfulness.

One may ask at this stage, know oneself at what level—at the body/physical level or at the mind/intellectual level? Or is there something more lurking behind these intuitively obvious categories? In our common usage, we tend to refer to these as "my body," "my mind," and "my intellect."

We do not say "I-body," "I-mind," "I-intellect." This is not just a linguistic contrivance or convenience but a fundamental distinction that goes to the very root of who we are. To refer to our body as "my" body and our mind as "my" mind is to say that I am not my body nor my mind. For example, we are used to saying "my body is strong/weak" or "my mind is sharp/clear," *et cetera*. In other words, "I" and "my body/mind" are two separate things. After all, I "experience" my body and mind. It is a fundamental law that "I am different from whatever I experience."

This intuiting of separation between "I" and my "body-mind-senses" apparatus is sometimes referred to as the awareness of "I-Amness," the awareness of our innermost being or presence. Come to think of it, this feeling of "I-Amness" is our only true capital. Everything else is either borrowed or construed knowledge/information. That we exist is the only thing we know beyond any shadow of doubt, for no one can deny one's own existence. To say that "I do not exist' is illogical for it presumes that *I had to exist* in order to claim that *I do not exist!* So this awareness reverses the Cartesian logic of "I think, therefore I am": it is not that "I think therefore I am"; rather, "I am, therefore I think!" This is the most essential point to grasp in approaching the question "who am I." It is also a master key that opens the door to the abode of meaning and fulfillment.

Mindful Moments: Searching for Our Sweet Spot!

1. What are my most vital strengths?
2. What am I most naturally good at? What are my innate gifts?
3. What activity gives the fullest expression to my innate strengths or gifts?
4. How often do I feel a sense of "Joy" during the day?
5. What will I continue doing if I win a lottery?
6. What would I like to be known for, my most significant contribution, my legacy?

It is important to bear in mind that our search has two aspects, as it were: internal and external. At one level, the search for our true nature has to take place *within,* that is, in the innermost recesses of our soul. This is the "seeking" part of our search. Yet, at another level, we have to engage ourselves fully in the humdrum of life *without,* armed now with self-knowledge and awareness. This is the "sharing" part of our search. Thus, the two words that capture the essence of our quest and speak admirably of our purpose of life are *seeking* and *serving.* By seeking perennially who we truly are and serving selflessly, we may redeem our existence and be fulfilled.

Self-Actualization, Peak Experience, and Being-Values[4]

As a celebrated prophet of human potential, Maslow believed that the realization of one's total potential (variously described as the need for self-actualization or self-realization) to be the ultimate goal of all humankind. He presented a taxonomy of five types of needs, starting with physical needs and culminating in the need for self-actualization. In his later research, Maslow enlarged the list of basic needs to include a still higher category of needs, called "metaneeds." He called the ultimate values sought by self-actualizing people as "being-values" or "B-values." These values were mentioned again and again in his research by self-actualizing people or by other people to describe their peak experience. According to Maslow, these are comprised of the following attributes: wholeness, perfection, completion, justice, aliveness, richness, simplicity, beauty, goodness, uniqueness, effortlessness, playfulness, truth, honesty, self-sufficiency, and meaningfulness.

Later, Maslow reclassified needs into D-Needs and B-Needs, with their correlates, deficiency motivation and growth motivation. The physiological, security, belonging, and esteemed needs may be termed as deficiency needs (D-needs) since they are activated by deficiency. Self-actualization needs and the B-needs may be called growth needs since they represent not so much of a deficiency as an unfolding of all those wonderful possibilities that lie deep within each human being, waiting to express themselves. Toward the end of his life, Maslow went beyond even self-actualization. He considered self-transcendence to be our deepest need and highest aspiration.

What holds us back from achieving true greatness? Like a true prophet of human potential, Maslow believed that we have unused and undeveloped capacities. Now, why would these possibilities, present in all, actualize themselves in only a few? Maslow wrestled with the question all his life. One impediment to growth he considered the "fear of one's own greatness" or "running away from one's own best talents"[5]:

> I have found it easy enough to demonstrate this to my students simply by asking, "Which of you in this class hopes to write the great American novel, or to be a Senator, or Governor, or President? Who wants to be Secretary General of the United Nations? Or a great composer? Who aspires to be a saint, like Schweitzer, perhaps? Who among you will be a great leader?" Generally, everybody starts giggling, blushing, and squirming until I ask, "If not you, then who else?" And in this same way, as I push my graduate students toward these higher levels of aspiration, I'll say, "What great book are you now secretly planning to write?"[6]

The easiest way to boost self-esteem, according to Maslow, is to become a part of something important, something bigger that transcends narrow personal limitations. Maslow held that all self-actualizing people have a cause they believe in, a vocation they are devoted to. "Self-actualizing people are, without one single exception, involved in a cause outside their own skin, in something outside of themselves. ... When they say, 'my work,' they mean their mission in life."[7]

Just having an important task is not enough: the self-actualizing person must also do it well. Substandard work is not a good path to self-actualization. Self-actualization means working to do the thing well that one wants to do. One must strive to be the very best in whatever one undertakes. Maslow considered this striving to be the best one is capable of becoming the *sine qua non* of human happiness.

In Buddhist literature, great emphasis is placed on choosing the right kind of work. One of the eight components of righteous living in Buddhism is called "right livelihood"—the kind of livelihood that fosters self-fulfillment, inner peace, and contentment. Maslow also believed that it is difficult to conceive of a feeling of satisfaction or self-pride if one were doing work that is bogus or shoddy.

It must be noted that self-actualization, according to Maslow, is not a matter of one great stride. Rather, it is a matter of degrees, little victories won and accumulated one by one over time. Self-mastery assumes self-understanding and self-knowledge. It also assumes a certain awareness of our true purpose in life. It requires hard work, patience, perseverance to stay the course. It also requires clear articulation of our aim in life. Without formulating our aim, we drift aimlessly amidst the sea of life, like a ship without rudder. Knowing who we are and what our purpose is, therefore, are the two fundamental questions that capture the essence of self-knowledge and personal meaning.

The Significance of Meaning in Life

What sustains us in the wake of life's toughest challenges? What keeps us from falling apart emotionally amidst life's most trying situations? What keeps us going in face of the inevitable suffering that life brings us through, such as illness, deprivation, and death? It is the knowledge, says Frankl, that "human life under any circumstances, never ceases to have a meaning and that this infinite meaning of life includes suffering or dying, privation and death."[8] Now, Frankl was no armchair psychologist—he was the survivor of four concentration camps! In his classic work titled *Man's Search for Meaning*, Frankl provides the inside story of a concentration camp and presents a concrete guide to support his unshakable view that "life holds a potential meaning under any conditions, even the most miserable ones."[9]

Could the trials and tribulations be seen as opportunities, as occasions life presents us with to help us discover and realize our true destiny, to fulfill our true purpose in life? Well, it depends upon how we approach them. Seen as occasions for self-growth and fulfillment, these challenges are opportunities that provide us the raw material to fashion the garment of our life. Taken with the disempowering "why me" attitude, however, they can dampen our spirit and stifle our soul. Frankl reminds us that "everything can be taken from a man but one thing: the last of human freedoms—to choose one's attitude in any given set of circumstances, to choose one's own way."[10]

When we cannot change the situation, "we are challenged to change ourselves!" And "it is this spiritual freedom—which cannot be taken away—that makes life meaningful and purposeful."[11] Frankl concludes that "there is nothing in the world, I venture to say, that would so effectively help one to survive even the worst conditions as the knowledge that there is a meaning in one's life."[12] He who has a *why* to live for, said Nietzsche, can bear almost any *how*.

Frankl finds existential vacuum—this feeling of utter meaninglessness—to be widespread in modern times and considers it to be the root cause of depression, aggression, and addiction in the modern Western society. For Frankl, every act of responsibility is an act of self-actualization. This emphasis on personal responsibility forms the very essence of Frankl's philosophy and ethical imperative: "Live as if you were living for the second time and had acted as wrongly the first time as you are about to act now."[13] He further clarifies: "Ultimately, man should not ask what the meaning of his life is, but rather he must recognize that it is he who is asked."[14] In the final reckoning, we are not in the pursuit of happiness but rather "in search of a reason to be happy"—aspiring to be worthy of our happiness.

Living Our Highest Purpose in Life

Our highest purpose is the true embodiment of who we are at the very core of our being. It is the most authentic expression of our innermost nature, our true self. We are at our creative best when we are in tune with our highest self. It represents our inner truth that seeks expression through myriad activities as life is happening to us. In Sanskrit, this truth of our innermost being is expressed by the word *svadharma*—one's deepest, innermost nature. In the Bhagavad Gita, the most revered Hindu scripture, we are told, "Better one's own dharma, however imperfect, than the dharma of another perfectly performed." Indian sage Ramana Maharishi said, "Be as you are." In the same vein, the great Jewish philosopher Martin Buber, in his book *Tales of Hasidism,* quotes Rabbi Zusya: "In the coming world, they will not ask me, 'Why were you not Moses?' They will ask me, 'Why were you not Zusya?'"[15]

These examples tell us that only by being true to our real self can we fulfill our destiny, our true purpose in life. We cannot have fulfillment any other way. We may not be always aware of our true purpose, but it is always there, ready to sustain us through the toughest challenges of our life. Only by discovering our unique gifts and talents can we hope to polish them and share them with our fellow beings.

How can we discover our true purpose in life that gives value and meaning to our existence? There is no direct path or ready-made answer to this vital question. There is no sure map or formula that can lead us to our life's true purpose. Nor can it be handed over to us by someone else. Besides, nobody can spare us the journey, the alchemic process of self-discovery and transformation, leading to the unfolding and fulfillment of this purpose.

Got Flow?

Csikszentmihalyi has been studying the psychology of optimal experiences, that is, flow, in various settings for the past 35 years.[16] *Flow* refers to a state of total immersion, effortless concentration, and rapt enjoyment in an activity in which one loses any sense of space, time, and self. According to Csikszentmihalyi, "Flow represents a state where skills required to perform a particular task match evenly with the challenges presented by the task." He explains,

> The metaphor of "flow" is one that many people have used to describe the sense of effortless action they feel in moments that stand our as the best in their lives. Athletes refer to it as "being in the zone," religious mystics as being in "ecstasy," artist and musicians as aesthetic rapture. Athletes, mystics, and artists do very different things when they reach flow, yet their descriptions of the experience are remarkably similar.[17]

Flow involves "being completely involved in an activity for its own sake. The ego falls away. Time flies. Every action, movement, and thought follows inevitably from the previous one, like playing jazz. Your whole being is involved, and you're using your skills to the utmost."[18]

Csikszentmihalyi identifies the following key elements accompanying flow:

1. A challenging activity that requires skills.
2. The merging of action and awareness.
3. Clear goals and immediate feedback.
4. Concentration on the task at hand.
5. The paradox of control.
6. The loss of self-consciousness.
7. Transformation of the sense of time.[19]

Life Founded on Purpose

Once we have found our highest purpose, it can stay in the background, as a substratum, a *raison d'être* for everything we do or undertake. The following story exemplifies this concept nicely:

Dividing 17 Horses among Three Children: The Case of the 18th Horse!

A father left a large inheritance of land, money, gold, and 17 horses to be divided as 1/2, 1/3, 1/9 among three children. Everything else got divided easily but they were confused how to divide the horses. In desperation, they contacted an old friend of their father. He came riding on his horse and offered to add his to the herd, to make the total=18 in all. Now they could easily divide it in 1/2, 1/3, 1/9, as (9+6+2) = 17. The friend still had his horse.[20]

Our true purpose in life is like the 18th horse in the story, without which life has no meaning.

Life presents itself to us as a series of challenges. With self-knowledge and the courage to be, we can rise to meet these challenges squarely. "The meaning of life," said Ouspensky, "is in eternal search. And only in that search can we find something truly new."[21] By undertaking this search, we plant our feet firmly on the path that leads to the full blooming of our potential, to self-fulfillment—the fulfillment of our true purpose and mission in life.

The Gift of Pure Motivation

Simply see that you are at the center of the universe, and
accept all things and beings as parts of your infinite body.
When you perceive that an act done to another is done
to yourself, you have understood the great truth.[22]
~ LAO TZU

Where Has the Pure Motivation Gone? A Personal Experience

Growing up in a small town in North India, I would pass by a doctor's office everyday on my way to high school. This doctor seemed to be the only physician in our town and hence had a very busy practice.

Ours was one large joint family with all three generations living happily under one roof. One day when I came back from school, I found out that my grandmother had just had a stroke. She must have been around 85 then and was in relatively good health. There she lay unconscious with everyone gathered around her bed. As soon as I walked in, my maternal uncle asked me to hurry and get the doctor. In India, it is not uncommon for a doctor to come to people's homes for an extra fee to prescribe medicine. I rushed to doctor's office and requested him to come with me to our house right away. Within minutes, I found myself walking beside the doctor on the way to our house, carrying his brief case.

(continued on next page)

(continued from previous page)

As soon as we walked in, everybody made room for the doctor to examine my grandma. The doctor just took one look at her and said, "She is gone!" She was not breathing, and there was no pulse. No further diagnosis was necessary. As I walked back with the doctor to his office, there was a grave silence between both of us. Before I bade him good bye, he turned around and said, "And do not forget to send my fee."

I was stunned!

As I walked back to my home, thoughts kept rushing through my disturbed mind: Is that all he had to say about my grandma? We were going to send him his fee anyway; why did he have to remind me about this? He could have also said, "I am so sorry" or something like that. No compassion? What happened to the Hippocratic Oath?

This was my first exposure to the importance and necessity of practicing pure motivation in everything we do and under all circumstances. Otherwise, one may be outwardly engaged in a noble profession and still be internally engaged in a self-centered mission.

At every turn, our life provides us opportunities for practicing both pure and impure motivation in what we do. When we act from the stance of "what is in it for me," we are operating from an impure motivation. And when we act with a view to benefit others, to help others, our motivation is considered pure and unselfish—regardless of what we do and its outcome.

The Importance of Practicing Pure Motivation

Since all conscious behavior has a motive, we begin at the beginning, namely, with the gift of pure motivation. Let's take two examples to illustrate the importance of pure motivation. In the first example, a wealthy man is going to a bank to deposit a large sum of cash. He is stopped by a fugitive in the parking lot and is forced to hand over the cash. During the fight, the fugitive stabs the rich man and runs away with cash. The rich man dies immediately. In the second case, a surgeon is preparing to perform open heart surgery on a patient. The surgeon also uses a knife to operate upon the patient. Unfortunately, the patient dies during the operation. In both examples, someone ends up dying; the outcome is the same, yet the fugitive and the surgeon were acting from two entirely different motives. In the first case, the intention was to harm, whereas in the second case, the intention was obviously to help. So the purity of motivation makes all the difference in finding significance in life. Whereas the success paradigm may argue that ends justify means, significance is about means justifying means and ends justifying ends.

Modern science tells us that from the standpoint of our brain activity there is no difference between hitting a person and merely thinking about the act. Our brain's limbic system, the part of our brain that is responsible for controlling motor function, releases all the muscle energy that would be required to actually hit someone just by thinking about it. Our brain just cannot tell the difference between thinking about hitting someone and actually doing it! However, based on the above observation, the Buddha would add that if we have been thinking about hitting someone, its effect on our happiness will be similar to actually hitting someone.

This works both ways, that is, for bad intentions as well as good intentions. Suppose you are getting off the freeway and you see a poor person asking for some spare change for lunch. As soon as you try to reach for your wallet to help this person, the light turns green and you have to go quickly, without being able to give this person any money. Gurdjieff, a Russian mystic, comments that since consciousness is interconnected, someone will stop by later and help this person. By your mere intention to help this person, you have triggered a series of events in the universe, so to speak, that would finally result in someone actually helping this person with money for lunch. This is how powerful our intentions are.

Therefore our intentions are very important. When we act from the pure intention of helping someone, we are in fact helping the universe. The wisdom traditions have known this secret all along, as expressed in the following set of refrains:

> ## Mindful Moments: Your Thoughts Control Your Destiny!
>
> Watch your thoughts; they become words.
> Watch your words; they become actions.
> Watch your actions; they become habits.
> Watch your habits; they become your character.
> Watch your character; it becomes your destiny.[23]

The Best Rationale for Practicing Pure Motivation

The operation of the law of *Karma* perhaps presents the best rationale for practicing the gift of pure motivation. The moment we commit to any action, the universal laws take over and process it according its proper motivation. In its simplistic form, this dynamic is generally presented as the law of action and reaction—or popularly as "what goes around comes around"—yet it is a highly developed principle of self-purification designed to put the seeker right on the path that leads to self-realization. When our actions are dedicated to a higher principle or a higher being, instead of being motivated by mere personal gain, they act as a purifying force to enable us to work selflessly for the benefit of all beings. This, in turn, prepares the heart to receive—and the mind to understand—the subtler spiritual teachings that are the beyond the ken of an acquisitive mind that is always busy with the business of "what is in it for me."

Indian philosophy takes the doctrine of *Karma* to its utmost development where it is seen as a highly sophisticated spiritual practice called *Karma Yoga*. *Karma Yoga* emphasizes proper action and proper attitude toward action. Under this scheme, the propriety of an action is not measured according to its capacity for giving material gain—which is incidental anyway—but according to its capacity for harnessing inner growth. It is a matter of common experience that the attitude with which an action is performed can change the quality of our action as well as the quality of our response to the outcome of an action. Therefore, attitude is at least as important as the action itself—all the more reason to practice pure motivation!

Pure Motivation: What Is in It for Me?!

The reader must have realized by now that the moment we ask the question "what is in it for me," our motivation ceases to be pure! As stated earlier, the whole idea about the practice of pure motivation is to act with the intention of helping others without expecting anything in return. This goes against our perennial conditioning that all actions are motivated by some desire to benefit the doer. Otherwise, why would someone act in the first place?

Many spiritual traditions of the world provide ample guidance in this regard. By and large, they urge us to dedicate all our actions to a higher being or principle. For example, the Bhagavad Gita teaches the gospel of selfless action in an oft-quoted verse as follows:

> Your right is to work only,
> But never to its fruits;
> Let not the fruits of action be your motive,
> Nor let your attachment be to inaction.[24]

The Gita urges us to do all actions selflessly *(nishkaama karma)* for the unification *(lokasamgraha)* and for the well-being of all beings *(sarvabhutahitae)* without anxiety about the outcome of our actions. It further exhorts us to dedicate the fruits of our actions to the divine. Even if we take the spiritual import of this teaching out of the picture, it still remains a highly pragmatic teaching to live by. For when we focus too intently on the results of our actions, we are not able to give our best to the task at hand. The following story admirably sums up the practical wisdom of this teaching:

Alas! It takes us longer to learn when we are too much obsessed with speed

Once, a young student approached a renowned piano teacher for lessons. He came from a far off country to learn the art of piano from this famous teacher. After a couple of weeks, the student asked the teacher how long it will take him to master the art of piano. The teacher replied, "Good 4–5 years." "But I have an ailing parent back home to take care of," explained the student. "How long will it take in this case for me to finish my lessons?" The teacher replied, "10 years." "You do not understand," objected the student, "I really have to finish my lessons as quickly as possible so I can go back and look after my ailing father and his business." "In that case, 20 years!" answered the teacher.

The student was quite perplexed. He wondered how inconsiderate of the teacher to keep on doubling the time required every time he had expressed some new urgency to finish quickly.

He asked the teacher the reason why.

"Because, when you are more focused on finishing lessons quickly—the results—than the lessons, you take much longer to learn!" replied the teacher calmly.[25]

If we reflect deeply about our actions, we realize that we do not really have any control over the results of our actions anyway. So a disinterested, detached action is all we can aspire to. Viewed in this light, the Gita presents a scientifically advanced and psychologically practical teaching of the highest order.

Other spiritual traditions also emphasize the virtue of dedicating our work to a higher power. For example, the great German composer, J.S. Bach, treated all his compositions as offerings to God. He called most of his studies for the keyboard "exercises for the spirit." He even named one of his compositions "A Musical Offering." It is quite natural for writers and artists to feel this way since most of them consider their finest creations to be divinely inspired, with the artist acting only as a mediating instrument in divine hands. Igor Stravinsky is reported to have said this of his finest creation: "I had only my ear to help me. I heard and I wrote what I heard. I am the vessel through which *The Rite of Spring* passed."

Below is an excerpt from the handwritten portion of Leo Tolstoy's will that he wrote 20 years before his death. In this document, he reflects upon his life work as follows:

> Furthermore, and in particular, I ask all people near and far not to praise me. (I know they will do so because they have done so in my lifetime in the most unseemly way.) But if they want to study my writings, let them look carefully at those passages in them in which I know the power of God spoke through me, and make use of them for their own lives. *There have been times when I felt I was becoming the bearer of God's will* [emphasis added].[26]

Tolstoy admits that, despite his acutely perceived shortcomings, the divine inspiration has sometimes passed through him, and that those have been "the happiest moments of [his] life." When our work becomes an offering, and we are able to set our little self aside to enable the higher Self to take over, we touch the depths of real existence where we experience a glimpse of true happiness in a most unexpected way. When we allow the divine inspiration to operate through us in this manner, we become faithful instruments in the hands of God—a vessel through which our creative undertakings pass. And we let ourselves be fashioned by the Divine Will, a higher creative principle in which all actions are at best impersonal and anonymous. We become in tune with the infinite.

Chinese sage Lao Tzu captures this state—a state that represents action in inaction—through two characters, *wu-wei*. All masters of poetry as well as the martial arts know this very well.

Concluding Story and Remarks

The Difference between the Window Glass and the Mirror Glass

Once a rich and very stingy man came to his rabbi to ask for a special blessing. The rabbi sat and talked with him for a while and then, all of a sudden, took the man's hand and brought him to the window.

"Tell me what do you see?" asked the rabbi.

The man answered, "I see people out on the street."

The rabbi brought him a mirror. "Now what do you see?" he asked.

"Now I see myself," the man replied.

The rabbi said, "Now let me explain the meaning of my actions. Both the window and the mirror are made of glass. The window is a clear glass but the mirror has a layer of silver on it. When you look through clear glass you can see people, but when you cover it with silver, you no longer see other people but only see yourself."[27]

The foregoing story has great implications for leaders. A wise person, well-versed in the ways of the life and leadership, once told me, "When you are going up—in an organizational hierarchy—be nice to people around you. You will surely meet them when you will be coming down." Modesty is probably the most important leadership quality that is honored more in breach than in observance in modern leaders. Organizational arrogance is the most fatal flaw that soon leads to cluelessness and triggers derailment of leaders. It is very easy to feel insulated and indulge in ego trips. One should always be on one's guard against such tendencies.

Outpourings of a Heart Gladdened with Gratitude

I am grateful ...

For this wonderful gift of precious human birth,
  for being blessed with good health and a kind, generous heart.
For my parents who were kind, loving, and spiritually-inclined.
For my teachers in life, in history, and in spirit,
  who sowed in my mind the seeds of insatiable curiosity
    about things inspired, eternal, and sublime!

For sparing me from the pangs of acute poverty and pain,
  with enough by way of food, clothing, and shelter;
But not too much to make me proud and vain,
  blissfully oblivious to life's real purpose and aim!

For sparing me from the servitude of transient fame,
  from trivial pursuits and shifting aims,
    from dizzy dignities, petty jealousies, and success tame.
Instead gracing me with the abiding treasure of taste sublime,
  for the finest in music, literature, and philosophy prime.

For granting me best opportunities to study, learn, and travel.
For the gift of noble work that I daily cherish and marvel!

For my family, and my children, and my friends
  who, despite my incongruities and idiosyncrasies,
    continue to bear with me kindly, with some amends.

Though at times I may not have acted in ways worthy of Thy Grace,
  yet You have always showered your blessings beyond trace,
    forgiving my transgressions like a kind parent and a loving sage.

Above all, I am deeply grateful for being blessed
  with an unquenchable yearning for learning,
    for seeking and sharing stories of Thy Glory!

Sitting here in my study, I am gratefully humbled to muse:
  "O, Radiant One! What did I do to deserve all this?"
    What did I do to deserve all this?!

        I seek Thy blessings till the end of my days,
        To serve Thy creation in innumerable ways!

CHAPTER FIVE

THE GIFT OF GRATITUDE

Many things threaten life, which is even more
Ephemeral than a bubble of water full of air.
How amazing is the opportunity to exhale
After inhaling and to awake from sleep.[1]

~ NAGARJUNA

If the only prayer you said in your whole life was, "thank you,"
that would suffice.

~ MEISTER ECKHART

Everything is a loan that is given as a gift.[2]

~ YAFFA LEIBOWITZ

There is no greater difference between people than between
grateful and ungrateful people.

~ R.H. BLYTH

For each new morning with its light,
For rest and shelter of the night,
For health and food, for love and friends,
For everything Thy goodness sends,
Father in heaven, we thank Thee.

~ RALPH WALDO EMERSON

We can only be said to be alive in those moments when our hearts
are conscious of our treasures.

~ THORNTON WILDER

Why Be Grateful?

Reflect on your present blessings, of which every man has many,
not on your past misfortunes, of which all men have some.

~ CHARLES DICKENS

At the deepest existential level, the gift of gratitude is our resounding tribute to the universe for all its anonymous blessings. At the interpersonal level, the gift of gratitude springs from a deep realization that our whole life depends on the kindness of others. These others could be our parents, our teachers, our friends, and other people who make our daily life possible. From dawn to dusk, almost everything we do or experience depends upon the anonymous efforts of countless people participating in a highly interdependent dance of life. In sum, all of the things that we are privileged to enjoy in our lives depend upon the kindness of others. By acknowledging and appreciating their kindness, we redeem our share in the mutual maintenance of our communal existence.

> ### *Blessedness of Gratitude!*
>
> *Gratitude unlocks the fullness of life. It turns what we have into enough, and more. It turns denial into acceptance, chaos to order, confusion to clarity. It can turn a meal into a feast, a house into a home, a stranger into a friend. Gratitude makes sense of our past, brings peace for today, and creates a vision for tomorrow.*
>
> ~ Melodie Beattie

The Parent of All Virtues!

Gratitude is not only the greatest of the
virtues but the parent of all others.
~ CICERO

Gratitude, rightly practiced, can change our orientation toward life beyond belief. It can help us become happier and more content. As you start recognizing the positive that already exists in your life, you will notice an inner shift reflected in your outer reality. You will find yourself bumping into abundance in situations and places where you least expected it or where you had previously felt a sense of lack in your life. This shift from scarcity to abundance will invariably create more opportunities to be grateful for and will slowly bring a more positive orientation to life's overall journey.

Taking Gifts for Granted

It is a common human tendency to take life's gifts for granted. In the insightful words of Huxley, "Most human beings have an almost infinite capacity for taking things for granted." We do not seem to realize how much we would crave the things we now have if we did not have them to begin with, and how much we would miss what we now have if we were to lose it—hence the well-worn cliché, "count your blessings." The following Hasidic story splendidly portrays the art of unconditional gratitude.

Story Time: Art of Thanking God When Bad Things Happen to Us?

Once Shmelke of Nikolsburg asked Dov Baer of Mezritch to explain the Talmudic commandment that we should praise God for evil as much as we praise him for good. Dov Baer said, "Go to the house of study and ask my student Zussya." Shmelke went to the house of study and found Zussya emaciated, filthy, clothed in rags. Shmelke asked, "How can we praise God for evil as much as we praise him for good?" "I can't tell you," said Zussya, "because nothing bad has ever happened to me."[3]

What Is Gratitude?

Put simply, gratitude is the art of noticing and appreciating our gifts. According to Robert Emmons of the University of California at Davis and Michael McCollough of Southern Methodist University in Dallas,

Texas, "The word *gratitude* is derived from a Latin root gratia, meaning grace, graciousness, or gratefulness."[4] Dr. Alex Wood, a postgraduate researcher in the Department of Psychology, University of Warwick, defines gratitude as "a life orientation towards noticing and appreciating the positive in the world." Researchers in the field of positive psychology have found that simple acts of gratitude practiced on a regular basis act as "happiness boosters" that contribute significantly to improved health and happiness.

Gratitude Boosts Well-Being

Emmons and McCullough, two pioneers in the field of gratitude research, have attempted to empirically test the popular assumptions regarding the effects of "grateful outlook" on psychological and physical well-being. Their initial studies indicate that gratitude plays some role in a person's sense of emotional, psychological, and social well-being. They also cite a 1998 Gallup survey of American teen and adults, according to which 90% of respondents indicated that expressing gratitude helped them to feel "extremely happy" or "somewhat happy." According to their findings, people who feel grateful are also more likely to feel loved. They also noted that gratitude promotes a positive cycle of reciprocal kindness among people. Grateful people are happier, less depressed, less stressed, and more satisfied with their lives and interpersonal relationships.[5]

Steven Toepfer of Kent State also found that expressing gratitude can improve levels of happiness and enhance quality of life. Toepfer enlisted students from different courses to write letters expressing deep sense of gratitude to people who have positively impacted their lives. The students were asked to write one letter every two weeks over a six-week period. After each letter, students completed a survey to gauge their moods, satisfaction with life, and feelings of gratitude and happiness. Toepfer reported, "I saw their happiness increase after each letter, meaning the more they wrote the better they felt."[6] Seventy five percent of the students said they intended to continue to write similar letters even after the study was completed. This is an excellent testimony to the age-old wisdom that "gratitude is double happiness because it blesses both the giver and the receiver."

Lyubomirsky, a psychologist at the University of California, Riverside, in her book *The How of Happiness: A Scientific Approach to Getting the Life You Want*, admirably presents "what the scientists currently understand about the causes and potential for abiding well-being."[7] She states that 50% of happiness is determined by genetics, about 10% by things pursued in the pursuit of happiness, while the remaining 40% is determined by deliberate habits, behaviors, and intentional activities such as expressing gratitude, practicing kindness, learning to forgive, and cultivating optimism.[8] Addressing the role of gratitude in happiness, Lyubomirsky observed, "The expression of gratitude is a kind of metastrategy for achieving happiness.... It is wonder; it is appreciation;... it is fathoming abundance; it is thanking someone in your life; it is thanking God; it is 'counting blessings.'"[9]

Counting Our Blessings

Let's take stock of our human endowments and blessings. For the sake of simplicity, we can divide our gratitude into three types of blessings:

1. Gratitude for the precious human birth.
2. Gratitude for the gift of wondrous nature.
3. Gratitude for the kindness of others.

Gratitude for the Precious Human Birth

To be born as a human being is a rare blessing. We seldom realize the precious rarity of our human status that is full of unique freedoms and fortunes. We mostly take it for granted as a matter of course, and live as if it is going to last forever. We are so dazed with the humdrum of life and so lost in the trivial pursuits that we tend to overlook the infinite preciousness and precariousness of our existence. Rarely does it occur to us that human birth is very difficult to get and very easy to lose.

The following Buddhist tale underscores the extreme rarity and supreme preciousness of human birth.

A Buddhist Parable on Human Condition (Blind Turtle)

A story is told in a Buddhist scripture of a blind turtle who dwells in the depths of a vast ocean, coming up for air only once every hundred years. On the surface of the same ocean floats a golden yoke. "When this turtle—which can come to the surface only once every hundred years—comes to the surface, can he put his head into the floating yoke even one time?" asked the Buddha.

The disciple answered, "It's impossible! Even if it took hundreds of millions of years or even millions of millions of years for the turtle to be able to put its face in the hole, it would be very hard to do it."

Then the Buddha said, "I know everyone thinks that it's impossible! But are you sure? To be born into this world as a human is infinitely more difficult than a blind turtle putting his face into the hole of the golden yoke!"

Then the Buddha put some dirt into his hand, opened his hand, and said, "The beings who have a human body are like the dirt in my hand, a very small amount, but the beings who fail to obtain a human body are like the huge ground. A human body is the hardest to come by. You monks need to listen and think about that."[10]

This is not an empty parable from the old Buddhist scriptures, but a true representation of the human condition. It is a clarion call to take stock of our situation.

Let's reflect on how rare our human birth is. As modern astronomy shows, the universe does not teem with life. It is a rare combination of conditions where life can emerge, and yet more unique to allow it to develop and reach the stage of self-aware human beings.

For every human form of life, there are billions of other life forms on this earth. Humans live on land that covers roughly 30% of the earth's surface, and the mighty oceans cover the remaining 70% of earth's surface. However, the creatures that live in the ocean vastly outnumber those on land. When we compare the number of humans to the overwhelming number of other species on earth, we come to understand why the human population is referred to as "the speck of sand on a fingernail."

According to reliable medical estimates, there are typically 40 million bacterial cells in a gram of soil and a million bacterial cells in a milliliter (gram) of fresh water. A few small colonies of ants can easily outnumber the entire population of human race on our globe! A *New York Times Magazine* article expressed it even more graphically: "There are more...intestinal bacteria in your colon at this moment than there are human beings who have ever lived."[11]

Our primary gratitude, therefore, is for the precious human birth which is very rare and full of fortunes and freedoms. *Vivekachudamani,* an eminent Hindu wisdom text of *Vedanta,* emphasizes that "among various living creatures on earth, being born as a human being is rare" *(jantunaam narajanma durlabham).* It then goes on to highlight the great rarity of three things—and only these three—the human birth, the desire for freedom from the limitation of conditioned existence, and the saving grace of sages.[12]

What makes our human birth so very unique and precious? According to the sages, it is our freedom of choice—a freedom attained only in the human condition—that leads to liberation from ignorance and limitations. The sages explain that, while all beings reap the fruits of their previous actions, humans initiate new actions, new *Karma.* If we look into the nest of a bird, we may find no change at all, even after thousands of years of nest-making. If that were the case with humans, we would still be living in caves. The supreme gifts of free will and creativity are uniquely human prerogatives. And these great gifts become available through a self-aware mind, which is only possible when one attains human status. And, yet, alas! it is so easily lost.

Human status—so hard to get, not so easy to be found;
My Gratitude is infinite, hard to recount!
When we fail to recognize it,
We verily fail to realize it!

Gratitude for the Wonderful Gift of the Human Body

Let's consider the wonderful gift of the human body, an information processing marvel. Werner Gitt, a German information scientist, concurs: "Without a doubt, the most complex information-processing system in existence is the human body. If we take all human information processes together, i.e. conscious ones (language, information-controlled, deliberate

The Wonder of the Marvelous Human Body

+ A pair of human feet contains 250,000 sweat glands.
+ We use 200 muscles to take one step.
+ The human nose can remember 50,000 different smells.
+ The human eye can detect more than 10,000,000 different colors!
+ The human body contains up to ten pints of blood; red blood cells are formed at a rate of 2 million per second.
+ The body requires 24 quarts of air per minute when walking; in a lifetime, the average person will breathe about 75 million gallons of air.
+ The human body has an automatic thermostat that regulates its heating and cooling systems at about 37°C (98.6°F).
+ It is believed that one human brain probably holds more electrical circuitry than all the computer systems of the world combined.
+ The spinal cord is less than two feet in length and is the same diameter as your index finger, yet the spinal cord contains over 10 billion nerve cells.
+ A human brain cell can hold five times as much information as the Encyclopedia Britannica.[13]

voluntary movements) and unconscious ones (information-controlled functions of the organs, hormone system), this involves the processing of 10^{24} bits daily. This astronomically high figure is higher by a factor of 1,000,000 (a million times greater) than the total human knowledge of 10^{18} bits stored in all the world's libraries."[14]

The rarity and preciousness of human birth cannot be established solely on the marvel of our physical body, however. Many animals have equally wonderful and versatile bodies. It is the gift of free will and resultant creativity that really seems to set humans apart from the rest of the species. It is self-knowledge and awareness that distinguish us among all creation. George Santayana once said that "even if the universe crushes me, I am still greater than the universe because I know that I am being crushed and the universe does not know that it is crushing me."

Human Status Is Rare: *Carpe Diem* (Seize the Day!)

To be born human is a rare blessing indeed.

What am I going to do with my life now that I have this precious and wonderful opportunity?

In the foregoing pages, the Buddhist parable of the blind turtle was presented to underscore the extreme rarity of human birth. Let's not treat the story of the turtle merely as an amusing little fable, but allow it to act as a vivid reminder of how rare our human status is. There are many good uses to which we can put our human life. When we are conscious of its true value, we will surely wish to choose the very best way to lead it. The Buddha also taught on many occasions that human life is only as long or as short as one breath because if we exhale, then do not inhale, we have already died and stepped over into a new lifetime.

How lucky we are to have this precious human life full of freedom and opportunity, freedom to practice goodness and opportunity to have access to the teachings on self-knowledge and personal transformation. Let's reflect on the rarity of being in a place and time and circumstance in which we are presented with real opportunities of developing self-wisdom and compassion.

The purpose of understanding the preciousness and rarity of our human life is to encourage us to realize the true meaning of our human existence and not squander it on trivial pursuits. We will be gravely remiss if we devalue this infinitely precious human birth and let it slide by for the accomplishment of transient goals and ephemeral desires. Our human life is fulfilled only if we apply it to obtain self-knowledge and attain supreme happiness of enlightened living, characterized by pure motivation, unconditional gratitude, altruistic generosity, complete harmlessness, selfless service, constant mindfulness, and total acceptance. This is truly seizing the day! Treasure yourself and cherish your privilege of precious human birth.

Thanksgiving Day! Now What Should I Do for the Other 364 Days?!

Celebrating Thanksgiving Day is one of the important cultural events in most Western countries. Like Mother's Day or Father's Day, such events remind us to formally express our gratitude for life in general and for our loved ones in particular. And certainly such celebrations bring their due share of satisfaction in their wake. However, in order to reap enduring benefits from the gift of gratitude, one has to develop an abiding orientation of gratefulness that extends itself in every aspect of our life, without waiting for some special events to sing our gratitude. Only then are we able to maximize the benefits of gratitude. The invitation here is to develop a disposition that notices and celebrates the positive gifts available to us at all the times.

The Great Art of Being Grateful!

A blind boy sat on the steps of a building with a hat by his feet. He held up a sign that said: "I am blind. Please help." There were only a few coins in the hat.

A man was walking by. He took a few coins from his pocket and dropped them into the hat. He then took the sign, turned it around, and wrote some words. He put the sign back so that everyone who walked by would see the new words.

Soon the hat began to fill up. A lot more people were giving money to the blind boy. That afternoon the man who had changed the sign came to see how things were.

The boy recognized his footsteps and asked, "Were you the one who changed my sign this morning? What did you write?"

The man said, "I only wrote the truth. I said what you said but in a different way."

What he had written was: "Today is a beautiful day and I cannot see it."

Do you think the first sign and the second sign were saying the same thing?

Of course both signs told people that the boy was blind, but the first sign simply said the boy was blind. The first sign simply told people to help by putting some money in the hat.

The second sign told people that they were able to enjoy the beauty of the day, but the boy could not enjoy it because he was blind.

The first sign simply said the boy was blind.

The second sign told people they were so lucky that they were not blind.

Should we be surprised that the second sign was more effective?

The moral of the story: *Acknowledge and be thankful for what you have. Be creative and innovative. Think differently and positively.*[15]

Gratitude for the Gift of Wondrous Nature

On the long list of things that we take for granted, the wondrous gift of nature can perhaps be placed next to taking our human status for granted. We feel that the world has always been there for us to experience. The beauty of a sunrise or sunset, the touch of soft grass on bare feet, the perfume of a flower that blooms in our backyard, the cool ambiance of a full moon—all these gifts go unnoticed or perhaps get lost amidst our daily economic grind of life. In the industrialized cities, we seldom really get to enjoy our kinship with Mother Nature. And yet, our biological clock is totally dependent on the biosphere that inhabits the space surrounding us.

When we wake up in the morning, the whole world lights up for us to experience all at once! The symphony of birds singing in natural harmony is ready to entertain us at no cost or effort on our part. The plants and trees are eager to generate the life-nourishing oxygen as a part of their natural contribution to the mutual maintenance of the universe. What a rare privilege to be able to experience this world!

We generally do not think in terms of paying back for the free gifts of sunshine and air that sustain our life. We cannot live even for a few minutes without the vital air we call breath. The sunshine sustains all plant life and food systems for us. When we develop a grateful disposition toward appreciating the dance of nature around us, we pay our rightful share for the services received generously and freely out of nature's bounty.

Gratitude for the Kindness of Others

At the interpersonal level, the gift of gratitude springs from a deep realization that our whole life depends on the kindness of others. In fact, the whole universe has to participate or collaborate to make our existence possible. With due reflection, an act as simple as having breakfast could be seen as a cosmic event! Just imagine all the steps, all the people, all the agencies involved in making our breakfast happen: the earth, the water, the sun, the air that nourished the grains, the farmers who harvested the crop, the cold storage facility, the baker, the trucker who transported it to the nearest supermarket, the bagger who joyfully bagged the groceries, and so forth. The whole universe seemed to have conspired just to make our breakfast happen! The same is true of all the things that we get to enjoy in our lives: they depend upon the kindness of others. By acknowledging and appreciating their kindness, we get to contribute our rightful share in the mutual celebration of our social and economic life.

In many wisdom traditions, it is believed that by our very birth we incur debt to our Mother Earth, to our parents, to our teachers, and to our common creator. We are indebted to the earth for giving us all kinds of food to sustain our lives and space to walk and live. We are indebted to our parents because they are responsible for our physical birth and our upbringing. (In one of his dialogues, the Buddha tells his disciples that even if one were to carry each of one's parents on both shoulders for the rest of one's life, still one will not be able to repay the debt one owes to one's parents.) We are indebted to our teachers, who are responsible for our psychological and spiritual birth. And we are indebted to our common creator for all known and unknown blessings.

Keeping a Gratitude Journal

Recent research on the salutary effects of gratitude upholds the practice of keeping a gratitude journal or appreciation journal on a daily basis. Lyubomirsky found that taking the time to consciously count their blessings once a week significantly increased subjects' overall satisfaction with life over a period of six weeks, whereas a control group that did not keep the happiness journal showed no such gain.[16] The idea is to consciously notice abundance in our life.

Gratitude exercises are more than just mood boosters. Emmons found these exercises to "improve physical health, raise energy levels, and for patients with neuromuscular diseases, relieve pain and fatigue." He further noted that "the ones who benefitted most tended to elaborate more and have a wider span of things they are grateful for."[17]

The recommendations for a gratitude journal are quite simple:

1. Have a small notebook readily available by the bedside.

2. Write five things you are grateful for each night before going to bed. These can be simple things such as family, friends, health, sunshine, nighttime, and the like.

3. Throughout the day, take mental notes of happenings from the standpoint of gratitude.

4. Start each day with a positive mindset, always taking note of simple joys that life brings. Every simple act of life holds some joy.

5. Focus on the positive side of things, even in situations normally considered negative. Remember, it can always be worse. This is the best way to deal with the "slings and arrows of outrageous fortune."

Mindful Moments: Five Things in Life to Be Grateful for!

I invite you now to take a moment to think of five things in your life that you are grateful for. For example, your friends, your family, your job, your health, your sense of smell, touch, taste, sight, and sound.

The list can go on and on. Imagine what your life would be like without any of these things.

Do this quite often and you will notice that your whole being is filled with gratitude.

If you want to feel rich, just count all the things that you have that money can't buy.

Concluding Remarks

The gift of gratitude is first and foremost an expression of the true joy of just being alive. "If you can digest your food and sleep well," says an Eastern adage, "sing your gratitude to sun and ask for no other blessing." When we approach our life with a deep sense of gratitude, it turns into a privilege and ceases to be a problem or a burden. Similarly, when we recognize that the whole universe of sight and sound manifests itself as soon as we open our eyes in the morning, we realize how privileged our position happens to be; our heart is overwhelmed with untold gratitude. Finally, at the interpersonal level, when we realize that our life depends entirely upon the kindness of others, our heart wells up with the expression of gratitude and goodwill for everyone and everything.

For countless eons, i have suffered
the slings of self-cherishing mind,
Ever living in the servitude of Ego-Supreme:
The vicious cycle of I, Myself, and Me.
Failing to recognize the great kindness of others ~
Our mother sentient beings.

CHAPTER SIX

THE GIFT OF GENEROSITY

Cultivate caring and generosity. Happiness is the natural state of a loving heart.[1]

There is a wonderful mythical law of nature that the three things we crave most in life—happiness, freedom, and peace of mind— are always attained by giving them to someone else.
                                                              ~ PEYTON CONWAY MARCH

Even if the world were to end tomorrow, I will still pay my debts and plant an apple tree.
                                                              ~ DR. MARTIN LUTHER KING JR.

Generosity is giving more than you can, and pride is taking less than you need.
                                                              ~ KHALIL GIBRAN

A human being is part of a whole, called by us "universe," a part limited in time and space. He experiences himself, his thoughts and feelings as something separated from the rest…a kind of optical delusion of his consciousness. This delusion is a kind of prison for us, restricting us to our personal desires and to affection for a few persons near us. Our task must be to free ourselves from this prison by widening our circle of compassion to embrace all living creatures and the whole of nature in its beauty. Nobody is able to achieve this completely, but the striving for such achievement is in itself a part of the liberation and of a foundation for inner security.[2]
                                                              ~ ALBERT EINSTEIN

Generosity is a state of heart. A generous heart is doubly blessed in the sense that it bestows goodwill on both the receiver and the giver. The gift of generosity is the best antidote to the inveterate human tendencies of acquisitiveness and resultant greed. It is motivated by a deep conviction that it is noble to give and to share. It flows directly from the gift of gratitude. When we reflect on our life and recount what we have and what we have been given, we realize how the generosity of our parents, relatives, teachers, friends, neighbors, and society at large has empowered and enriched our life. Our heart wells up with untold gratitude at the very thought of it and we feel inspired to return the favor. Through the gift of generosity, we get to share our abundance with others as a direct expression of our gratitude. Quite simply, the gift of generosity signifies giving more than we get, for the more we give the more we grow in fulfillment.

It is not necessary to have a lot to spare in order to practice generosity. As pointed out earlier, it is more a condition of the heart that wants to share regardless of one's means or ability to give. More often than not, those who have less to spare are observed to be more keen to share. It is all about the sheer joy of giving. The following story splendidly illustrates this condition.

The Joy of Giving Joy to Others

Two men, both seriously ill, occupied the same hospital room. One man was allowed to sit up in his bed for an hour each afternoon to help drain the fluid from his lungs. His bed was next to the room's only window. The other man had to spend all his time flat on his back. The men talked for hours on end. They spoke of their wives and families, their homes, their jobs, their involvement in the military service, where they had been on vacation.

Every afternoon when the man in the bed by the window could sit up, he would pass the time by describing to his roommate all the things he could see outside the window.

The man in the other bed began to live for those one-hour periods where his world would be broadened and enlivened by all the activity and color of the world outside. The window overlooked a park with a lovely lake. Ducks and swans played on the water while children sailed their model boats. Young lovers walked arm in arm amidst flowers of every color, and a fine view of the city skyline could be seen in the distance. As the man by the window described all this in exquisite detail, the man on the other side of the room would close his eyes and imagine the picturesque scene.

One warm afternoon, the man by the window described a parade passing by. Although the other man couldn't hear the band, he could see it in his mind's eye as the gentleman by the window portrayed it with descriptive words.

Days and weeks passed. One morning, the day nurse arrived to bring water for their baths, only to find the lifeless body of the man by the window who had died peacefully in his sleep. She was saddened and called the hospital attendants to take the body away.

As soon as it seemed appropriate, the other man asked if he could be moved next to the window. The nurse was happy to make the switch, and after making sure he was comfortable, she left him alone.

Slowly, painfully, he propped himself up on one elbow to take his first look at the real world outside. He strained to slowly turn to look out the window beside the bed. It faced a blank wall. The man asked the nurse what could have compelled his deceased roommate who had described such wonderful things outside this window.

The nurse responded that the man was blind and could not even see the wall. "Perhaps," she said, "he just wanted to encourage you."[3]

Cultivating an Abundance Mentality

When we learn to give, we develop the mind-set of having more than enough. We move away from the scarcity mentality of "I don't have enough" to the abundance mentality of "I have enough to share." This may include giving a smile, helping an elderly person, giving your time for a noble cause, giving affection and encouragement, being patient, giving forgiveness, sharing your knowledge freely, helping someone in financial need, or just listening and understanding. We begin to feel that we are giving from an infinite reservoir of abundance. Realizing that we have more than enough gives us the freedom to share what we have and to live a life full of meaning and authenticity. When we live authentically, we feel better connected to the life around us. We walk, radiating the joy of abundance. We discover that the more we give, the richer and happier we become!

Mutual Maintenance of the Universe

The gift of generosity springs from a high sense of sharing—that is, sharing our gifts, time, expertise, and blessings. At the very face of it, this may seem counterintuitive. One may ask, "Why should I share my fortune that I have worked so hard to acquire?" Peripherally, it may seem that existence is so designed that we come wired with self-interest and self-reference. We like to work hard for our self-preservation and self-propagation. In just about every interaction, the underlying question is always, what is in it for me? The suggestion to share may seem at first to run counter to our precious self-interest.

However, if we look around carefully we find that, on a cosmic scale, everything exists for something else. The sun and the moon, the wind and the air, the plants and the trees, the birds and the animals exist to serve a larger purpose beyond their own limited sphere of existence. The universe seems to be set up on the principle of mutual sharing and collaboration among all its participants. Gurdjieff, a Russian mystic, used to call it the principle of "mutual maintenance of the universe." Thus, according to this understanding, contributing our rightful share as human beings would seem be the logical thing to do. And yet the gift of generosity does not always come naturally to all of us. It has to be consciously formulated, conscientiously cultivated, and concertedly practiced.

Generosity and the Wisdom Traditions of the World

Many wisdom traditions suggest that one should give away a certain portion of one's income regularly to those less fortunate and those in need. Some traditions even specify that their adherents contribute a certain percentage (5–10%) of their respective income to charities and/or religious institutions of their preference. Though it may seem a bit prescriptive to most modern minds, it does show a high degree of awareness on the part of spiritual traditions about the importance of the need to share for the proper functioning of human communities. It also indicates a deeper understanding about human nature. In their greater wisdom, such spiritual traditions realize the importance of practicing generosity as a sure remedy for addressing societal disparities and inequities. After all, when left to its own resources, the need for self-preservation may not leave much room for concern for the preservation of the greater common good. Therefore, it really is better to give than to receive.

In Buddhism, for example, generosity is recommended as an antidote to the self-inflicted mental poison of greed. Wanting and hoarding more than what we have or need are seen to be the twin maladies responsible for much of humanity's ills. Greed is both the cause and effect of self-centeredness that manifests in tendencies such as hoarding, self-indulgence, and deceitfulness. It ultimately leads to undue attachment to things that are inherently fleeting and time-bound. So by developing a generous heart, we not only overcome our inveterate greed but also reduce our attachment to transient things. Being less self-centered, we become more open, caring, and compassionate toward others. A generous heart also leads to contentment through discovering joy by bringing joy to others.

Again, we have to check the purity of our motivation. We should not give to seek acceptance, admiration, recognition, power, or even gratitude. Secondly, it is the need of the recipient that should determine the choice of recipient rather than considerations such as religion, nationality, or ethnicity. In other words, we should base our decision purely dictated by the privation and not the credentials of the recipient. We should learn to give out of the sheer joy of giving and because we believe we have more than enough to share. Only a life guided by generosity and compassion is a life worth living.

Three Types of Generosity

The Buddha speaks of three kinds of generosity or giving:

a. Stingy giving, which is giving something you were going to throw out anyhow.

b. Ordinary giving, which is giving something of value, but still expecting a return of some kind.

c. Kingly giving, which is giving what is most precious to you with no expectation of any kind of return—no favors or any particular response. It is just something that is given in a completely open-handed way.[4]

As stated above, giving can happen in many ways, including sharing of material goods and money. It can also involve giving our time for a noble cause, sharing our expertise with people in need, or serving a charitable organization. The key again is pure motivation. It is not what we give that matters; it is how we give.

The Best Antidote to Greed

Unquestionably, greed is a constant factor in human affairs, irrespective of what we have, as illustrated in the following folk tale.

Aladdin's (Talking) Lamp!

A story is told of a person who possessed the like of an Aladdin's lamp. This lamp granted every wish of its owner. After a while, the owner got kind of bored with the lamp. Someone told him that there was another person in the town who had an even better lamp—this lamp doubled the wish of its owner. After searching for this luckier owner of the lamp, the man inquired if the owner of the doubling lamp would like to make an exchange. To the surprise of the first owner, the owner of the lamp that promised double wishes agreed to an exchange.

Now, the first owner hurried back to his home to test his new lamp. He closed all the doors and put the lamp on its pedestal, ready to make a wish. "Give me a large, beautiful house," commanded the owner. "Why not two?," replied the lamp. Then the man said," Give me a sports car." The lamp replied, "Why not two?" After a few more similar tries, the owner discovered to his dismay that it was only a talking lamp, programmed to reply "Why not two?" to every request made. But it was too late. The owner of the talking lamp had already left town. So much for greed![5]

Greed runs rampant in modern society, causing glaring inequities and untold exploitation. The modern capitalistic lifestyle seems to thrive on three maxims:

1. The next thing we buy will satisfy us.
2. You can never be too rich.
3. He who dies with the most toys wins.

Adam Smith (1723–1790), author of the classic *Wealth of Nations*, is often recognized for his celebrated "invisible hand" expression, which he used to demonstrate how overall, the pursuit of self-interest in a free market ensures society's best interest. However, many believe that a more nuanced understanding of Smith's idea would be that an unfettered pursuit of self-interest and capitalistic greed do not always promote society's best interests. As a matter of fact, Adam Smith anticipated this in his earlier work *Theory of Moral Sentiments,* in which he counseled that "We must become the impartial spectators of our own character and conduct."[6] Can we, then, legislate greed? Well, we can't! It is far better to rely on the deep springs of human wisdom to keep one's head than to count on the not-so-reliable invisible hand. After all, the grand invisible hand can also use some help from all of us!

Buddhist psychology recognizes that, the way we normally live, our mind is stained by three unwholesome psychological states—the "three poisons": greed, hatred, and delusion. Buddhism believes that "the cause for the endless competition, conflict, injustice, and oppression does not lie outside the mind. These are all just manifestations of intentions, outcroppings of thoughts driven by greed, by hatred, by delusion."[7] The goal of the Buddhist approach to life is to eliminate these unwholesome states by transforming them into their wholesome counterparts: greed into generosity, hatred into loving kindness, and delusion into wisdom.

Generosity Boosts Happiness

There is tremendous happiness in making others happy despite our own situations. Research in positive psychology reveals that lasting happiness comes from making others happy. A life devoted to making only one's own wishes come true makes a very small, insignificant package. According to the findings of positive psychology, giving boosts happiness. Generosity, it seems, brings more happiness than selfish indulgence. Giving just a few dollars or a few minutes to someone else may help you live longer, happier, and healthier. *LiveScience* staff writer Jeanna Bryner reported on this research, "Statistical analyses revealed personal spending had no link with a person's happiness, while spending on others and charity was significantly related to a boost in happiness."[8]

The alchemy of giving seems to work like this: When we share something with others, the joy of sharing takes our attention away from our preoccupation with little worries and petty annoyances. Too much self-focus and self-brooding can lead to constriction of spirit. Often, the best way to transcend our worries is to help others overcome their worries. A young man once approached a Zen master with this question: "I feel very discouraged, what should I do?" The Zen master replied, "Encourage others who are discouraged." When we share with others words of hope and encouragement, they also uplift our spirits. It has been rightly said that "shared grief is half the sorrow, but happiness when shared, is redoubled."

Cultivating Generosity: *Points to Ponder*

a. *Personally speaking, what do you think makes for deep gratification—achieving your own goals or helping others to reach their goals?*

b. *Can you think of a situation or an event in which your main focus was to help others, without expecting anything in return? How did you feel having gone through it?*

c. *Recall a situation where you were solely motivated by your own gratification. How long did the euphoria of self-satisfaction last? (Hint: You may discover that the joy of helping others lasts much longer than self-indulgence.)*

Smile, the Most Beautiful Human Gift!

It is said that we use 33 facial muscles when we frown and only 13 facial muscles when we smile. Why waste extra muscular effort frowning?!

When life gives you a hundred reasons to cry, show life that you have a thousand reasons to smile. Perhaps the most beautiful thing in human interactions is to see a person smiling. And even more beautiful is knowing that you are the reason behind it!

In the coming week, give a smile to everyone you meet. Whether it's the homeless person asking for some change, the hurried driver who cuts you off on the freeway, the police officer writing you a ticket, the customer who is complaining about the service, the cashier at the grocery store who mistakenly charged you twice for an item, or the stranger who scared you by making a face at you. Then just watch the magic wrought by it!

Hidden Benefits of Giving

Although true giving is an altruistic act at best, there are natural benefits that accrue from practicing selfless generosity. For one, we become free from our self-constrictive motives and open up to the world of mutuality and interdependence. We see our life as a collaborative flow of impersonally interlinked experiences. In this flow of life, there are no unrewarded acts of random kindness. When we see others as an expression and extension of our own self, paradoxically, we discover every true act of giving brings back manifold blessings in its wake. And since in the final reckoning there are no others, we find life unexpectedly rewarding us with seemingly random windfalls and surprise bonanzas.

The following story illustrates beautifully how a generous act done many decades before can bear an unexpected boon at the right moment.

What Goes Around, Comes Around

A young, 18-year-old student was struggling to pay his fees. He was an orphan, and not knowing where to turn for money, he came up with a bright idea. A friend and he decided to host a musical concert on campus to raise money for their education.

They reached out to the great pianist Ignacy J. Paderewski. His manager demanded a guaranteed fee of $2,000 for the piano recital. A deal was struck, and the boys began to work to make the concert a success.

The big day arrived. Paderewski performed at Stanford, but unfortunately, the boys had not managed to sell enough tickets—the total collection was only $1,600. Disappointed, they went to Paderewski and explained their plight. They gave him the entire $1,600, plus a check for the balance, $400. They promised to honor the check as soon as possible.

"No," said Paderewski. "This is not acceptable." He tore up the check, returned the $1,600, and told the two boys, "Here's the $1,600. Please deduct whatever expenses you have incurred. Keep the money you need for your fees. And just give me whatever is left." The boys were surprised and thanked him profusely.

It was a small act of kindness. But it clearly marked out Paderewski as a great human being. Why should he help two people he did not even know? We all come across situations like these in our lives. And most of us only think, "If I help them, what would happen to me?" The truly great people think, "If I don't help them, what will happen to them?" They don't do it expecting something in return. They do it because they feel it's the right thing to do.

Paderewski later went on to become the Prime Minister of Poland. He was a great leader, but unfortunately when the World War began, Poland was ravaged. There were over 1.5 million people starving in his country and no money to feed them. Paderewski did not know where else to turn, so he reached out to the US Food and Relief Administration for help.

At the head there was a man called Herbert Hoover, who later went on to become the US President. Hoover agreed to help and quickly shipped tons of food grains to feed the starving Polish people. A calamity was averted. Paderewski was relieved. He decided to go meet Hoover and personally thank him.

When Paderewski began to thank Hoover for his noble gesture, Hoover quickly interjected and said, "You shouldn't be thanking me, Mr. Prime Minister. You may not remember this, but several years ago you helped two young students go through college in the US. I was one of them."[9]

This is a true story that had happened in 1892 at Stanford University. Its moral will always be relevant because it illustrates the wisdom of generosity and caring for others. This story also reveals an important aspect of the operation of law of *Karma*: what goes around comes around!

Abiding in the Wisdom of Generosity

At a deeper level, the wisdom of generosity is about freeing oneself from the cocoon of "I, my, me, and mine." It is about freeing oneself from the unending servitude of greed and self-centeredness in one's quest for lasting happiness. It is about understanding that no matter how much money, power, or fame I may be able to amass for myself, it is never going to enough because there is always going to something more that my mind will crave to acquire. Besides, all human structures are essentially impermanent and hence ultimately unfulfilling. But if I come out of the self-imposed limitation of "I-servitude" and move toward "we-orientation," I may unexpectedly discover abiding joy and fulfillment.

Robert Louis Stevenson (1850–1894), the Scottish novelist, poet, and essayist, beautifully conveys the essence of generosity as follows:

> To be rich in admiration and free from envy,
> to rejoice greatly in the good of others,
> to love with such generosity of heart that your
> love is still a dear possession in absence or unkindness—
> these are the gifts which money cannot buy.

The following story captures the heart of the matter by conveying the wisdom of generosity.

Preciousness within and Preciousness without

A wise woman who was traveling in the mountains found a precious stone in a stream. The next day she met another traveler who was hungry and the wise woman opened her bag to share her food. The hungry traveler saw the precious stone and asked the woman to give it to him. She did so without hesitation.

The traveler left, rejoicing his good fortune. He knew the stone was worth enough to give him security for a lifetime. But a few days later he came back to return the stone to the wise woman. "I've been thinking," he said, "I know how valuable the stone is, but I give it back in the hope that you can give me something even more precious: Give me what you have within you that enabled you to give me the stone."[10]

This is a wonderful story with multiple layers of deep meaning. It tells us that the wise woman had something in her—a deeper understanding—that enabled her to part with what was considered precious in the worldly sense. At best, the message is symbolic: Unless we have something precious inside us, we are not able to share precious things outwardly! The story also portrays that the wisdom of the wise lies in understanding the impermanence and precariousness of human valuables and structures. We are told that we cannot take anything with us. But we can certainly leave something behind. Only a life guided by a wise mind and a generous heart is a life capable of leaving something worthwhile behind. When the Buddha was asked to describe the hallmarks of an awakened person, he simply said: "Cool mind and a warm heart!" By cultivating a cool mind and a warm heart, we may discover a genuine way to pass on our gifts to others.

The following short poem by English Evangelist John Wesley (1703–1791) truly conveys the essence of the art and science of generosity:

> Do all the good you can,
> By all the means you can,
> In all the ways you can,
> In all the places you can,
> At all the times you can,
> To all the people you can,
> As long as ever you can.

Concluding Remarks

There seems to be a striking similarity between the findings of positive psychology and Buddhist psychology on this essential point: the road to lasting happiness is paved by a selfless, caring concern for others. It is cultivated by harnessing our intrinsic goodness, by developing the spiritual qualities of mind and heart—qualities of kindness and compassion, generosity, gratitude, and altruism. It has been observed that if we cannot change the course of the winds, we can always adjust our sails. A Buddhist perspective on pure motivation, gratitude, and generosity is not only in harmony with the findings of positive psychology and wisdom traditions on this subject, it also seems to present the most compelling case for adjusting our sails.

CHAPTER SEVEN

THE GIFT OF HARMLESSNESS

If all the insects on earth disappeared, within 50 years all life on earth would disappear. If all humans disappeared, within 50 years all species would flourish as never before.

~ JONAS SALK

*I visited all quarters with my mind
nor found I any dearer than myself;
self is likewise to every other dear;
who loves himself may never harm another.*

~ THE BUDDHA

Tse-kung asked, "Is there one word that can serve as a principle of conduct for life?" Confucius replied, "It is the word 'shu'— reciprocity. Do not impose on others what you yourself do not desire."[1]

~ CONFUCIUS

The highest realms of thought are impossible to reach without first attaining an understanding of compassion.

~ SOCRATES (469 BC–399 BC)

At the center of non-violence stands the principle of love.

~ MARTIN LUTHER KING, JR.

If we practice an eye for an eye and a tooth for a tooth, soon the whole world will be blind and toothless.

~ MAHATMA GANDHI

Harming neither by Thought, Word, nor Deed

At its core, the gift of harmlessness represents honoring and celebrating the preciousness of life and signifies non-harming by thought, word, and deed. When we understand that a harm done to others is essentially a harm done to ourselves—*since there are no others*—we have understood the real import of harmlessness. It is true that the very process of living involves a certain amount of violence and that it is perhaps not possible to eliminate violence completely. What we have to do is to seek to minimize its extent as much as possible. Only then we can truly claim our heritage as evolved beings. Thomas Edison put it well: "Non-violence leads to the highest ethics, which is the goal of all evolution. Until we stop harming all other living beings, we are still savages."

However, it must start with us, one person at a time. Harmlessness, like charity, also begins at home. Dalai Lama said, "The atmosphere of peace must first be created within ourselves then gradually expanded to include our families, our communities, and ultimately the whole planet."[2]

Psychology of Violence

There are four primary reasons that prod people to violence. The first reason seems to be ignorance. The person causing the harm is not aware that his or her actions are causing harm to others. Most mental harm takes place when the person supposedly causing such harm is ignorant of the real impact of his or her actions. This brings to us to the second cause of violence, insensitivity. Most religious violence emanates from a certain lack of sensitivity toward other people's belief system. Developing empathy and understanding can go a long in addressing such violence. The third reason for violence is anger, and the fourth is hatred; unaddressed anger leads to hatred. Both anger and hatred are responsible for most of the harm done in the world. Cultivating compassion through understanding seems to be the best antidote to violence born out of anger and hatred.

If we carefully look at the psychology behind these four causes of violence, we discover that they all emanate from a common factor of self-centeredness. It is a direct cause of insensitivity toward others and the operative cause of anger leading to hatred. Developing patience, understanding, kindness, and compassion can go a long way in dealing with violence at the personal as well as global level.

Forget Everything—Remember Your Humanity

Russell's enjoinder to be mindful of our humanity can help us avoid an all-too-common source of conflict. When asked who we are, mostly we find ourselves answering this question by stating our profession, nationality, culture, race, or gender. Some of us even like to be known by our particular political, social, cultural, or organizational affiliation or orientation. Who are we, really? Are we nothing more than our nationality, profession, race, culture, or orientation? Is that all? Aren't these identifiers rather incidental and accidental and thus, secondary at best? Most of these frames of reference have to do with where we are born and raised, over which we have no choice or control at all. Our birth is a biological or geographical accident, so to speak. Very often, such identifiers lead to artificial differences and divisions. We know from experience that everything that divides creates conflict. This is rather a disempowering position to operate from.

Dalai Lama's observation is quite enlightening in this regard: "Before I am monk, I am a Tibetan; and before I am a Tibetan, I am a human being." This is an empowering stance to live by.

A Great Cosmic Joke

We're all the same. We think we're different.
~ Peter Vaill

If we reflect deeply on who we are, we will find more commonalities than differences among us. I recall an interesting encounter with Julius Shulman that underscores this important point.

> ## A Great Cosmic Joke: We Think We are Different!
>
> Among my meetings with remarkable people, my encounter with Mr. Julius Shulman, the great architectural photographer, has a special significance. He had recently donated a portfolio of 60,000 images to the Getty Museum. He was 95 at the time and had only few more months to live. His body was frail, but his mind was still solid.
>
> It was quite impressive to hear his progressive views on sustainable housing, world peace, and mesmerizing photography. Then in the middle of the conversation, Mr. Shulman paused and asked me, "So, what is the difference between you and me?" I do not know what possessed me at the time, but without even thinking much about the question, I replied, "Nothing!" "How so?" he inquired. Without missing a beat, I said, "Because we both have problems!"
>
> Mr. Shulman burst into laughter and extended his hand again and said, "Now, we can truly be friends."

Who Loves Himself Should Never Harm Another

Our self is the most dear to us of all. It comes as a natural endowment that perhaps has its roots in the instinct of self-preservation. An important verse in one of the ancient Hindu wisdom texts, Upanishads, states that it is not for the sake of husband, wife, son, or any other beings that one loves, but for one's own sake.[3] However, in our bid to get our self-interest across, we often tend to forget the simple fact that, likewise, everyone's self is also most dear to him or her. According to the teachings of the Buddha, every creature holds itself most dear of all; every being wants to live and thrive.

Our Self Is Most Dear to Us All

Pasenadi, the king of Kosala, strolls with his queen, Mallika. In an intimate mood, King Pasenadi asks his wife, "Is there anyone who is more dear to you than yourself?" This surely not meant as a philosophical inquiry; the King no doubt expects the Queen to reply, "You, of course, my dear." But the Queen is in a very frank mood, and she answers, "No." Then she returns the question to the King, asking, "Is there anyone who is more dear to you than yourself?" Her candor is disarming; the King has to be frank too. "I also know no one who is more dear to me than myself," he says. Not long after this troubling conversation, the King sought the counsel of the Buddha.

Buddha, understanding the true meaning of this, pronounced these inspired verses: "If you thoroughly search in ten directions with your mind, nowhere will you find anything more dear to you than yourself. In the same way, the self is extremely dear to others. Therefore, one who loves himself should cause no harm to another."[4]

Live and Let Live!

The ideal of harmlessness finds a great parallel in the Sanskrit word *ahimsa*. The word is derived from the Sanskrit root *himsa*, meaning injury. *A-himsa*, therefore, means non-injury or non-harming or simply nonviolence. *Ahimsa* as a Hindu and Buddhist principle represents a belief in the sacredness of all life that signifies non-injury in thought, word, and deed. The ultimate purpose of practicing nonviolence is to lessen the overall suffering in the world by fostering peace and harmony.

In his autobiography *The Story of My Experiments with Truth*, Gandhi has stated that the phrase "passive resistance," then current in Europe, was too narrowly conceived. It could be interpreted as a cover for cowardice. Or else, it could be disguised hatred and could finally manifest itself as violence. Gandhi believed that mere non-retaliation without love and compassion toward the attacker was not true *ahimsa*. For Gandhi, *ahimsa* signified universal love and an indirect means to the spiritual end of realization of the ultimate truth. This is why he called his peaceful movement *Satyagraha*—firmness in the abode of truth.

According to Gandhi, nonviolence is not a weapon of the weak, but it is the supreme virtue of the brave. For him, the practice of non-violence required far greater bravery than that of swordsmanship. As a principle, it is far more profound than a simple injunction to cause no physical harm. In its original meaning, it denotes dynamic peaceful-ness that undergirds our essential mutuality with one another and with rest of the existence. It is important to remember that in Gandhi's life nonviolence did not just mean causing no harm; rather, it permeated his whole character and emanated from his deeper being as a positive force to help others in the most natural ways.

Mahatma Gandhi's cardinal principle of nonviolence *(ahimsa)* was a true expression of this gift. It emanated from a deep conviction about the essential oneness of all life and served as a true-north orientation in the life of that great leader. It sustained him well during India's long struggle for its independence. Per his own acknowledgement, he learned it from his readings of Tolstoy, the Bible, and the Bhagavad Gita. Gandhi believed that *ahimsa* without compassion is worthless. *Ahimsa* should begin in self-discipline and must end in love and compassion. So harm-lessness does not simply entail not doing harm; it also occasions doing good through loving kindness and compassion. This principle also later inspired a host of other moral leaders, including Martin Luther King Jr., Rosa Parks, and Nelson Mandela.

The following story illustrates the power of Gandhi's gentle being and shows that doing good came to him naturally as well.

My Life Is My Message!

Once Gandhi was boarding a train, and a journalist stopped him in the doorway to ask him some questions. As he was finishing his interview, the train started to take off very slowly. The journalist got off the train and started walking along with the slowly moving train, trying to ask his last set of questions. He finally asked Gandhi, "What is your message?" Gandhi simply replied, "My life is my message!"

As Gandhi was leaving the doorway of the train, one of his sandals slipped from his foot and landed near the railway track. Suddenly the train began pulling away quickly, leaving him no time to retrieve it. Immediately, Gandhi removed the other sandal and tossed it back to lie with the other along the track.

When his astonished fellow passenger asked why he did this, Gandhi replied, "Now the poor man who finds it will have a pair he can use."[5]

Reverence for Life

Deeply influenced by Indian religious thought, especially the principle of nonviolence, Albert Schweitzer (1875–1965), a Christian theologian, organist, philosopher, physician, and medical missionary, developed his doctrine of "reverence for life," for which he was awarded the Nobel Peace Prize in 1952. He considered this principle both a universal frame of ethics for our times and an evolutionary imperative. Simply stated, the principle of reverence for life finds its expression in "unconditionally respecting the wish of other beings to exist as one does towards oneself." Schweitzer strove hard to put this principle into practice in his own personal life as well as in his work as a medical missionary in central Africa.

Schweitzer acknowledged that in nature one form of life must always prey upon another. However, he believed that a self-aware, ethical human being respects the will of other beings to live and endeavors hard to minimize the unavoidable harm as far as possible:

Standing, as all living beings are, before this dilemma of the will to live, a person is constantly forced to preserve his own life and life in general only at the cost of other life. If he has been touched by the ethic of reverence for life, he injures and destroys life only under a necessity he cannot avoid, and never from thoughtlessness.[6]

Making a Difference—One Fish at a Time!

Any change at a personal or social level requires commitment, hard work, and patience. Sometimes we feel disheartened in wake of the enormity of the undertaking. We feel overwhelmed. We start entertaining thoughts such as "what difference does it make? I am just one person." The following story illustrates the point that when we choose to follow the right course of action, it does make a difference.

You Can Make a Difference

Once upon a time, there was a wise man who used to go to the ocean to do his writing. He had a habit of walking on the beach before he began his work.

One day, as he was walking along the shore, he looked down the beach and saw a human figure moving like a dancer. He smiled to himself at the thought of someone who would dance to the day, and so, he walked faster to catch up.

As he got closer, he noticed that the figure was that of a young man, and that what he was doing was not dancing at all. The young man was reaching down to the shore, picking up small objects, and throwing them into the ocean.

He came closer still and called out "Good morning! May I ask what it is that you are doing?"

The young man paused, looked up, and replied, "Throwing starfish into the ocean."

"I must ask, then, why are you throwing starfish into the ocean?" said the somewhat startled wise man.

To this, the young man replied, "The sun is up and the tide is going out. If I don't throw them in, they'll die."

Upon hearing this, the wise man commented, "But, young man, do you not realize that there are miles and miles of beach and there are starfish all along every mile? You can't possibly make a difference!"

At this, the young man bent down, picked up yet another starfish, and threw it into the ocean. As it met the water, he said, "It made a difference for that one."[7]

Help Ever—Hurt Never

The great Indian epic, *Mahabharata*, contains 100,000 verses and is considered to be the world's longest epic poem (it is more than seven times the combined size of Homer's *Iliad* and *Odyssey*). Its claim to greatness, however, does not rest only on its quantity but also in the quality of its message. It has been rightly said, "What is found in *Mahabharata*, one may find elsewhere in other works, but what is not found in it will not be found in any other book at all." The great English critic A.R. Orage felt that there were absolute truths embodied in the *Mahabharata*. Orage considered it to be the greatest book ever written and "a touchstone of literary style and quality." The Bhagavad Gita, the world's loftiest spiritual poem, forms a part of this epic.

The legendary author of this epic, Ved Vyasa, presents all conceivable human tendencies in the form of certain characters. When someone asked him to select the most important single verse that represented the essence of this work, he is reported to have stated, "The gist of a million treatises is expressed in half a verse: The highest merit is helping others; the highest wrongdoing is hurting others."[8]

It is important to reflect why the learned author of this great work singled out hurting others as the highest possible spiritual demerit. In order to understand the depth of this observation, we have to dig further into the truth of our existence. Consider the following illustration: At its most basic level, all existence—from a piece of rock to a most developed specimen of living beings—is composed of five fundamental elements: earth, water, fire, air, and space. Each of these elements within our body, for example, exists with reference to the totality of its corresponding element outside our body. Take, for example, the element of air. The air that we breathe in exists by virtue of its relationship and interaction with the totality of air that exists outside in the environment. Likewise, the water that exists in our body in the form of various liquids cannot exist without the totality of water that exists outside. The same is true of the remaining elements: they exist in the microcosm of our body by virtue of their relationship with the totality of these elements in the macrocosm. So far, so good! If this is true regarding these physical elements, how much more so the consciousness that is the fundamental building block of all existence?

This short excursion into the interconnected nature of reality perhaps provides the simplest compelling reason yet to understand the oneness of the whole of existence. In our human terms, it means that we are inseparably one with the rest of existence. So, in effect, to hurt others is to hurt ourselves. That is why sages of humanity have always insisted on helping others, because they understood that, essentially, there are no others, and all life is inseparably interlinked and interconnected.

Why is this simple existential fact not obvious to everyone? Why are we not naturally able to sense it and warm up to this view of reality? Perhaps in the perennial fight for self-preservation, this type of thinking does not further any evolutionary agenda. Perhaps by some sort of optical illusion, we are not able to see beyond the façade of self-centered, separately existing objects vying for their survival and flourishing. This leads to self-defeating strategies that disempower at best and seriously impinge upon the mutual preservation of everyone's interest, the mutual maintenance of the universe. Albert Einstein captures the issue succinctly and suggests a solution to come out of this prison of separateness, as follows:

A human being is part of a whole called by us "Universe," a part limited in time and space. He experiences himself, his thoughts and feelings, as something separated from the rest…a kind of optical delusion of consciousness. This delusion is a kind of prison for us, restricting us to our personal desires and to affection for a few persons nearest to us. Our task must be to free ourselves from this prison by widening our circle of compassion to embrace all living creatures and the whole of nature in its beauty.[9]

David Bohm, Einstein's colleague and successor at Princeton, believed that the quantum theory reveals the "unbroken wholeness of the universe."[10] According to Bohm, this is the natural state of the human world—separation without separateness.

However, we continue to delight in differences and fail to see what is essentially the same in all of us. It is abundantly evident that the divisions of race, religion, color, creed, and culture have contributed to the most heinous horrors of humankind. This will continue unabated, as history testifies, until we see the tyranny of our disempowering stance. Let's seek and share the underlying truth of mutuality that does not lead to unnatural differences and disharmony. That is the truth of our identity behind diversity—the essential oneness of all that exists. By seeking the truth that is equally good to all, we will be able to revere all life and truly redeem our human existence. Only then can we ensure equally the happiness and welfare of all beings. That will be our true gift of harmlessness to the universe.

Harmlessness and Vegetarianism

Ahimsa is the basis for the vegetarianism within Hinduism and Buddhism though it goes well beyond just being vegetarian. This core principle is derived from the Vedic injunction *"ma himsyaat sarva-bhutani"*—do no harm to living creatures. This recommendation is also repeated to the seeker after truth in the Upanishads. According to the Chandogya Upanishad (7.26.2), "If the food is pure, the mind becomes pure. If the mind is pure, memory becomes firm. When memory becomes strong, one is released from all knots of the heart and liberation is attained."[11]

> ## The Perspective of a Buddhist in China
>
> When a scholar named Chou Yu was cooking some eel to eat, he noticed one of the eels bending in its body such that its head and tail were still in the boiling point liquid, but its body arched upward above the soup. It did not fall completely in until finally dying. Chou Yu found the occurrence a strange one, pulled out the eel, and cut it open. He found thousands of eggs inside. The eel had arched its belly out of the hot soup to protect its offspring. He cried at the sight, sighed with emotion, and swore never to eat meat.[12]

According to the Hindu Vedic tradition, all creatures form the limbs of a single, all-pervading divine being. To benefit one limb is to benefit the divine being and to harm one limb is to harm the integrity of the divine being. Therefore, all of our actions should be performed for the welfare of all beings. All the great spiritual traditions of India, drawing upon this root idea, dictate that a spiritual aspirant must abstain as much as possible from causing any harm to any living being. However, at the same time, it was recognized that life inherently involves harm of some form or another. As a Vedic verse puts it, "life lives by living off of another life" *(jeevo jeevena jeevati)*. It is true that vegetarians too cause harm by killing plants or using animals to plough the fields. One may also inadvertently harm other beings in the process of raising crops. However, this seems minimal compared to the routine cruelty that is involved in raising, transporting, and slaughtering animals for food.

It is true that no one in reality can have a completely harmless existence. But that does not mean that we should abandon the core value of harmlessness. We must minimize the harm we cause to other creatures as far as possible. Clearly no one is arguing that Eskimos and others who have no other means of sustenance should adopt a vegetarian diet. However, abstaining from eating meat is possible for nearly all of us, given the choices that the modern life accords. And, in the process of adopting our vegetarian diets, we may atone for some harm we might have caused inadvertently in the process of adopting a vegetarian diet!

The great scientist Albert Einstein has reported to have declared vegetarianism to be the only viable solution for the sustainable way of living on this planet. Likewise, Gandhi observed, "I do feel that spiritual progress does demand at some stage that we should cease to kill our fellow creatures for the satisfaction of our bodily wants."

It is well beyond the scope of this work to recount the health hazards of eating meat. They are very well documented in the current scholarly and popular literature on health and nutrition. In the final reckoning, it all depends upon our personal beliefs and choices. These choices, being habit-driven, are not always easy to change, even if one is willing. The spirit is willing, says the Bible, but the flesh is weak. Observation and reflection make it clear that as human beings we are not the most rational creatures when it comes to forming our beliefs and making our choices. If life were rational, everyone would quit smoking. For some, the decision to become vegetarian happens instantly. They read some study on the risks of eating meat or watch documentary footage of a factory farm, and meat is off their menu for good. For others, the decision may come in fits and spurts.

We can choose to become vegetarian as a healthy decision both for ourselves and for the environment. We can also choose not to eat meat guided by the pure motivation of harmlessness—by becoming vegetarian out of kindness and compassion. Preventing the suffering of living creatures to satisfy our taste buds and appetite is the minimal expression of compassion we all can offer. The choice is always ours.

Harmlessness in a Darwinian World

The reader must be wondering if it is really possible to practice harmlessness in this dog-eat-dog world. People often argue that harmlessness can be perceived as a weak stance and one can be taken advantage of as a result. As the following parable states, harmlessness should be practiced with tactful diligence so as to deter manipulative people who would walk all over you.

A Parable of a Snake and a Holy Man

There was once a holy man who came to a village. The villagers warned him that he must not go on a certain path because a venomous snake that had killed many people always lay there. "It won't hurt me," said the holy man and continued on his way. Sure enough, the snake approached, reared its head, hissing and ready to strike, but when it saw the holy man it prostrated itself humbly at his feet.

The sage taught it to give up the idea of biting and killing. Soon the boys of the village discovered the change in the character of the snake. Knowing that it was now harmless, they would attack it with sticks and stones whenever it came out of its hole—but the snake would never strike back.

When next time the holy man came to that village, he went to the snake's hole and called it. Hearing its teacher's voice, the snake came squirming out, crippled from the blows it had received from the village boys. The holy man questioned it about the reason for its condition.

"Revered sir, you asked me not to bite or kill anyone." The sage replied, "I told you not to bite. Did I tell you not to hiss?"[13]

This story is an excellent answer to the objection that meekness and humility have no place in this Darwinian world. By pointing out the difference between "biting" and "hissing," the story illustrates that it is still possible to practice kindness and meekness wisely. Accordingly, harmlessness should not be allowed to become a position for the unwise to take advantage of. It must be practiced with tactful awareness and discernment.

Harmlessness and Fulfillment

What is the relationship between harmlessness and fulfillment? Why should one who is seeking fulfillment practice harmlessness? The simplest and the most obvious answer to this question is based on the understanding that it is hard for someone to experience lasting joy while engaged in causing harm to others rampantly. As indicated above, harmlessness is related to the doctrine of *Karma*. This principle teaches us that what goes around comes around. When we treat the universe in a non-harming way, the universe in turn treats us accordingly. A Chinese proverb puts it this way: A little perfume stays with the hand that gives flowers to others. The converse is true as well for the hand that carries thorns for others.

However, for a person seeking fulfillment, *Karma* may not even be the most compelling reason for practicing harmlessness. In fact, the real reasons for practicing harmlessness are kindness and compassion. This compassion is borne with our deep understanding about the unity of the web of life. When one has understood the underlying oneness of all existence—when one has realized that the harm done to others is really the harm brought upon oneself—then harmlessness becomes a most natural expression of our innate kindness and compassion. It then leads to purity of mind that can finally help us realize the highest truth about ourselves—the final goal of our finite existence. In his autobiography, Gandhi similarly states that the only means for the realization of truth is *ahimsa*.

A Tale of Universal Pity

The Legend of the Moslem Saints abounds in tales of pity shown to animals, birds, and even insects. It is related that Bayazid purchased some cardamom seed at Hamadhan, and before departing put into his gabardine a small quantity which was left over. On reaching Bistam and recollecting what he had done, he took out the seed and found that it contained a number of ants.

Saying "I have carried the poor creatures away from their home," he immediately set off and journeyed back to Hamadhan—a distance of several hundred miles![14]

Concluding Remarks

So who are we, in essence, truly?

When one considers oneself as a human being, one develops kinship with all the human beings regardless of their color, race, religion, and culture. And when one realizes oneself to be a sentient being, one develops one's kinship with the whole of existence, with all creation. In fact, there are no "others." All are "I" or "We." With this realization, one is able to offer the greatest possible gift to all existence: the gift of complete harmlessness! Ultimately, harmlessness is about making peace with all that exists. And when we make peace with all creation, we make this world a better place to live just by being in it! In sum, the practice of harmlessness arises out of a deep understanding of the oneness and the unity of life: living is not just about me, but about everything that exists.

The purpose of this understanding of oneness is, therefore, highly practical: to live a life of harmlessness born of the understanding of oneness of all existence, remaining ever established in the realization of one's identity with the highest unitive principle in the universe.

Just imagine how different things would be if a few members of a community took a vow of harmlessness. Just imagine how different our workplaces would be if a small fraction of their members decided to live by the principle of harmlessness. And just imagine how much peace we could foster if we could elevate this gift to a macro level. Our planet is plagued by mindless exploitation, rampant destruction, dogged self-centeredness, and unbridled greed that has manifested in terrorism, war, and violence. If there is one thing that can save our species from the mad self-destruction of war and violence, it is the gift of harmlessness.

CHAPTER EIGHT

THE GIFT OF SELFLESS SERVICE

I don't know what your destiny will be, but one thing I know: the only ones among you who will be really happy are those who will have sought and found how to serve.

~ ALBERT SCHWEITZER

The best way to find yourself is to lose yourself in the service of others.

~ MAHATMA GANDHI

Wealth, like happiness, is never attained when sought after directly. It comes as a by-product of providing a useful service.

~ HENRY FORD

I slept and dreamt that life was joy. I awoke and saw that life was service. I acted and behold, service was joy.

~ RABINDRANATH TAGORE

One does not have to be an angel in order to be saint.

~ ALBERT SCHWEITZER

A student once asked Phillip Kapleau, an American Zen Teacher, if the Bodhisattva of Compassion, Avalokitesvara, actually existed. "To meet (her) face to face," answered Kapleau, "all you have to do is to perform a selfless deed."[1]

The Joy of Selfless Service

This gift flows naturally from the gift of gratitude and the gift of generosity. When we truly understand the interconnectedness of all life, we devote ourselves to finding joy in selfless service. It has been observed that life is like the game of tennis; in order to win, we have to be good at service. Our desire to serve must be pure; it should emanate from the sheer joy of service without expecting any reward, self-recognition, or self-gratification. When service emanates from a self-centered motive, it ceases to be service and becomes a business transaction.

Under the guise of the Darwinian struggle for survival, we frequently discern that self-interest is placed before service in the relentless race to accumulate wealth, possessions, power, and fame—all geared entirely toward personal benefit alone. This unbridled pursuit of self-gratification inevitably leads to excessive greed, competition, and materialism that reign supreme in the world today. As an antidote to rampant self-centeredness, selfless service is absolutely paramount, individually and collectively, without which there can be no real progress or harmony in society.

Selfless service to others can be offered in numerous ways, ranging from financial assistance to physical help. Real self-growth depends upon transcending the ego, ennobling the spirit, and revering all life, expressed in actions guided by selfless service without any thought or expectation of reward whatsoever—always working selflessly in oneness of spirit for the common good. In fine, service is a way of being where one approaches life as an offering rather than viewing it from the standpoint of entitlement.

The lives of moral leaders, such as Mahatma Gandhi and Mother Teresa, bear ample testimony to the power of selfless service. Gandhi devoted all his life in serving his country and its people and found deepest fulfillment through serving. According to Gandhi, "The best way to find yourself is to lose yourself in the service of others." His life serves as a beacon of light to all humanity. Likewise, Mother Teresa was a prime example of selfless service. Her entire life revolved around helping others in need—the poorest of the poor. As a result, she experienced a great deal of affection and self-fulfillment in her life.

In this chapter, we primarily focus on the path of detached action *(Karma Yoga)* as a framework for performing selfless service. We believe that, as a practical teaching, *Karma Yoga* furnishes the best set of guidelines to put service before self and to perform actions for the well-being of all beings. The principal Hindu sacred book, the Bhagavad Gita, will be our key guiding text in this terrain. Regarding its efficacy, we have the testimony of Mahatma Gandhi, who tested its teachings in every sphere of his life with great success. He called the Bhagavad Gita the "Gospel of Selfless Action" and referred to it as his "spiritual dictionary." As a matter of fact, the Bhagavad Gita's emphasis on selfless service was the prime source of inspiration for Mahatma Gandhi's life and leadership.

The Bhagavad Gita expounds a three-fold path to self-realization: (1) the path of selfless action *(Karma Yoga)*; (2) the path of devotion *(bhakti yoga)*; and (3) the path of knowledge *(jnana yoga)*. Meaning literally "Lord's Song," the Bhagavad Gita unfolds as a dialog between Sri Krishna, the divine incarnation, and his warrior-disciple, Arjuna, on the eve of a historic battle of cosmic proportions.

The Bhagavad Gita consists of 18 chapters comprising 700 verses. Different commentators have read different meanings in interpreting the text based on their own tradition *(sampardaya)* and philosophical leanings. Some say that it teaches *Karma Yoga* (path of selfless action), others observe that it teaches *Bhakti Yoga* (the path of devotion), and still others state that it teaches *Jnana Yoga* (the path of self-knowledge). Some commentators believe that the 18 chapters of the Bhagavad Gita cover three broad categories of themes: (1) the first six chapters, called *karma-shatkam,* deal with the concept of selfless actions as a path to liberation; (2) the next six chapters, called *bhakti-shatkam,* deal with the topic of love of the personal God as a path to liberation; and (3) the final six chapters, called *jnana-shatkam,* deal with the path of self-knowledge as a means to spiritual liberation.

Commenting on *Karma Yoga* as enunciated in the Bhagavad Gita, Mysore Hiriyanna explains, "The object of the Gita is to discover a golden mean between the two ideals...of action and contemplation...

preserving the excellence of both. Karma-Yoga is such a mean…. [It] stands not for renunciation *of* action, but for renunciation *in* action."[2]

The Path of Enlightened Action

These words, *Karma* and *Yoga,* have become a regular part of the daily discourse in the West. In order to understand the true import of *Karma Yoga,* the path of selfless action, we need to take a short excursion into the realm of Indian philosophy—especially the system of *Advaita Vedanta.* This system takes the ultimate reality to be one only, without a second, and represents the end or culmination of Vedas, the sacred books of knowledge. A proper understanding of *Karma Yoga* also assumes a clear grasp of the operation of the law of *Karma* as conceived within the framework of the Indian spiritual paradigm. This section is presented as a self-contained, complete module and assumes no prior knowledge of Indian philosophy on the part of the reader.

All systems of Indian philosophy take it as axiomatic that the primary cause of our bondage (in the form of suffering or misery) is due to a special type of ignorance *(avidya).* This ignorance does not denote lack of information or knowledge in any general sense. The ignorance that is referred to here is actually the ignorance of our essential nature, that is, self-ignorance. A person may be highly literate or educated but may still be operating under the spell of self-ignorance. Therefore, the *summum bonum* of all Indian philosophy is to eradicate this ignorance, root and branch, through self-knowledge—the knowledge of our true nature.

Advaita Vedanta[3] is the most widely known system of Indian philosophy, both in the East and the West. It presents perhaps the clearest formulation of the human predicament and the means to address it. The be-all and end-all of *Advaita* (non-duality) is the absolute non-difference of the individual self *(Atman)* and the ultimate reality *(Brahman).* It starts with rather lofty assertion that the absolute *(Brahman)* alone is real, and the individual self is none other than the absolute. The ultimate reality is called *Brahman* because it is all-pervasive. The *Brahman* is undifferentiated pure consciousness, devoid of parts, attributes, form, changes, or limitations. It is self-luminous and non-dual—one only, without a second. It is the source and substratum of all and everything.

Advaita postulates that at no time ever is our individual self not one with the absolute. Due to ignorance *(avidya)*, however, we do not realize our true identity with the absolute *Brahman*. When this ignorance is removed through the realization of our true self—which is ever identical with the absolute—we attain liberation from the bonds of our conditioned existence. To achieve this freedom through selfless action is the real purpose of *Karma Yoga*. Thus, *Karma Yoga* serves as a preamble to self-knowledge through self-renunciation. Indian philosophy makes it clear that *Karma Yoga* purifies the mind and prepares it to receive the wisdom of self-knowledge, which alone leads to spiritual freedom.

What is *Karma*?

Etymologically speaking, the word *Karma* is derived from a Sanskrit word *Karman*, which means *action* or *deed*. As a moral principle, *Karma* means at once the *deed* and the *result of deed*. The doctrine of *Karma* states that "whatever action is done by an individual leaves behind it some sort of potency which has the power to ordain for him joy or sorrow in the future according as it is good or bad."[4] The moment an action is performed, the universal law of *Karma* takes over and processes it according to its proper nature.

According to this law, nothing is chaotic or capricious in the moral realm. As we sow, so we reap: Sow a thought and reap an act. Sow an act and reap a habit. Sow a habit and reap a character. Sow a character and reap a destiny. Put simply, what goes around comes around. "A man becomes good by good deeds," says the Brhadaranyaka Upanishad (4.4.5), "and bad by bad deeds." Thus, *Karma* becomes at once the law of cause and effect and also nature's way to restore lost harmony.

Types of *Karma*

Indian philosophy divides all *karmas* into three types: *Sanchita*, *Agami*, and *Prarabdha*. This is a most useful classification to understand the workings of the law of *Karma*. *Sanchita* is *Karma* accumulated in the past; *Agami* is *Karma* to be worked out in the future; and *Prarabdha* is *Karma* that has begun to fructify in the present lifetime. All actions as normally undertaken entail results or outcomes that have a binding effect; that is, they bind the doer with their results, good or bad. *Karma Yoga*—the *yoga* of selfless action—is the enlightened art of performing actions in such a way that actions *lose* their binding power. This is accomplished through performing actions with the spirit of self-renunciation and by way of submission to the divine will so that one remains unattached inwardly while being fully engaged in actions outwardly. This is the alchemy of *Karma Yoga*.

It is when one can so restrain oneself as to only perform actions in the spirit of self-renunciation that one ceases to accumulate any new *Karma* for fresh results. One only has to experience the results of one's previous *Karma* that have ripened for giving fruits. If in the meantime one attains true knowledge of one's real self, all past accumulated actions are destroyed. In sum, once certain actions have become fit for fruition, these can't be avoided—like an arrow that has already been shot toward the target. However, those actions that have not yet matured are annulled once and for all if the person attains self-knowledge in the meanwhile, as advocated by Vedantic philosophy.

Does *Karma* Teach Passive Resignation?

Some critics remark that the doctrine of *Karma* is fatalistic. So that such teachings are not misconstrued as a doctrine of passive resignation—and a license for laziness—the sages have always advised seekers to first do their part diligently and then trust in God. The following Sufi story illustrates this point admirably.

> ## Doing Our Rightful Share First and Then Trusting in God
>
> Once a novice seeker paid a visit to a Sufi master to learn something about the art of living. The master lived in a small tent in a remote part of the desert. The young seeker entered the tent intently and after paying respects took his place among the select audience seated quietly around the Sufi.
>
> The Sufi greeted the young man with a smile and asked him how he got there. The young man said that he had come riding on a camel.
>
> "Where is your camel now?" asked the Sufi. "I left it outside under Allah's care," replied the young man, trying to impress the master.
>
> "Go! First tie the camel and then place your trust in God," replied the Sufi.[5]

This story also demonstrates that the strength of a teacher lies in using mundane occasions of life to illustrate the deeper lessons of life.

Moral Balance Sheet or Sure Path to Sagehood?

Hindus find *Karma* very useful in explaining the experiences of life: it is seen as a law of moral harmony. It provides a highly plausible explanation of inequities in life and thus destroys the cause of envy and jealousy and consequent ill will (for example, our neighbor is more fortunate because he or she has earned it). It also seems to remove impatience (for example, whatever is mine shall come to me sooner or later). It must be noted that the doctrine of *Karma* does not negate the idea of personal freedom. Though our present seems to be largely determined by our own past, the future seems to be dependent on the propriety of our present actions. In the words of Sir Radhakrishnan, "The cards in the game of life are given to us. We do not select them. They are traced to our past *Karma*, but we can call as we please, lead what suit we will, and, as we play, we gain or lose. And there is freedom."[6]

In Indian philosophy, the law of *Karma* is used to explain the cause of human bondage as well as the means to attain liberation from bondage. When actions are performed with a selfish motive, they bind; when actions are performed with the spirit of self-renunciation—and by way of submission to divine will—they liberate. Performance of actions selflessly purifies the mind and renders it worthy to receive the liberating spiritual wisdom. Ethics is thus considered a necessary prelude to spiritual freedom. According to a well-known Indian dictum, "Scriptures do not cleanse the ethically unworthy."

According to *Karma Yoga*, it is not what one does, but the motive or intention behind the act that produces the binding effect of *Karma*. "God cares more for adverbs than for verbs."[7] Accordingly, it is not necessary to renounce any activity. All that is needed is to act with pure unselfishness. In the following pages, this path of enlightened action is explored in greater depth as the alchemy of sagehood—the realization of one's highest self.

Key Teachings Regarding *Karma* Yoga

The Bhagavad Gita starts with Arjuna's admittance of his confusion with regards to what is decidedly "good" *(shreya)* in life (2.7).[8] This is the basic human dilemma—the conflict between duty and desire. Arjuna admits that he is confused about the right thing to do, surrenders to the Supreme, and humbly asks for the guidance on the path (2.7).

The teachings regarding *Karma Yoga* are presented throughout the Gita, although chapters 2–5 specifically deal with it. Chapter 3 is specifically designated as the path of action. Sri Krishna provides an important clue about this path, starting with the two succinct verses in chapter 2, as follows:

Your right is to work only, but never to its results. Let not the fruit of action be your motive, nor let your attachment be for inaction.

Do your duty to the best of your ability, O Arjuna, with your mind steadfast in equanimity, abandoning worry and selfish attachment to the results, and remaining equanimous in both success and failure. This equanimity of mind is called yoga. (2.47–48)

Sri Krishna presents all the foundational elements of *Karma Yoga* in these two verses. The first verse (47) presents an existential fact: we have no control over the results of our actions. This is true whether we are talking about actions in the secular or the sacred sense. Even our control over our actions *per se* is also very limited, given that all actions are performed by force of our nature.[9] This crucial point is also elaborated later in chapters 3 and 5 of the Gita. So that we do not therefore resign ourselves to inaction, verse 47 clarifies that the teaching here is about renunciation of results and not renunciation of actions themselves, that is, renunciation *in* action and not *of* action.

Verse 48 exhorts us to perform our actions to the best of our capacities, abandoning any concern for their results, remaining equanimous in both success and failure. This evenness of mind in both success and failure is called *Yoga*. However, remaining unconcerned about the results is not a license for sloppiness. One has to perform one's actions remaining steadfast in the *yoga* of equanimity. This *Yoga* (equanimity) is in fact the dexterity *(kaushlam)* in the performance of actions (2.50). This dexterity works in two ways: it frees actions from their inherent binding power, while at the same time transforming actions into effective means of spiritual freedom. "The *Yogis* perform actions," says the Gita, "unattached, for the purification of their mind" ("*Yoginah karam kruvantey, sangg tyagttva, aatma-shuddhey,*" 5.11).

Chapter 3 of the Gita, titled the path of action *(Karma Yoga)*, begins with a clarification that there are two paths: the path of knowledge for the contemplative and the path of works for the active (3.3). It adds, however, that no one attains perfection merely by giving up actions (3.4) without possessing self-knowledge. After all, no one can remain without action even for a moment; everyone is driven to action by nature (3.5). One cannot even maintain one's body without action (3.8); therefore, one attains the supreme by performing actions effectively, without attachment, as a matter of duty (3.19). Only actions in the spirit of renunciation do not bind (3.9). The wise act for the unification of the world at large (*loka samgraham,* 3.20, 3.25).

Then come two verses that provide perhaps the greatest *raison d'etre* of all actions performed by force of inherent qualities:

> All actions are performed by gunas [qualities] of primordial nature [Pakriti]. One whose mind is deluded by egoism thinks, "I am the doer."

> But one, with true insight into the respective domains of gunas and action, knowing that gunas as senses merely move among gunas as objects, does not become attached. (3.27–28)[10]

These verses state that we perform all actions by the energies of three qualities *(gunas)*—purity *(satvic),* activity *(rajasic),* and inertia *(tamasic).* Acting upon *gunas* via senses, and deluded by our ego sense *(ahamkara),* we take ourselves to be the doers. But those who understand the respective domains of these *gunas* and their actions do not get attached to them:

> The knower of Truth, [being] centered [in the Self] should think, "I do nothing at all"—though seeing, hearing, touching, smelling, eating, going, sleeping, breathing, speaking, letting go, holding, opening and closing the eyes—convinced that it is the senses that move among sense objects.[11] (5.8–9)

The above verses state that the seer of reality *(tattva-vit)* is firm *(yukto)* in his or her belief *(manyeta)* that "I do nothing at all" *(na eva kinchit karom iti)*, realizing that the senses are moving among the sense objects. Sankara explains in his commentary that one who has the knowledge of the actionless Self sees inaction in action (4.18) for he or she realizes that in all actions the senses operate upon objects (sense objects), while the Self remains immutably inactive.

The Bhagavad Gita tells us that "for one who knows the self, who rejoices solely in the Self, who is satisfied with the Self, and who is content in the Self alone,—for him there is nothing more left to do" (3.17). In other words, the Self is ever actionless, as action in nature *(Prakriti's gunas)* is inaction in the Self *(Atman)*. Ultimately, the Self is beyond both action and inaction for, as we do with action, we also incorrectly attribute inaction to the Self, as we see, for example, in the phrase, "Quiet and doing nothing, I sit happy."[12]

A question may be asked here: If, for the knower of the Self, nothing remains to be done, then how do we explain the apparent actions of the enlightened ones? In his commentary on the Bhagavad Gita, Sankara (788–820 AD), the greatest Indian philosopher, presents at least four explanations. The sages act:

1. with a view to set an example to the masses, so the unwary do not go astray (3.26);

2. for the unification of the world at large *(loka samgraham, 3.20, 3.25)*;

3. for the welfare of the world at large *(sarva bhuuta hitae, 5.25)*;

4. for the purification of the self *(atmasuddhaye, 5.11)*.

In verses 5.25 and 12.4, a liberated person is described as "most naturally and intently engaged in seeking and promoting the welfare of all beings" *(sarva bhuuta hitae ratah)*. Sri Krishna, using himself as an example of a liberated being, tells Arjuna, "there is nothing in all the three worlds for me to do, nor is there anything worth attaining unattained by me, yet I continue to work" (3.22). Then in verse 3.25 we find the clearest practical advice to live by: "As the unwise act with attachment, so should the wise, seeking maintenance of the world order, act without attachment."

In sum, the seers act for the well-being of all beings (*sarva bhuuta hitae ratah*, 5.25, 12.4) and for the unification of the world (*loksamgraha*, 3.20, 3.25). At the highest level, they spontaneously embody the virtues of universal morality, such as selflessness, compassion, desirelessness, forbearance, peace, and harmony. This is the culmination of *Karma Yoga*.

Conducting Our Affairs without the Tag of Doership

The alchemy of *nishkaama Karma,* selfless action, lies in neutralizing the binding power of *Karma*. When an action is performed with an egoistic feeling, the pride of doership, then the *Karma* binds us in two ways. First, it reinforces our false sense of ego, thus making the egoic grooves deeper. Second, it sows the seeds of reaping the good or bad results of our actions. From the absolute standpoint, it makes little difference whether the so-called results of our actions are good or bad since both are ultimately binding in the sense that both will require the agent—the ego entity—to be there to experience the results. It will create more occasions for further *Karma* to be generated, which is precisely what conditioned existence *(samsara)* entails—the cyclic rounds of endless births and deaths. This does not, therefore, involve complete spiritual freedom *(Mukti)* from all phenomenal existence, once and for all—the *summum bonum* of all Indian spiritual pursuits. Viewed in the light of Indian doctrine of *Mukti*, all of our selfish actions suffer from the defect of tainted results *(vipreet dosha);* that is, they lead to bondage. Only selfless actions purify the soul and prepare it to receive the spiritual wisdom that alone leads to liberation in due course of time.

This is then the gist of *Karma Yoga*: perform all actions as offerings *(arpana)* to the supreme and accept all results as graceful gifts *(prasaad)* from the supreme, that is, performing all actions in the spirit of service to the Lord *(Ishvara-arpana bhavana)* and accepting all results as gracious gifts from the Lord *(Ishvara-prasaad bhavana).*[13]

The following story clearly illustrates how one can discharge one's duties most diligently without any sense of personal agency.

Source of Our Misery and Sorrow: False Sense of Ownership

Once, a king decided to celebrate his birthday in an unusually generous manner. He announced that on his birthday he would organize an exhibition in which traders from far and wide would be invited to display their goods for sale. However, on the day of his birthday, anyone could come to the exhibition and get anything they wanted for free. This was the best deal ever. So people rushed from everywhere to get things for free on the day of the king's birthday.

Toward the evening, a sage was seen walking through the stalls. He did not seem to be interested in anything that was displayed. Instead, he had been asking for the whereabouts of the king who organized the unusual exhibition. Some people surmised that he might have a special wish that he wanted to express directly to the king.

He was soon directed to the king's court. As the sage walked into the court, the king greeted him respectfully and asked him if he found anything worth getting from the stalls in the exhibition. The sage indicated what he wanted was not available in the exhibition. The king readily agreed that he would be most happy to give him anything he wished for. "Anything?" asked the sage, just to make sure. The king replied, "Yes, I would be happy to give anything that you would like to have."

The sage said, "Actually, I want your kingdom!"

(continued on next page)

(continued from previous page)

At first, the king was very surprised at the sage's unusual request. Then, being true to his word, the king said, "I will be happy to fulfill your wish. You can have my kingdom and everything that goes with it. It is all yours. Kindly come forward and be seated on the throne." Everyone in the court was stunned to hear this, and there was dead silence for several minutes. They had never seen or heard something like this before.

Everyone present was even more surprised when they heard the sage address the king, thusly: "I am very pleased with your generous sense of renunciation. However, I have no desire to claim this or any other throne. I am a forest-dweller and have no attraction for such worldly things. I ask you only this. From now onward, please rule your kingdom as before but with the understanding that it really belongs to me; you are just a caretaker. This way, you will be able to conduct all its affairs without your usual sense of 'me and mine.' Above all, you will always be happy and content because all worries and misery come from our false sense of ownership and undue attachment to things that are ultimately transient and subject to change."

The sage left the court.

The king's perspective on life and leadership had been changed forever![14]

Freedom from the Ego

The knower of Self has achieved complete freedom from the shackles of egoism, that is, from the false sense of doership. In a most telling verse, the sage Astavakra analyzes the malady of egoism and prescribes the fitting medicine: "Do you who have been bitten by the great black serpent of egoism 'I am the doer,' drink the nectar of the faith 'I am not the doer,' and be happy" (Astavakra Gita 1.8).

Finally, we present a story that crystallizes the burden of false ego in a powerful manner. This story was first told by Swami Brahmatmananda Ji Saraswati of Rishikesh:

The Irony of Carrying the Deadweight of Imposter Ego

A man was travelling in a train. He was alone in the train compartment. He was enjoying the moving scenery outside until another passenger got into the compartment and took the seat right in front of him. Outwardly, this passenger looked rather wealthy and was carrying a big long suitcase—a heavy trunk made of iron—that he put right beside himself. Because of its heavy weight, he could not put it up on the berth. The first passenger was watching it rather intently wondering what could be in the suitcase. He mused that this fellow seemed very wealthy (judging from the clothes and the golden watch etc. that he was wearing); he must have something really precious in the suitcase, like gold bricks or diamonds. That is why probably he did not even put it up on the berth! Such thoughts were racing through his brain like crazy as he was watching very carefully every gesture of the mystery passenger.

The train stopped at the next railway station and the mystery passenger asked the first passenger: "I am going to get a cup of coffee for myself. Do you want me get you something? Would you kindly watch my luggage until I come back?" "Sure, I will be happy to," said the first passenger. As the mystery passenger got off the train to get a cup of coffee, the first passenger's mind started working in a turbo mode, wildly imagining all sorts of things that could be in the suitcase.

In the meanwhile, the train started! Anxiously, he got up to look for the mystery passenger through the window. The

(continued on next page)

(continued from previous page)

mystery passenger was not to be seen anywhere. The first passenger thought that, may be, the mystery passenger got on in another train compartment due to the train taking off quickly. So, he waited for him till the next train stop. But the mystery passenger did not come back.

Now, his greedy mind again started spinning all sorts of thoughts about the contents of the suitcase. And then he suddenly saw the ticket collector—called the "Guard" in India—get in the train compartment to check tickets. He asked this passenger: "Whose suitcase is this and why is it placed on the seat and not placed on the berth?" A million thoughts raced through this passenger's mind....the ticket collector does not know anything about the mystery passenger...what if I say this suitcase is mine...and then I can have it when he leaves and be rich for the rest of my life, so on and so forth...

The ticket collector asked him again: "Whose suitcase is this?" "It is mine, sir!" "And why did you put it on the seat?" asked the ticket collector. "Because it is a bit heavy and I did not have the strength to put it up on the berth. Besides the compartment was all empty; no one was here besides me so I thought it is okay to leave it on the seat." "Okay, so what is in it?" asked the ticket collector. The passenger was not ready for this question. Trying to look genuine, he immediately blurted: "Just the clothes, shoes, utensils—the usual house hold stuff." "Can you please open it for me? I want to see what is in it," asked the ticket collector. "Sure!" said the passenger, confused, anxious, and a bit worried but still trying to maintain a false look of confidence.

As the passenger opened the suitcase for the ticket collector to see, he was stunned to find out that there was a dead body inside!

The ticket collector asked the passenger: "What is this and who is this person?" The passenger, who was still in a state of complete shock, tried to explain that he did not know anything about the dead body and that the suitcase did not in fact belong to him. But the ticket collector told this person that he had been lying and arrested him on the spot and put him in prison for a crime that he did not really commit.[15]

Swami Sri Brahmatmananda Saraswati's comment on this story is noteworthy:

> This is the common plight of man. All his life, man carries the burden (dead body) of the imposter ego, which he falsely calls his own. And because of this false attribution/identification, he remains in bondage (prison), so to speak, and suffers all his life.[16]

The story of course is symbolic and has subtle layers of meaning. The mystery passenger in the story is a metaphor for *jivanmukta*—a being who is liberated while living—who has abandoned the dead weight of the false ego and has been awakened to the reality of the pure, action-less Self. The false identification with body, mind, and senses—and becoming a doer-enjoyer *(karta-bhokgta)* as a result—is what is called ignorance *(ajnana)* in *Advaita Vedanta*. The realization that "I am not doer"—since all actions are performed by qualities *(gunas)* born out of Nature *(Prakriti),* the Divine Illusion *(Maya),* is called Knowledge *(jnana).* In the Vedantic scheme of things, this is the final end and purpose, the *summum bonum,* of human existence. In a categorical verse of the Ashtavakra Gita: "Neither doer nor enjoyer—you are verily ever free" *(Na kartaasi na bhogrtaasi, mukktt evaasi sarvadaa,* 1.6).

Selfless Service and Servant Leadership

The gift of selfless service has a great application in the realm of leadership. First and foremost, leadership is a responsibility—a call to serve—and not a position to wield power or influence. The power that is bestowed upon the leader by the followers is of the nature of trust and good faith. In other words, it is a fiduciary relationship. Viewed in this manner, the only reason a leader exists is to enable and empower the followers. Great leaders approach their work as a contribution, as a service, without any sense of entitlement whatsoever.

Practicing servant leadership is deceptively simple: one is led by the deep desire to serve others. It is also about putting others' interest first. History is a testimony to the fact that true leaders, above all, are servant leaders. When all is said and done, there is no human ideal higher than the gift of selfless service. For in serving others, we find our true joy and fulfillment.

Concluding Remarks

In this chapter we approached the gift of selfless service as a discipline of *Karma Yoga,* mainly as presented in the Bhagavad Gita. It is important to realize the true import of these teachings. The most striking feature of our human existence is the sense of doership, the feeling of "me, my, and mine" in all that we undertake. These teachings strike at the very root of our fundamental existential illusion, namely, the false sense of doership. It invites us to consider a revolutionary viewpoint. Since all actions are performed by the three modes of Nature, they do not really originate as deliberate acts of volition in our mind. This understanding frees us from the clutches of imposter ego and paves the way for the realization of our true self. For as long as we operate within the false paradigm of "me, my, and mine," real Self-knowledge will elude us.

In elucidating what is called the doctrine of selfless action *(nishkaama Karma),* the Bhagavad Gita urges us to renounce selfish actions and fruits of actions. In the ultimate analysis, renunciation is an inner, mental act and should not be confused with outward tokens of relinquishment. It is about renunciation of results and not renunciation of actions themselves.

That is, renunciation *in* action and not *of* actions. True renunciation is the renunciation of *kartapann*—the deeply ingrained sense of doership. In one word, the alchemy of *Karma Yoga* lies in performing actions without the tag of doership. This is the master key!

When actions are performed with the spirit of self-renunciation and by way of submission to the divine will so that one remains unattached inwardly while being fully engaged in actions outwardly, they serve as harbingers of sagehood—the realization of one's highest Self.

Arousing the Mind of Compassion

May my life become a suitable vessel
of Loving-Kindness and
a Gateway to Great Compassion.
Mind ever-pure, established in Serene Joy,
Always refraining from doing harm,
Forever abiding in doing good~
Inspire me thus!

For countless eons, i have suffered
the slings of self-cherishing mind,
Ever living in the servitude of Ego-Supreme:
The vicious cycle of I, Myself, and Me.
Failing to recognize the great kindness of others~
Our mother sentient beings.

Wake me up from the slumber of Ego-Grasping,
And guide me in the Wisdom Supreme—
The noble path of the Enlightened Ones...
The path of Buddhas and Bodhisattvas...

For the sake of others
Arouse in me the precious Bodhichitta~
The altruistic mind of enlightenment.
May all my actions be guided by the
sole desire to serve and benefit all beings~
Inspire me thus!

May i exchange myself with others,
By developing the mind of equanimity.
Recognizing that, like myself, everyone
desires happiness and shuns sorrow.
May i become the cause of their happiness,
and benefit all beings equally~
Inspire me thus!

CHAPTER NINE

THE GIFT OF TOTAL ACCEPTANCE

He is a wise man who does not grieve for the things which he has not, but rejoices for those which he has.

~ EPICTETUS

I accept life unconditionally. Most people ask for happiness on condition. Happiness can only be felt if you don't set any condition.

~ ARTHUR RUBINSTEIN (1887-1982)

Nobody needs to go anywhere else. We are all, if we only knew it, already there. If I only know who in fact I am, I should cease to behave as what I think I am; and if I stopped behaving as what I think I am, I should know who I am. What in fact I am, if only I think I am would allow me to know it, is the reconciliation of yes and no lived out in total acceptance and the blessed experience of Not-Two. Conflicts and frustrations—the theme of all history and almost all biography. "I show you sorrow," said the Buddha realistically. But he also showed the ending of sorrow—self-knowledge, total acceptance, the blessed experience of Not-Two.[1]

~ ALDOUS HUXLEY (1894-1963)

A student once asked Zen teacher Steve Allen, "If you were given a wish-fulfilling jewel, what would you wish for?" "To stop wishing," replied Allen.[2]

When I am in New York, I want to be in Europe, and when I am in Europe, I want to be in New York.

~ WOODY ALLEN

In winter, we think summer is the best season; in summer, we think winter is the best season. Such is human logic.

~ MULLA NASRUDDIN

Accepting Life, Warts and All!

One of the sweet "catches" of life is that we become wiser after the event, and hindsight is always 20/20. We are often reminded that everything is exactly the way it should be in the cosmic scheme of things. The Zen masters have told us all along that everything is on schedule in the universe. They express their zany wisdom as follows: No appointment, no disappointment. There seems to be a certain inevitability in every incident in our life. To wit, life just happens to us amidst our planning and projections. Although things may work out in the end after all, accepting them the way they are *en route* is very hard to come to grips with.

True acceptance stems from understanding life's profound reality and entails surrendering to its wisdom. It is about realizing our proper place in the universe—accepting our relative existence with all its vulnerability, precariousness, and transience. Suzuki Roshi, a remarkable Soto Zen master, said it well: "Without accepting the fact that everything changes, we cannot find perfect composure. But unfortunately, although it is true, it is difficult for us to accept it. Because we cannot accept the truth of transiency, we suffer."[3]

It is important to remember that the gift of total acceptance, more often than not, pertains to accepting ourselves and others as such so as to bring peace and harmony in human relationships. A careful reflection on the human plight reveals that two things that most spoil our peace and harmony are self-regret and blame for others. We keep on blaming

ourselves for something we did not do that we could have or should have
done. Likewise, we tend to blame others for something they should have
or could have done for us. As long as we remain trapped in the cocoon
of resentment and blame, there is no possibility of any real peace and
happiness. So the real secret of bringing true peace and harmony in our
relationship is just this: total acceptance—accepting ourselves as we are
and accepting others as they are.

The gift of kindness and the gift of forgiveness serve as the warp
and woof for the gift of acceptance and can really prove life-empowering
in their own right. I recently attended a seminar regarding the health
benefits of super foods. After extolling the virtues of such super foods as
acai berries, goji berries, broccoli sprouts, organic vegetables and fruits,
and probiotic supplements, the speaker concluded his two-hour talk by
saying that "the one best thing that you could do to restore your health
is this: If you are holding some grudge against someone in your life,
forgive them." Huxley, at the end of his illustrious career as a celebrated
writer of perennial philosophy, had only this to say: "It is a bit embar-
rassing to have been concerned with the human problem all one's life
and to find at the end that one has no more to offer by way of advice
than 'Try to be a little kinder.'"[4]

Strangely enough, accepting ourselves as we are may the hardest
part of the equation. As long as there is any aspiration to become something different than what we are, life remains a struggle. Krishnamurti
(1895–1986), a modern sage, once surprised his audience by saying,
"Let me tell you my secret: I do not compare and I do not mind what
happens." In the short space of a sentence, Krishnamurti has provided
the secret to the art and science of fulfillment: non-comparison and
acceptance of what is. By relinquishing the need to be different from
what we are, we step out of the cycle of becoming and enter into the
peaceful abode of being, which is always available to us in the present.
Being ourselves involves no struggle; it is the most easy and natural
thing in life and requires no time. It is always available to us right here
and now, effortlessly, through the medium of acceptance.

Acceptance out of Helplessness or Understanding

Acceptance can happen in one of the two ways: acceptance due to utter helplessness in wake of the inevitable or acceptance due to deep understanding about life as it really is. In the first case, there is a sense of helplessness or disillusionment that creates inner resistance and acts as a constant drain on our energies. This is called unhealthy acceptance because there is an unaddressed, nagging sense of victimization, injustice, or even hatred in the face of the inevitable.

Acceptance of what has happened, said William James, is the first step to overcoming the consequences of any misfortune. It is possible only when there is acceptance without resistance or expectation. It is a common fact of life that we soon adapt to whatever experience life brings to us. As Leo Tolstoy (1828–1910) observed, "There are no conditions to which a man cannot become accustomed." Psychologists call this tendency of becoming accustomed to our experiences "hedonic adaptation." According to this theory, we tend to maintain a relatively stable level of happiness despite major positive or negative events.[5]

The second type of acceptance is the result of clear understanding of the real nature of our existence and its props—finite, precarious, and time-bound. The idea is not just growing accustomed to life conditions, helplessly, but accepting their inevitability without preference or denial. This is called happy acceptance. It has a transformative power that transmutes the misfortunes into opportunities of self-growth and development. It is perhaps this type of acceptance that Katherine Mansfield (1888–1923) had in mind when she observed that "everything in life that we really accept undergoes a change." The most important point to remember here is that, with some reflection, the first type of acceptance can be transformed into the second type of acceptance. However, it is not always the case that pain in our life gives way to understanding; but when it does happen, the inner resistance is replaced by life-affirming wisdom.

Healthy acceptance is beautifully expressed in what is known as the "Serenity Prayer":

O Lord…

Grant me the serenity to accept what I cannot change,
Grant me the courage to change what I can change; and
Grant me the wisdom to know the difference.

The prayer bestows the three virtues of acceptance, courage, and discernment: balance of mind to accept what cannot be changed, courage to transform what can be changed, and the discerning wisdom to know what can or cannot be changed in life.

Expect Nothing—Accept Everything

It has been observed that the sure road to contentment is paved by expecting nothing and accepting everything. At first this may sound like a counsel of perfection. The following story splendidly illustrates the wisdom of acceptance in life, as it unfolds, without resistance or expectation.

Good Luck or Bad Luck? How Do We Know?

An old man was living with his son at an abandoned fort on the top of a hill, and one day he lost a horse. The neighbors came to express their sympathy for this misfortune, and the old man asked, "How do you know that this is bad luck?" A few days afterwards, his horse returned with a number of wild horses, and his neighbors came again to congratulate him on this stroke of fortune, and the old man replied, "How do you know this is good luck?" With so many horses around, his son began to take to riding, and one day he broke his leg. Again the neighbors came around to express their sympathy, and the old man replied, "How do you know this is bad luck?" The next month, there was a war, and because the old man's son was crippled, he did not have to go to the front.[6]

Total Acceptance: Not a Passive Resignation

We should not, however, misconstrue the gift of total acceptance as the recipe for doing nothing and accepting passively whatever life brings to us. If there arises a spontaneous urge to change what is, then total acceptance also means accepting that urge and acting on it. Total acceptance is not a recipe for laziness but a philosophy of spontaneous engagement with the flow of life, without preference or rejection. Walt Whitman (1819–1892), in his poetry collection *Leaves of Grass,* takes this to be a great life-lesson: "Here the profound lesson of reception, *nor preference nor denial…*" (emphasis added).

Total Acceptance: Letting Things Be!

Total acceptance also means letting things be or, as Chinese wisdom puts it, not *legging* the snake. As the story goes, participants in a painting competition were asked to paint a snake. One participant finished his painting rather quickly and as he looked around, he realized that everyone else was still busy with their paintings. Wondering if he had left something out, he started drawing legs under the snake without realizing that snake has no legs! Chinese wisdom tradition, called Taoism, refers to this principle as *wu-wei*—non-doing—which means doing nothing unnaturally or forced. It is about refraining from an undue interference with the natural flow of things. In his book *Zen in the Art of Archery,* Eugen Herrigel was gently reprimanded by his Zen master for trying to force the results too willfully, thusly: "What stands in your way is that you have a much too much willful will. You think that what you do not do yourself does not happen."[7]

The gift of total acceptance also serves as the best antidote to impatience. Sometimes, in our bid to hasten the process of life, we end up hurting it permanently, not unlike the farmer who, in order to help the plants grow faster, ended up killing them by trying to pull them up a bit. As they say in Zen, "Don't push the river." Here is another story that illustrates the deleterious effect of trying to help the course of nature without really understanding the sacred wisdom of its natural course:

The Need and Importance of Struggle

A man found a butterfly cocoon. One day a small opening appeared. He sat and watched the butterfly for several hours as it struggled to force its body through that little hole. Then it seemed to stop making any progress.

It appeared as if it had gotten as far as it could, and it could go no further. So to help the butterfly, He took a pair of scissors and snipped off the remaining bit of the cocoon.

The butterfly then emerged easily. But it had a swollen body and small, shriveled wings. The man continued to watch the butterfly because he expected that, at any moment, the wings would enlarge and expand to be able to support the body, which would contract in time. Neither happened! In fact, the butterfly spent the rest of it's life crawling around with a swollen body and shriveled wings.

It never was able to fly. What the man, in his kindness and haste, did not understand was that the restricting cocoon and the struggle required for the butterfly to get through the tiny opening were God's way of forcing fluid from the body of the butterfly into its wings so that it would be ready for flight once it achieved its freedom from the cocoon.

Sometimes struggles are exactly what we need in our lives. If God allowed us to go through our lives without any obstacles, it would cripple us. We would not be as strong as what we could have been. We could never fly.[8]

The Problem with Having No Problems!

In our search for the ideal haven, we sometimes fail to realize that life isn't perfect. Actually it isn't meant to be perfect. In fact, it is good that life is not perfect or even near perfect for if it were so, we would lose any inspiration to better our best, and soon we would lose any desire to live out of sheer boredom. Life's little annoyances, silly irritations, and discomforting imperfections are responsible for all of humanity's progress. So to ask for perfection is to ask for the impossible and to ask for the impossible is the surest way to nonfulfillment, as the following story splendidly illustrates.

The Problem of Expecting No Problems

A tale is told about a man who came to the Buddha for help. He was unhappy with his life. There was nothing overwhelmingly terrible about it, but it always presented him with endless succession of little disappointments and complaints.

He was a farmer. And he enjoyed farming. But sometimes it didn't rain enough, or it rained too much, and his harvests were not the best.

He had a wife. And she was a good wife; he even loved her. But she sometimes nagged him too much. And sometimes he got tired of her.

And he had kids. And they were good kids. He enjoyed them a lot. But sometimes....

The Buddha listened patiently to the man's story until finally the man wound down. He looked at Buddha expectantly, waiting for some word to fix everything. The Buddha said, "I can't help you."

The man was startled. He said, "I thought you were a great teacher. I thought you could help me.'

"Everybody has got problems," said the Buddha. "In fact, we always have eighty-three problems, each one of us, and there's nothing we can do about it. If you manage to solve one problem, it's immediately replaced by another. You will always have eighty-three problems...."

The man became furious. "Then what good is your teaching?" he demanded.

> "Well," said the Buddha, "it might help you with the eighty-fourth problem."
>
> "The eighty-fourth problem?" said the man. "What's the eighty-fourth problem?"
>
> "That you do not want any problems," replied the Buddha.[9]

Acceptance Means Not Asking for the Impossible!

Realizing that problems are a part of being alive and not asking for the impossible is the true expression of the gift of acceptance. It is important to note that healthy acceptance is born out of understanding the way things are: transient, subject to change. Expecting permanent fulfillment from things, objects, and situations that are inherently impermanent is a sure recipe for discontentment. Too often, we expect the impossible and then complain that life is not fair. Consider the following tale:

> ### Asking for the Impossible
>
> A person died and the God of rebirth appeared before him to grant him a boon. The man said that he had lived a virtuous life and, therefore, would like to have several boons. He started his list as follows: I will like to be reborn in the richest country of the world and have a very comfortable childhood—no teething troubles, no mumps, no measles. I will like to go to the best schools and study under the best teachers who do not insist on homework.
>
> When I grow up, I want to marry the most beautiful woman in the world who will not grow old. I want to have several children who are respectful and obedient to me. I want to live in a place where there is no pollution, where there are no earthquakes, no tsunamis, no wars, and so
>
> (continued on next page)

> (continued from previous page)
>
> *forth. I will like to have a mansion in every big city of the world without having to make mortgage payments. I want to live a very long life, without any illness or impending old age. The list continued....*
>
> *After hearing the laundry list of wants, God replied to this man, "If there exists such a place on earth as you have asked for, why would I send you there? I will like to go there myself!"[10]*

This tale clearly illustrates the inevitable frustration resulting from unreasonable expectations. Understandably, the story writer has used the art of exaggeration to make a point. But isn't this how we keep unconsciously priming the pump of our expectations? When we approach life in this manner, we ask for guaranteed disappointment. There is no fulfillment in expecting the impossible.

Healthy acceptance is based on the understanding that somehow whatever happens, happens for good and that things have a way of working out in the end. There may be an invisible cosmic hand guiding the course of our destiny and choreographing the events of our life. As the following story beautifully illustrates, very often, what we consider unfavorable event in the beginning turns out to be blessing in disguise:

> ### Whatever happens, happens for good!
>
> *There was once a king who had a wise counselor whom he respected a lot. In every sacred and secular endeavor, the king used to consult with him. The king held him in high regard. The counselor had a peculiar habit, though. His patent response to all situations in life was always the same: "Whatever happens, happens for good."*
>
> *One day, both went hunting in the forest. Accidently, the king hurt his thumb due to mishandling of one sharp*

arrow. While the king could have used some sympathy, the counselor merely said: "Whatever happens, happens for good." When they reached the palace, the royal physician was called in. He examined the thumb and said that the wound had become infected and recommended cutting the thumb. The king was alarmed. The counselor again said: "Whatever happens, happens for good!"

This really upset the king. He flew into a rage and angrily said, "You are fired from your position as a counselor." The counselor simply said, "Whatever happens, happens for good" and left. Months went without the wise counselor by king's side. One day, the king went hunting again. This time he was alone since he had already fired his trusted counselor. Towards the end of the day, the king was captured by a tribal group and was brought in front of their master. The master was delighted to see all this. He announced, "Today is a very special day. On this day we offer a human sacrifice to our chosen god. I am glad that you brought this person. We can offer him at the altar of sacrifice tonight." Little did anyone know about the true identity of the king.

So, they started making preparations for the sacrifice. The king was getting frightened beyond measure. The custom is such that only that human being is offered as a sacrifice who does not have a mutilated body part. So, when they examined the king they found out that his one thumb was missing. The master said that they cannot offer the king in sacrifice. So, they let him go the next morning.

The king had a sigh of relief when he came back in his palace. He remembered his counselor's words: 'Whatever happens, happens for good.' He now realized the wisdom behind these words. He called one of his officers and sent

(continued on next page)

(continued from previous page)

him to bring his counselor back. To win the counselor back, the king even offered the salary for the time when the counselor was unemployed.

When the counselor came back, the king told his story to him. The counselor once again said the same thing: "Whatever happens, happens for good." The king addressed the counselor thusly: "I now realize the wisdom behind this observation. But I am curious to find out how losing a job was a good thing for you." The counselor said, "Your Majesty! Losing job was a blessing on three counts: First, if I still had a job we both would have been captured by the fugitives. And being able-bodied, I would have been sacrificed at the altar. Secondly, my losing job was a blessing in disguise since I have received salary for a few months even without working. Thirdly, and most importantly, Your Majesty, you have learned the most important life-lesson: 'Whatever happens, happens for good!'"[11]

Concluding Remarks

The gift of acceptance invites us to consider that there may be some fairness about the situations we find ourselves in. In the final reckoning, there is no randomness in the hand life has dealt us. If we can change our circumstances, we should certainly try to do so. We should also reflect on our previous experiences about the effect of changing the external situation on our psychological well-being. At the same time, there is no benefit in arguing with the inevitable.

The Serenity Prayer mentioned in this chapter represents a healthy form of acceptance. Composure, courage, and discernment are three virtues that accompany fulfillment and pave the road to self-knowledge. Healthy acceptance is borne out of understanding life's profound reality and entails surrendering to its unfolding wisdom. It is about realizing our proper place in the universe—accepting our relative existence with all its vulnerability, precariousness, and transience. As long as we are not happy with what is and pine for what is not, the supreme joy of contentment will elude us.

Simple Joys of Acceptance

Whatever gifts life brings, unasked as matter of course,
I embrace joyfully and whole-heartedly,
Without imposing my naïve preferences!
For how do I know what is good what is bad for me,
Unless life has run its full course!

Accepting everyone and everything as is,
We move away from surface likes and dislikes!
To submit to life's abiding wisdom in granting
What is best for us in life's long strides!

Accepting things and people as they are
Does not mean passive submission or deference!
Being open to change what we can, and
By patiently bearing what we can't,
With wisdom that knows the difference!

By accepting myself and others as is,
I let life's wisdom shape greater ends!
Never expecting life to accord to my whims,
I let Existence to suit,
Nature's divine trims!

Less and less I fret and frown
At peoples' nature-driven behavior
I concern myself in ensuring that
My boat is secure of drown.

By affirming everyone and everything
I embrace all life in its diversity,
Making my willful will mute,
I open to the Oneness of the Absolute!

CHAPTER TEN
THE GIFT OF PRESENCE

We were speaking of awareness, and splitting hairs as to its nature, when suddenly we felt a jolt. We paid no attention to it and continued our conversation. A few seconds later, Krishnaji turned around and asked us what we were discussing.

"Awareness," we said and immediately started asking him questions about it.

He listened, looked at us quizzically, and then asked, "Did you notice what happened just now?"

"No."

"We knocked down a goat; did you not see it?"

"No."

Then with great gravity he said, "And you were discussing awareness."

No more words were necessary. It was devastating.[1]

~ PUPUL JAYANKAR

It is easy to be mindful. What is difficult is to remember to be mindful.

~ THANISSARO BHIKKHU

To be awake is to be alive. I have never yet met a man who was quite awake.

~ HENRY DAVID THOREAU

Everything you need for your life and your practice are directly in front of you in the present moment.

~ A ZEN SAYING

"There are two ways to wash the dishes," Thich Nhat Hanh once told a student. "The first is to wash the dishes in order to have clean dishes. The second is to wash the dishes in order to wash the dishes."[2]

Mindfulness is the miracle by which we master and restore ourselves…it is the miracle which can call back in a flash our dispersed mind and restore it to wholeness so that we can live each minute of life.[3]

Being Wherever We Are with All Our Mind!

The gift of presence is the culminating gift in the sense that it facilitates the practice of all other gifts by reminding us to remain alert from moment to moment. Only when we are awake to our inner and outer reality can we ensure the observance of the gifts of pure motivation, gratitude, generosity, harmlessness, selfless service, and total acceptance. Practices such as mindfulness and silence can bring about greater awareness in everything we do and enable us to share the gift of our presence. This chapter begins by presenting an overview of the essential elements of Buddhist psychology as a mental discipline, the Buddhist practice of mindfulness as it is found in the earliest Buddhist writings. This overview is followed by a detailed description of my recent experience with a form of Buddhist meditation called *Vipassana*.

Right mindfulness, right concentration, and right effort constitute the Buddhist mental discipline. The mind is trained, disciplined, and developed through these three practices, which aim at cleansing the mind of impurities and disturbances, such as lustful desires, hatred, ill-will, indolence, worries and restlessness, skeptical doubts, and cultivating such qualities as concentration, awareness, intelligence, will, energy, the analytical faculty, confidence, joy, tranquility; leading finally to the attainment of the highest wisdom which sees things as they are, and realizes the Ultimate Truth, Nirvana.[4]

How does Buddhist philosophy and psychology help us attain lasting happiness and fulfillment? As must be evident by now, Buddhism is more a way of life, a philosophy, than a religion in the traditional sense. It is a "do-it-yourself psychology" by way of "to whom it may concern." The Buddhist viewpoint aims at achieving abiding happiness through mind training, development, and control, irrespective of our external circumstances. Through the wisdom of seeing things as they are, it helps us in the cultivation of unconditional loving kindness toward all existence.

The best gift we human beings can give others is the gift of our presence, our attentive listening, our empathy, our kindness and compassion. This is possible only if we are truly present in all our engagements and interactions. A sign in Las Vegas says, "In order to win, you have to be present." Likewise, in order to be successful at the game of life, we have to be alertly present in everything we do. Being present requires the development of a special faculty called self-awareness. Intrinsically, our being is of the nature of pure awareness—of the nature of "wisdom-seeking wisdom"—always available to all of us right here and right now, whenever and wherever we need it, if only we open ourselves to it unconditionally.

If we observe our mind we discover that it hops from past to future and from future to past, endlessly. It rarely, if ever, dwells in the present. This phenomenon can be called, half-jokingly, the Law of Elsewhere: our mind always likes to be elsewhere! Interestingly, "now" is rightly called "present"—it truly is a "gift" from gods. As with our other gifts of fulfillment, we must make a habit of this one by learning to be alertly present in the present moment—to be keenly attuned to the current reality. It is a strange realization that even past and future can only be experienced in the now, the eternal present moment. The ability to be in the present moment, from moment to moment, is the master key to enjoy small pleasures that life accords us unexpectedly. Most of the time our mind is roaming elsewhere when we outwardly seem engaged in an activity. For example, when taking a shower or eating our breakfast, our mind may be worrying about a meeting that is not going to happen until later during the day. So if we are thinking about our meeting while eating our breakfast, we are actually eating our meeting and not our breakfast! Perhaps that is why we have modern day reminders such as "Live the moment! or "Seize the day!"

The Art of Paying Attention to Attention

The opening story about mindless driving splendidly illustrates the importance, and the resulting challenge, of cultivating mindfulness in our life. In the same vein, a modern Zen story talks about a novice approaching a Zen master, inquiring about the most important thing in life. "Attention," said the master. The student persisted: "What is the second most important thing?" "Attention," replied the master. "And the third thing?" asked the student. "Attention," the master added firmly. "Anything else?" continued the student. "You do not seem to be paying attention!" roared the master.

The faculty of self-awareness has been prized by various wisdom and spiritual traditions. While Hindu, Sufi, Hassidic, and Christian traditions employ some form of awareness to attune to current reality, it is the Buddhist meditative tradition in which mindfulness has really played a key role in developing awareness of the present moment. Perhaps in no other tradition has mindfulness received such a comprehensive treatment as it has in Buddhist doctrine and discipline, both in the ancient manuals and in the modern Buddhist writings.

The term *mindfulness* has come to be used in a variety of ways and contexts in the modern times. Starting as a meditation technique more than 2,500 years ago, mindfulness has found its way in recent times into health clinics, prison houses, wellness centers, government offices, law firms, and corporate boardrooms. In its original Buddhist form, the practice of mindfulness refers to the technique of developing awareness of the body and the mind in the present moment.

Underscoring the universal importance of mindfulness, Buddha observed, "Mindfulness, I declare, is helpful everywhere."[5] Various other wisdom traditions of the world also underscore the importance of garnering a heightened sense of awareness of present reality by focusing on a chosen object with intense absorption, meditation, contemplation, concentration, remembrance, and recollection. For example, Sufi masters use a special form of meditation called *Zikr* to develop "yearning for the divine" through constant remembrance and recollection.

Christian desert fathers likewise used the royal art of "the prayer of the heart" to garner the knowledge of the divine. The Philokalia, a collection of texts written between the fourth and fifteenth centuries by masters of the Greek Orthodox tradition, speaks of the virtue of developing mental silence and inner attention in the service of the divine. In modern times, Russian mystics Gurdjieff and Ouspenksy have placed special importance on "self-remembering" as a unique way to psychological self-evolvement. And Krishnamurti popularized the phrase "choiceless awareness" to denote a state of pure alertness where we are fully aware of the moment-to-moment reality "as it is," yet our awareness is not focused on any particular physical or mental object.

Samatha and *Vipassana* Meditation

There are two main types of Buddhist meditation: *Samatha* meditation, which facilitates the development of serenity or calm, and *Vipassana* meditation, which facilitates the development of insight. Calm meditation aims to provide the mind an essential clarity to make it serene, stable, and strong. By preparing the mind to see the things as they really are, it serves as a necessary foundation for insight meditation. Together, calm meditation and insight meditation form the Buddhist path that leads to the realization of final awakening or enlightenment. Explaining the role and relationship of calm and insight meditation, Peter Harvey observed:

> Calm meditation alone cannot lead to *Nibbana* [Sanskrit: *Nirvana*], for while it can temporarily suspend, and thus weaken, attachment, hatred, and delusion, it cannot destroy them; only Insight combined with Calm can do this.... Calm "tunes" the mind, making it a more adequate instrument for knowledge and insight.... Insight meditation is more analytical and probing than Calm meditation, as it

aims to investigate the nature of reality, rather than remaining fixed on one apparently stable object.[6]

Buddhism believes the mind to be intrinsically pure, but sometimes it is stained or defiled by extrinsic impurities, such as greed, hatred, and delusion. The purpose of meditative practice is to expunge these adventitious impurities and to help restore the pristine purity of our natural mind so that it can see things as they truly are. The practice of meditation, therefore, starts with stilling or calming the mind to enable it to attain a measure of serenity, and then turns it toward insight into reality.

The Practice of Mindfulness

Mindfulness refers to a special form of awareness or presence of mind. Although we are always aware to some degree in a general way, this awareness rarely goes beyond the familiarity level to reach the mind's deeper layers. However, with the practice of mindfulness, normal awareness or attentiveness is applied with greater intensity and at a special pitch.

Renowned Buddhist scholar-monk Bhikkhu Bodhi explains the practice of right mindfulness:

> The mind is deliberately kept at the level of *bare attention,* a detached observation of what is happening within us and around us in the present moment. In the practice of right mindfulness the mind is trained to remain in the present, open, quiet, and alert, contemplating the present event. All judgments and interpretations have to be suspended, or if they occur, just registered and dropped…. To practice mindfulness is thus a matter not so much of doing but of undoing: not thinking, not judging, not associating, not planning, not imagining, not wishing. All these "doings" of ours are modes of interference, ways the mind manipulates experience and tries to establish its dominance.[7]

The most important and original discourse on the subject of meditation delivered by the Buddha is called *Satipatthana Sutta,* as it occurs in the collection of Long Discourses (Digya Nikaya No. 22) and in the collection of Middle Length Discourses (Majjhima Nikaya No. 10). Right mindfulness also constitutes the sixth step in the Noble Eightfold Path, the Buddhist path to awakening, so much so that the Buddha regarded *satipatthana* ("presence of mindfulness" or "attending with mindfulness") to be "the direct path to realization."[8]

The *Satipatthana Sutta* (Sanskrit: *Sutra*) is divided into four sections that list "four foundations of mindfulness," the four spheres in which to develop mindfulness:

1. Contemplation of the body through observing breathing.

2. Contemplation of the feelings through mindfulness.

3. Contemplation of the states of mind through observing different emotions.

4. Contemplation of the mental objects, especially the Four Noble Truths.[9]

As is clear from the above classification, we start with the contemplation of the body, the first sphere of mindfulness, and move through contemplations of the next three spheres of the mind. We begin with the body because it is our most immediate experience and is most accessible to us. From the body, we proceed to the contemplation of feelings and note their emotive and ethical qualities. Then we observe the mental states and objects, reflecting upon the Four Noble Truths—the truth regarding the reality of suffering, the cause of suffering, the cessation of suffering, and the path leading to the cessation of suffering.

It is important to keep in mind that, although the Pali word *sati* originally meant *memory* or *remembrance*, in its general Buddhist usage it mostly connotes a certain quality of attentiveness to or awareness of the present that the Buddhist doctrine specifies as good, wholesome, skillful, or right. It is not just bare attention referred to here; rather, it is appropriate or wholesome attention, connoted by the Pali word *yonisomaniskar*a. In Buddhism, the term *mindfulness* always implies *right mindfulness*—the adjective *right* connoting a state emanating from wholesome roots of mind such as kindness, compassion, joy, and equanimity.[10] In this sense, right mindfulness *(samma-sati)* forms the seventh factor of the Noble Eightfold Path.[11]

Mindfulness of Breathing *(Anapanasati)*

All forms of *Samatha* meditation start with an object or phrase to gain one-pointedness of mind. In most meditation traditions, breath is used as a choice object for concentration of the mind because it is closely linked to mind and "it is always available to us."[12] For example, in the Sufi and Greek Orthodox Church traditions, breath is employed as a primary vehicle to immerse the mind into the heart through a special prayer called "Prayer of the Heart." Similarly, Patanjali, the famous author of *Yoga-Sutras*, realized like Buddha that the "breath had close connection with the mind and that was the reason why excitement, anger, agitation, *et cetera* led to short and irregular breathing."[13]

The meditation practice most respected by Buddhists is called "mindfulness of breathing" *(Anapanasati)*. Referring to its great importance, Bhikkhu Bodhi observed, "By itself mindfulness of breathing can lead to all the stages of the path culminating in full awakening. In fact, it was this meditation subject that the Buddha used on the night of his own enlightenment."[14] Accordingly, the practice of mindfulness of breathing is considered to be the supreme meditation in Buddhism to awaken the mind to its full potential. The basic Buddhist practice here is being mindful of our breathing. It is said that proper breathing is more important than food. Proper breathing holds a special place in the practice of *Yoga*, as breathing provides the conscious connection between our body and our mind. It is common knowledge that when we are agitated, we breathe differently than when we are calm and relaxed. Our breath has a wonderful capacity to help us awaken to complete awareness.

Getting the Knack of Mindfulness

Here is the basic practice of mindfulness of breathing, in the words of Rahula:

*Breathe in and out as usual, without any effort or strain.
Now, bring your mind on your breathing in and breathing
out; let your mind be aware and observe your breathing in and
breathing out.... Your mind should be so concentrated on your
breathing that you are aware of its movements and changes.
Forget all other things, your surroundings, your environment;
do not raise your eyes or look at anything. Try to do this for
five or ten minutes.*[15]

After some practice, we are assured, we develop a knack for being
mindful so that we can extend this awareness to all spheres of our life.
Whatever we happen to be doing at the moment—eating, washing dishes,
walking, *et cetera*—we should try to become fully aware and mindful
of the act we are performing at the moment. This is called living in the
present moment or the present activity.

The idea is to be fully present to one activity since our mind can only
competently handle one function at a time. When informed about the
English expression of "killing two birds with one stone," Suzuki Roshi
said: "...our way is to kill just one Bird with one stone."[16]

Nhat Hanh, the modern Zen Master, uses the term *mindfulness* to
refer to "keeping one's consciousness alive to the present reality.... We
must be conscious of each breath, each movement, every thought and
feeling, everything which has any relation to ourselves."[17] He further
clarifies the miracle of mindfulness by providing these practical guidelines:

Keep your attention focused on the work, be alert and ready
to handle ably and intelligently any situation which may
arise—this is mindfulness: Mindfulness is the miracle by
which we master and restore ourselves...it is the miracle
which can call back in a flash our dispersed mind and restore
it to wholeness so that we can live each minute of life.[18]

How can we practice mindfulness, we may object, when modern
life seems to be maddeningly hectic and when so many activities clamor

to claim our precious little time? Ajahn Chah, a renowned Thai meditation master, provides the perfect answer: "If you have time to breathe, you have time to meditate."

Insight Meditation

As noted above, mindfulness of breathing occupies a prominent place in the practice of calm and insight meditation. Although each religious tradition has some form of serenity meditation as a part of its spiritual repertoire, the practice of insight meditation is the distinctive contribution of Buddhism to the spiritual heritage of humanity. Mindfulness of breathing is employed in both calm meditation and insight meditation with a different purpose and emphasis. In calm meditation, the purpose of employing mindfulness is to gain a certain measure of clarity and serenity of mind through the power of concentration. However, in insight meditation, concentration achieved through mindfulness of breathing is employed in a more analytical manner to gain insight into the very nature of the phenomenon, that is, seeing reality in the light of its three signs of existence, namely: impermanence, unsatisfactoriness, and not-self. In sum, insight meditation is practiced to gain direct insight into the very nature of ultimate reality.

What is the benefit of gaining this insight into the real nature of things? What does a person gain through this hard-won understanding? In two words: spiritual freedom, that is, freedom from dependence and clinging. In the words of the recurring refrain of *Satipatthana Sutta*, the Buddha states it thusly: "He lives independent, clinging to nothing in the world."[19]

Vipassana Meditation: My Recent Experience

I had the blessed opportunity to participate twice in a 10-day *Vipassana* meditation course during July 16–July 27, 2008, at North Fork, California, and during December 20–Decemeber 31, 2009 at the Northern California Vipassana Center. It was a life-transforming experience in the most complete sense of the word, as if the Buddha's teachings came vividly alive after 2,600 years![20]

The daily schedule of *Vipassana* meditation course was as follows:

4:00 a.m.	Morning wake-up bell
4:30–6:30 a.m.	Meditation in the hall or in your room
6:30–8:00 a.m.	Breakfast break
8:00–9:00 a.m.	Group meditation in the hall
9:00–11:00 a.m.	Meditation in hall or in your room
11:00–12 noon	Lunch break
12:00–1:00 p.m. 1:00–2:30 p.m.	Rest, and interviews with the teacher Meditation in hall or in your room
2:30–3:30 p.m.	Group meditation in the hall
3:30–5:00 p.m.	Meditation in the hall or your room
5:00–6:00 p.m.	Tea break
6:00–7:00 p.m.	Group meditation in the hall
7:00–8:15 p.m.	Discourse
8:15–9:00 p.m.	Group meditation in the hall
9:00–9:30 p.m.	Question time in the hall
9:30 p.m.	Retire to your room; lights out[21]

The following pages present a synopsis of my recollection of this wonderful experience. I have made a sincere attempt to convey the essence of meditation instructions imparted during the course as clearly and as faithfully as possible (see italicized portions below). The description that follows is offered only with a view to share what the reader could expect during such a course. Ideally, interested spiritual aspirants would attend the course themselves, as there is really no substitute for learning the *Vipassana* meditative practice firsthand.

Day One

Develop awareness of the process of respiration: Focusing only on the spot where the breath enters and leaves the nostrils (that is, the nostrils and upper lip area*), concentrate on the triangular area starting from the base of the nostrils and covering air passages of the nostrils. Observe incoming and outgoing breath, naturally and purely.*

Why use breath as an object? Breath is neutral and non-sectarian: Everybody breathes and breathes all the time, whether awake, sleeping, sitting, walking, standing, and so on. Most importantly, breathing takes place only in the present, in the now. So to bring our mind back to the present, focusing on breathing is the most natural and effective way.

Watch the breath entering the nostrils; feel the "touch" and be aware of it within the triangular area. Breathe normally and naturally. The Buddha's instructions are: The meditator should breathe naturally, without attempting to change the length or depth of the breath. If the breath is short, the meditator should simply observe that the breath is short. If the breath is long, the meditator should simply observe that the breath is long. (Note that it is not about controlling or regulating the breath, as in the case of *Pranayama. Pranayama* is a *yogic* practice in which breath is regulated to control the mind.) Just be aware of the bare breath in its most natural, pure state. Observe, notice, and be aware if it is passing through the left nostril or the right nostril or at times passing through both nostrils. That's all. Feel distinctively at what point the breath touches the area above the upper lip or the outer rings of the nostrils or inside the air passages (inner walls) of the nostrils.

Day Two

Continue with the awareness of breath entering the triangular area. Additionally, try to feel the touch—the point where the incoming or outgoing breath touches anywhere within the triangular area. Try harder to feel it: *The touch is always there, we are just not aware of it yet.* (If you still cannot feel the touch, try breathing a little harder than normal; you are bound to feel it.)

Day Three

Continue with the awareness of the touch of the breath. Additionally, be aware of any sensations that you may experience within this triangular area. Some examples of sensations are tingling, pulsating, vibrating, heat, cold, perspiration, heaviness, lightness, contraction, expansion, prickling, numbness, pain, pressure, itching, hardness, softness, and so on. Do not try to look for any specific sensations. Just be naturally aware of any sensations if and when they crop up in this area.

Day Four

Reduce the triangular area of your focus to the moustache line (the area below the nostrils and above the upper lip). First, try to feel, to be aware of the touch of air, and then feel and be aware of any sensations in this small area. The smaller area will sharpen your focus: the smaller the area, the sharper the focus. The idea is to improve the concentration and to make it the sharpest. *You need the sharpest concentration to dissect and scan the subtle, deeper layers of your mind. This and the prior exercises will prepare the mind for* Samadhi—*the state of meditative absorption.*

Days Five through Ten: *Vipassana* Meditation

Day Five

Vipassana *means seeing things as they really are. It is a process of self-purification by self-observation. One begins by observing the natural breath to concentrate the mind. With sharpened awareness one proceeds to observing the changing nature of body and mind, and experiences the universal truths of imper-manence, suffering, and egolessness. This truth realization by direct experience is the process of self-purification.*[22]

Vipassana **Technique:** With sharpened focus and concentration, *Vipassana* technique is pursued after practicing *anapana* (mindfulness of breathing) meditation. *Vipassana* means insight into reality. It is a technique whereby one scans the entire body—from head to toe and from toe to head—with razor-sharp awareness, looking for any and every sensation experienced anywhere on the body.

Start with scanning (moving your attention through) the scalp; move down to the face, part by part, piece by piece. Then move your attention through the right shoulder, upper arm, elbow, forearm, wrist, palm, fingers, and finger tips. Likewise, move your attention through the left shoulder down to the finger tips. Then scan the throat area, upper chest, and abdomen area; then the neck, upper back to lower back; then the right thigh, knee, leg, foot, and toes; then, likewise the left thigh, knee, leg, foot, and toes.

Every part of our body has changing sensations at all times; we are just not aware of them yet. If you cannot feel any sensations in any part of the body, spend a minute or two on that part by concentrating on your natural sensations. Observe and just be aware of your sensations. Do not choose for the pleasant sensations and do not try to avoid the unpleasant sensations. This is the habitual pattern of mind that we are trying to change at the deepest level.

While moving through the entire body like this, be aware of *anicca*—the law of impermanence. Every sensation is arising and passing away, changing, and changing again. Nothing is constant even for a few seconds. Observe with a balanced and equanimous mind, an objective mind—a mind that is balanced and observes reality as it is. Become aware at the deepest level of this universal law of change working with your body and mind. This is what the Enlightened One found out. And *when you would have experienced and know it through the experience of your own body and mind, you would have experienced the truth of the first turning of the wheel of* Dharma. *This is what Buddha called* bhavana-maya pannya—*wisdom based on experience of insight meditation or wisdom based on direct personal experience.*

According to S. N. Goenka, "*Vipassana* is about two things: awareness and equanimity. It is about changing from *Vedana-paccaya tanha* to *Vedana-paccaya pannya*—from sensations leading to craving to sensations leading to wisdom." Our habit pattern at the very deepest level is the automatic generation of *sankharas*[23] by reacting through craving and clinging if the sensations are pleasant, and through aversion and anger if the sensations are unpleasant. An awakened, equanimous mind understands that every formation is impermanent *(sabbe sankharas anicca)*. In other words, it understands the universal law of impermanence. Hence, it does not react as usual to sensations by developing craving or aversion. By helping us become constantly aware and equanimous about our sensations, moment to moment, *Vipassana* cuts at the very root, that is, at the sensation *(vedana)* level.

The evening discourse on the fifth day by Goenkaji was wonderful. I felt that this man's every word is worth its weight in gold! While explaining 12 links of dependent co-arising, Goenkaji commented that from this point—the point of *vedana* sensations—onward, there are basically two paths, one path leading to *Samsara (Bhava Sansaar)* and the other leading to *Nirvana*, the path of liberation born out of wisdom generated by insight meditation.

If we keep on reacting to sensations with craving and aversion, we will keep on adding to our cyclic misery. However, through *Vipassana* we develop a faculty of constant awareness and understanding of the universal law of impermanence—that sensations are not eternal but arise and pass away. This awareness and understanding allows us to respond to sensations with equanimity. By not reacting to craving and aversion, we cut at the very root of the problem. This is what Buddha was referring to:

> *The house builder (that is, craving) has been recognized…. At the sensations level, no more new* Sankharas *are created by reacting with craving and aversion to pleasant and unpleasant sensations respectively, and the old* Sankharas *have been purified, so no more rebirth—the* Nirvanic *peace of being liberated from craving and clinging has been achieved.*

There are three basic attachments to be aware of: the attachment to "I," the attachment to "mine," and the attachment to "my" beliefs or "my" views. *The greater the attachment, the greater the misery at the time of separation.*

Days Six and Seven: Continuing with *Vipassana* Meditation

The sixth day continued with moving our awareness throughout our body from the top of the head to the tip of the toes and from the tip of the toes to the top of the head, with a calm, equanimous mind noticing any and every sensation on any part of the body; always remembering the nature of every sensation—it arises, it passes away; not reacting to pleasant sensations with craving and to unpleasant sensations with aversion, and thus not generating any new *sankharas*. When we do this, no new *sankharas* are made. *It is the law of nature that the old* sankharas *that lie very deep in our mind get eradicated through this mind-purifying process.* Through the practice of *Vipassana*, sensations do not generate craving or aversion but generate the *pannya*, that is, the wisdom born out of insight into the nature of reality—reality that is changing all the time and whose very nature is impermanence. *The whole idea of* Vipassana *is to change the habit pattern of mind that automatically reacts with craving to pleasant sensations and with aversion to unpleasant sensations.* By experiencing the truth of impermanence within one's body through *Vipassana*, one sees through the madness and is able to stop this automatic response mechanism at the deepest level of the mind.

> *Learn to work with a calm and quiet mind, alert and attentive mind, equanimous and balanced mind. Learn to work objectively with your sensations without identifying with the pleasant ones with craving and unpleasant ones with aversion. Remember the nature of all sensations—whether solidified, gross, or subtle—they arise and pass away. So, observe them objectively without the feeling of I, my, and mine.*

> *Remember* anicca—*impermanence—the changing nature of phenomenon and work diligently to experience this truth within your body-mind complex. If you do not identify with pleasant sensations with craving and unpleasant sensation with aversion, you do not generate any new* sankharas. *And working objectively without a sense of I, my, and mine, the old ones get eradicated automatically. This is a law.*

Move your attention from head to toe and from toe to head:

✦ Top of the head to abdomen area, back of the head to the lower back.

✦ Both shoulders down to the fingertips of both hands.
✦ Hips/thighs to the toes of both feet and back up.

Instructions: For areas that are blank—that is, areas where no sensation is felt—move your attention slowly, part by part, piece by piece. If you experience vibration-like subtle sensations through entire portions of the body, you will be able to sweep *en masse* through areas that are experiencing subtle sensations. After two or three such sweeps, go back to blind areas or blank areas where sensations were hazy. If you continue like this, you will soon experience subtle sensations throughout the body. But do not crave for subtle sensations. Work patiently but persistently. You are bound to succeed. You are bound to succeed. Remember:

> *In this essenceless, substanceless, ephemeral mind-matter phenomenon, there is nothing that is permanent; there is nothing that is not changing. This sensation or that sensation does not make any difference. All sensations have the same characteristic—of arising and passing away—of* anicca. *So, what's the use of reacting with craving to something that is temporarily pleasant and with aversion to something that is temporarily unpleasant? With this understanding, always maintain equanimity. This way you will not generate new* sankharas. *No* sankharas *means no misery! This is liberation! And this is the purpose of insight meditation.*

> *The equanimity is the wisdom* (pannya) *of not reacting through craving and aversion to pleasant and unpleasant sensations but remaining equanimous. It is the insight that is developed through* Vipassana *by being aware of one's breath and sensations all the time. By remaining equanimous, one does not generate new* sankharas. *And when one does not generate new* sankharas, *then the old* sankharas *start coming to the surface. Through observation and remaining aware, one eradicates them slowly and slowly until they are fully wiped out. This is the Nirvana* Buddha *talked about—Nirvana of total extinction!*

Always be aware of your breath or your sensations: either breath or sensations. In whatever you are doing—sitting, standing, walking, working or sleeping—always be aware of your breath or sensations. This is Buddha's unique contribution to help sentient beings to come out of dukkha, *to come out of deep misery. Everything else he taught was already present in the then-prevalent teachings of India. By developing awareness of our breath and sensations, we start living in the present because breath and sensations can only happen in the present. This is the* Dhamma *he taught for 45 years, the* Dhamma *that is good in the beginning, good in the middle, and good in the end* (aadi kalyankaari, madhaya kalyaankari, and anntah kalyaankaari).

Day Eight: The Wonderful Teaching of *Dhamma* Continues

Recorded instructions by Shri S.N. Goenka and *Vipassana* teachers:

Your progress on the path of Vipassana *is measured by only one yardstick: the degree of equanimity you have developed, the mental equilibrium, the equipoise. Always remember that every experience—however pleasant or unpleasant at the moment—is impermanent. So by not reacting blindly to sensations, one does not generate new* sankharas. *Fewer* sankharas, *less misery. No* sankharas, *no misery.*

An important Note: The whole purpose of moving attention throughout the body and observing different sensations is to develop one's awareness and to train one's mind to always remain equanimous toward our experience by remembering the law of impermanence. With the mind deeply established in equanimity, whenever deep-seated old *sankharas* come to the surface during meditations, they are eradicated: thus, pleasant *sankharas* do not result in craving, and unpleasant *sankharas* do not result in aversion.

The Alchemy of Purification of Mind through *Vipassana* Meditation

This is the alchemy of purifying the mind: No new sankharas *are generated, and accumulated old* sankharas *get eradicated through* Vipassana. *Although it is clear that* when we respond with equanimity to our pleasant as well as unpleasant sensations, we do not develop any craving or aversion toward them. Hence, no new *sankharas*; no new misery!

But how does *Vipassana* help to eradicate old *sankharas*? This requires some further explanation. When we are equanimously observing our sensations in *Vipassana* meditation—especially when we get to the point where we can sweep our attention with a free flow up and down throughout our body—we come across areas where we may have coarse or solidified sensations. Generally speaking, one is able to do a quick sweep when one is experiencing subtle sensations. And for the areas that are blank/blind where one is feeling coarse sensations, one has to go back and work on them, part by part, piece by piece. Now it is the old, habitual pattern of mind to react with aversion to gross or coarse (unpleasant) sensations and to react with craving to subtle (pleasant) sensations. If we keep an equanimous mind, we counter mind's habitual pattern and thereby disempower its habit of reacting blindly. Our old *sankharas* sit as latent psychological tendencies at the deepest level of our mind. During *Vipassana* meditation, the latent mental tendencies born out of accumulated past *sankharas* come to the surface. *By observing them with equanimous mind and not reacting to them, we do not give them the opportunity to reestablish themselves.* And hence they are eradicated at the root level.

It is not uncommon during *Vipassana* meditation for some past experiences buried deep into our subconscious mind to resurface. If the experience had been pleasant and resurfaces again as a pleasant sensation, generating a craving for reliving it, then the grooves of *sankharas* deepen. *Vipassana* meditation teaches us to remain equanimous in wake of such sensations in order to eradicate these old, deep-seated *sankharas*. Success on the path of *Vipassana* meditation does not depend upon experiencing this sensation or that sensation. *Vipassana* teaches us that all sensations—pleasant or unpleasant—are of the nature of arising and passing away; hence, they are impermanent. What is important is to keep an equanimous mind, a balanced mind.

During his *Dhamma* discourse on the eighth day, Shri Goenkaji summed up the *Vipassana* technique with a bird analogy: Just as a bird has two wings, likewise the two wings of the bird of *Vipassana* are awareness and equanimity. To explain how deep-seated, old *sankharas* come to the surface when you stop making new *sankharas*, Goenkaji gave the example of burning of a pile of firewood. *On a pile of burning firewood, if we add new pieces of wood on the top, the new ones will start burning first. But if we stop adding the new pieces of wood to the fire, then the old ones have to burn themselves up.* Another example Goenkaji gave was of fasting: if you fast one day and then fast the second day and still another day—that is, when you stop putting new food in the body—the body starts using what it has stored in the past. Goenkaji also made a categorical statement: *Sensations are always in contact with the deepest level of the mind. By not reacting with craving or aversion, we purify our mind at the deepest level.*

Day Nine: The Most Detailed Instructions on the Path of *Vipassana* Meditation

The morning meditation instructions on the ninth day were most detailed and profound. The instructions mentioned three types of experiences pertaining to sensations. On the path of *Vipassana* meditation, the meditator experiences

1. coarse, gross, solidified sensations denoted by hazy or blind areas;
2. some areas with gross sensations and some with subtle sensations;
3. subtle sensations.

+ If you are feeling subtle sensations, then sweep your attention *en masse* two to three times with a free-flow sweep from head to toe and from toe to head.

+ Go back and survey, part by part, the areas that were left out during the free-flow sweep. Make sure that you do not leave out any areas, even a tiny part of the body, without scanning for sensations.
+ If you feel solidified, gross, blank, hazy, or misty areas, do not feel discouraged. Use them as tools to uncover your hidden *sankharas* of craving and aversion accumulated over countless lifetimes. With practice observing these areas patiently and objectively, you will find them becoming full of subtle sensations.

Bhanga Nyana: Collapse of the Entire Physical Structure as We Know It!

From time to time, now or in future, you may experience a flow of very subtle sensations throughout your body. You will feel that the entire structure of physical body is nothing but a field of subtle vibrations—wavelets of ripples of energy vibrating, like electric current, at the speed of light. There is nothing solid, so to speak, in the entire physical structure of your body, only a whirling dance of the subatomic particles (tiny kalapas). At that time, you may experience that the entire physical structure collapses into a field of vibrations; there is nothing solid in this constantly changing field of vibrations, nothing substantial or permanent. This is bhanga nyana—the wisdom (nyana) of dissolution (bhanga). This is when you experience two important aspects of reality according to Buddhism: anicca and anatta—impermanence and no-self.

Basically, *Vipassana* mediation has four progressive steps. The first three steps basically involve scanning the external part of the body, the skin area, moving the attention during these three steps vertically, up and down. The fourth step is an internal scan.

1. Slow scan: Moving attention slowly from top of the head to the tip of the toes and back, part by part, piece by piece.

2. Free-flow sweep: Sweeping attention freely *en masse* upward and downward where subtle sensations are experienced, then going back to observe those areas that have solidified coarse sensations or the areas that were initially left blank.
3. Spot check: Being able to quickly take your attention to any fingertip-size spot and move back and forth. Try only four or five spot checks and then go back to normal scan and sweep.
4. Penetrate and pierce: Scanning internally, moving attention inside the body areas, left to right, right to left, front to back, back to front. This is a highly advanced technique, reserved for advance-level practitioners who work under the close guidance of an experienced teacher during 20- to 90-day meditation retreats.

In the practice of all of these techniques, the meditator is reminded of the universal law of impermanence, to always maintain perfect equanimity, and not to generate new *sankharas* by reacting with craving or aversion to pleasant or unpleasant sensations. It is the old habit of our unconscious mind to react with craving to pleasant sensations or with aversion to unpleasant sensations; after all, *sankhara* is reacting mind! If we react to unpleasant sensations as we sweep or scan, we not only create new *sankharas* but also multiply the effects of the old *sankharas* of aversion, which means multiplying our misery! However, when we remain equanimous, understanding the wisdom of impermanence, not only do we not create any new *sankharas* of aversion, we also dissolve or help eradicate the accumulated old *sankharas*. The same applies to responding with equanimity to pleasant sensations. Remember, sensations are in contact with the deepest level of our mind, always. This is the insight into wisdom that the Buddha taught: the wisdom of *upekha*, the wisdom of equanimity. And this is the culmination of the path of insight meditation.

Day 10: *Metta* (Loving Kindness) Meditation

Metta is a Pali word that means loving kindness. The last day of the *Vipassana* meditation course is devoted to practicing *metta* meditation, which involves filling the mind and body with thoughts and feelings of goodwill for all beings. The practice begins with cultivating a deep sense of loving kindness toward oneself and then extending it toward one's loved ones, friends, teachers, strangers, enemies, and finally toward all beings. *Metta* meditation serves as a great antidote to the feeling of anger and contention. The whole atmosphere is filled with sharing the feeling of joy and goodwill with the whole of creation—a befitting grand finale to nine days of intense meditation!

Concluding Remarks

It has been said that the "order or confusion of society corresponds to and follows the order or confusion of individual minds."[24] Our modern civilization, which excels in "manufacturing irrelevances" (to use Huxley's phrase) has splendidly managed to shorten our attention span through myriad trivial pursuits geared toward instant gratification. In this age of "continuous partial attention," mindfulness has a great role to play in developing clarity through attentiveness and in sharpening the power of concentration by ensuring immunity from distraction and delusion. The practice of mindfulness accords greater value and presence to the activity at hand and thereby enhances our performance of the task and the resultant fulfillment.

When we carry out all activities in our usual daily life with mindfulness, with conscious presence, then every task becomes special, every act becomes a rite and a ceremony. And our whole life becomes a wondrous celebration! "If we practice the art of mindful living," says Thich Nhat Hanh, "when things change, we won't have any regrets. We can smile because we have done our best to enjoy every moment of our life and to make others happy."[25] And in making others happy, moment to moment, we discover the true secret to our happiness!

Mindfulness has tremendous potential in enhancing workplace well-being through improved communications, efficient meetings, optimum performance, better decisions, and greater understanding. If "change within is a prerequisite to a change without," then mindfulness accords the best place to begin the journey of inner transformation, personally and professionally. It is said that the proof of the pudding is in eating it. In the ultimate analysis, one can only determine the efficacy of the practice of mindfulness by practicing it diligently. *"Ehipassiko,"* said the Buddha, "Come and see for yourself."

Putting the World into Place

Every night, when a certain man came home from work, his little boy would run and jump up into his arms and ask, "Daddy, will you play with me? Will you, Daddy, will you?" And, almost every night, this man played with his son, sharing games and books and toys and talk.

But one night the father was very tired. So instead of rushing to play with his son, he sat down in his chair, opened his newspaper and began to read. As on every other night, his son asked, "Daddy, will you play with me?" But on this night the father replied, "Oh, not tonight, I'm just too tired." The little boy kept asking, but the father's reply did not change.

Finally, to keep his son occupied—and frankly, to get a little peace and quiet—the father took a whole page out of his newspaper. Printed on the page was a map of the world. He took a scissors and cut the map into many small pieces and said to his son, "Here is a puzzle of a map of the world. Why don't you go into your room and put the puzzle together?"

The father thought that the son would be gone for a long time, but the boy was back in just a few minutes. The father was amazed. He said, "How did you finish the puzzle so quickly? The map of the world is so large and complicated. How did you put it together so soon?"

And the little boy replied, "It was easy. You see, on the back of the picture of the world was a picture of a man. I just put the man together and the world fell right into place."[26]

CHAPTER ELEVEN

THE UNIVERSAL QUEST FOR SIGNIFICANCE

To look behind or to look upfront is not as important as to look inside.

~ RALPH WALDO EMERSON

A Cherokee elder sitting with his grandchildren told them, "In every life there is a terrible fight—a fight between two wolves. One is evil: he is fear, anger, envy, greed, arrogance, self-pity, resentment, and deceit. The other is good: joy, serenity, humility, confidence, generosity, truth, gentleness, and compassion."

A child asked, "Grandfather, which wolf will win?"

The elder looked him in the eye. "The one you care to feed."

~ A TRADITIONAL NATIVE AMERICAN TALE[1]

As Thoreau lay upon his death bed in 1862, a friend asked him whether he had made his peace with God. The poet responded, in Zen-like fashion: "I was not aware we had quarreled."[2]

What we are looking for is what is looking.

~ ST. FRANCIS OF ASSISI

Within you there is a stillness and a sanctuary to which you can retreat at any time and be yourself.

~ HERMANN HESSE

Why are you unhappy?

> *Because 99.9 percent*
> *Of everything you think,*
> *And of everything you do,*
> *Is for yourself—*
> *And there isn't one.*

~ WEI WU WEI[3]

Gertrude Stein, American author, poet, art collector who lived most of her life in France, died in 1946 at the age of 72 from stomach cancer. As she was being wheeled into the operation room for surgery, she asked her associate, Alice Toklas: "What is the answer?" When Toklas did not answer, Stein said, "In that case, what is the question?" These were her last words of wisdom.

Right self-effort is a part of divine will.

~ YOGA VASISHTHA

The first 100 years are the hardest.

~ A PERSIAN SAYING

What your mind does not know, your eyes do not see.

~ A HINDU SAYING

Integrating the Seven Gifts

In the foregoing pages, we have presented seven gifts as habits of mind that lead to significance and fulfillment in life. We started with pure motivation because it serves as a necessary foundation to all other gifts. If our motivation is impure, we will not really be able to practice gratitude, generosity, harmlessness, and selfless service because our self-interest will always be lurking in the background. The gift of pure motivation, therefore, acts as a salutary check on the deeply ingrained human tendency toward self-centeredness. The key to fulfillment lies in freeing oneself from the shackles of this fundamental human disability. Most great spiritual traditions of the world are in agreement on this vital point.

Pursuing our self-interest in everything we do comes naturally to all of us. It is hard-wired into our psyche due to millions of years of biological struggle for self-preservation. To a point, it has served us well, albeit in the biological sense. However, even when our self-preservation is not at stake, it remains operative in myriad, subtle ways. It is responsible for much of humanity's suffering through deception, greed, exploitation, and war. In nature, however, cooperation plays at least as important a role as competition in the so-called struggle for existence. It is possible to outgrow our rampant tendency of self-centeredness by practicing the gifts of gratitude, generosity, harmlessness, and selfless service. Paradoxically, in sharing these gifts with others, we ultimately bestow them on ourselves. Pure motivation is the master key that opens the door to all other blessings.

The Dichotomy of Being and Becoming

As human beings, we are caught in the constant dichotomy of being and becoming. The world of becoming operates outside and is swarmed with competition, comparison, and conflict. It is a race with no visible finish line. The world of being lies within us and is infused with self-knowledge, contentment, and contemplation. It is already within our reach and ever-attained. Struggle for becoming eventually leads to unhappiness, anxiety, stress, strain, and strife. Steady abidance in our being is the road that verily leads to happiness, peace, serenity, and fulfillment.

This, then, is the real irony: We squander our precious human life in the sole servitude of the economic grind called "making a living" without really finding much time to live—a classic case of all "becoming" and no "being," and a sorry sacrifice of abiding ends for transient means.

What Really Matters Most: The Art of Being!

Where should one begin if one were to attain what really matters in life? We are repeatedly told that if we seek the big things first, all other things will be added unto us. In the following pages, we will explore this vital subject from different angles through the medium of wisdom stories. The following story presents a valuable message in this regard and serves as a good starting point in our quest about what really matters in life.

Art of Time Management: Get the Big Rocks in First!

A philosophy professor stood before his class with some items on the table in front of him. When the class began, wordlessly he picked up a very large and empty mayonnaise jar and proceeded to fill it with rocks, about 2 inches in diameter.

He then asked the students if the jar was full. They agreed that it was.

So the professor then picked up a box of pebbles and poured them into the jar. He shook the jar lightly. The pebbles, of course, rolled into the open areas between the rocks.

He then asked the students again if the jar was full. They agreed it was.

The professor picked up a box of sand and poured it into the jar. Of course, the sand filled up everything else.

He then asked once more if the jar was full. The students responded with a unanimous "Yes."

"Now," said the professor, "I want you to recognize that this jar represents your life. The rocks are the important things—your family, your partner, your health, your children—things that if everything else was lost and only they remained, your life would still be full.

"The pebbles are the other things that matter—like your job, your house, your car.

"The sand is everything else. The small stuff.

"If you put the sand into the jar first," he continued "there is no room for the pebbles or the rocks. The same goes for your life.

"If you spend all your time and energy on the small stuff, you will never have room for the things that are important to you. Pay attention to the things that are critical to your happiness.

> *Play with your children. Take your partner out dancing. There will always be time to go to work, clean the house, give a dinner party, and fix the disposal.*
>
> *"Take care of the rocks first—the things that really matter. Set your priorities. The rest is just sand."*[4]

Reality: A Mere Reflection of Our Own Self

Seeking the right things assumes being the right seeker first. We create our own reality and carry it with us wherever we go. It has been observed that we do not see the world the way the world is, we see it the way we are. The world is merely a reflection of who we are. If we have an abundant mind and a generous heart, life invariably draws us toward circumstances where these qualities can be reinforced and nurtured. The converse is equally true. The following two stories admirably underscore this essential point.

> ### We Carry Our Reality with Us
>
> *An old man sat outside the walls of a great city. When travelers approached, they would ask the old man, "What kind of people live in this city?" The old man would answer, "What kind of people live in the place where you came from?" If the travelers answered, "Only bad people live in the place where we came from," the old man would reply, "Continue on; you will find only bad people here." But if the travelers answered, "Good people live in the place where we came from," then the old man would say, "Enter, for here too, you will find only good people."*[5]

This story is also an excellent illustration, albeit indirectly, of Gandhi's great maxim on change: Be the change you want to see in the world. If we want to see more goodness and harmony around us, we have to first enshrine goodness and harmony in our own life. The following Japanese folktale reinforces the message that all our experiences are mere reflections of who we are!

House of 1,000 Mirrors!

Long ago in a small, far away village, there was place known as the House of 1,000 Mirrors. A happy little dog learned of this place and decided to visit.

When he arrived, he bounced happily up the stairs to the doorway of the house. He looked through the doorway with his ears lifted high and his tail wagging as fast as it could. To his great surprise, he found himself staring at 1,000 other happy little dogs with their tails wagging just as fast as his. He smiled a great smile, and was answered with 1,000 great smiles just as warm and friendly. As he left the house, he thought to himself, "This is a wonderful place. I will come back and visit it often."

In this same village, another little dog that was not quite as happy as the first one decided to visit the house. He slowly climbed the stairs and hung his head low as he looked into the door. When he saw the 1,000 unfriendly looking dogs staring back at him, he growled at them and was horrified to see 1,000 little dogs growling back at him. As he left, he thought to himself, "That is a horrible place, and I will never go back there again."

All the faces in the world are mirrors, and the world is a mere reflection of our own self.[6]

Peace of Mind

It seems that happiness is related to peace of mind as success is related to significance. In our quest for our own happiness, we try to devote our talents to make ourselves happy; as in our quest for success, we try to pursue success for ourselves. Peace of mind, on the other hand, represents a state of significance that results from devoting ourselves unconditionally to the well-being of others. As mentioned in the beginning of this book, happiness and success, as commonly interpreted, have to be pursued; peace and significance have to ensue.

In his classic book titled *Peace of Mind*, Joshua Loth Liebman records an interesting conversation with his old friend on what matters most in life:

> Once, as a young man, I undertook to draw up a catalogue of the acknowledged "goods" of life. I set down my inventory of earthly desirables: health, love, talent, power, riches and fame. Then I proudly showed it to a wise elder. "An excellent list," said my old friend, "and set down in reasonable order. But you have omitted the one important ingredient, lacking which your list becomes an intolerable burden." He crossed out my entire schedule. Then he wrote down three syllables: peace of mind. "This is the gift that God reserves for his special protégés," he said. "Talent and health he gives to many. Wealth is commonplace, fame not rare. But peace of mind he bestows charily."[7]

Peace as Our Natural State

Peace is our natural state. That is perhaps why whenever we are in pain or distress, we want to get out of the pain or stress as quickly as possible and get back to our natural state of peace and comfort, whereas when we are happy and peaceful, we do not want that state to ever end. But how do we get to that still point within, one is tempted to ask. There is nothing that one has to do to reach it, we are told. One has just to be—to be in touch with that innate state. This seems to be the ultimate paradox of human life.

Ultimate Paradox: Accomplishing the Accomplished

I once asked a sage, "How can one attain a state of stillness, a state of abiding inner peace. What spiritual practice or discipline should one engage in to get to it?"

The sage clarified the point with a counter-question: "Throughout your life you play myriad roles such as a father, a son, a husband, a teacher, a friend, and so forth. But underneath of it all, you know that you are a human being."

"What spiritual practice/discipline do you need to realize that you are a human being?" asked the sage.

I stood speechless. The sage looked me in the eyes. There was an unspeakable intensity in his gaze. In that split second, which felt like an eternity, time stood still, and something significant had been conveyed forever!

No further words were necessary!

In fact, anything we do with our volitional mind takes us away from this innate state of being. In Indian philosophy, this natural state is expressed as the being-consciousness-bliss absolute *(Sat-Chit-Ananda):* Abiding or being in our natural state of pure, witnessing consciousness—awareness—is the key to bliss, peace, and harmony. Happiness, as we normally understand it, comes from outside, and we have to do something to obtain it. Peace of mind, on the other hand, is our natural inner state, and we do not have to do anything to revel in it.

The peace we experience during deep sleep every night is a testimony to this amazing discovery. During deep sleep, we are devoid of our awareness of body, mind, and senses. We are blissfully oblivious to all our possessions of the waking state such as wealth, power, fame, *et cetera*. And yet, we all experience a deep peace during sleep unlike any other experience that we have. Everyone looks forward to it every night, night after night. This is nature's gentle reminder that peace is our very nature.

The purpose of the sleep analogy is not to suggest that one should pass one's life in blissful slumber, experiencing unalloyed peace. The idea is to live one's waking life with the keen understanding that peace is an inner condition—our natural state—and that we do not have to do anything special to attain it except just be it. With a nod to Shakespeare, we can agree: "To be or not to be"—that is *the* question.

Does Happiness Reside in the Objects of Desire?

The basic assumption behind all pursuits of happiness is the belief that happiness resides in a desirable object or situation.[8] A little reflection will show that happiness does not reside in the object or the situation. If it were so, then that object or situation would always be the source of happiness for everyone. It is common knowledge that the same object or situation evokes different responses in different people. Even the same object or situation can evoke a different response in the same person at different times. If happiness were a quality inherent in objects, then everyone would desire all objects in the same manner all the time, and all the people who possess those objects would be universally happy. Our experience and observation tell us this is not the case. This analysis can apply to people, places, and situations. Thus, through proper enquiry, we should clearly determine that abiding fullness, peace, security, and happiness cannot come from objects or things that are themselves subject to change.

If happiness does not reside in objects or situations, could it then be a quality of the mind? Since the mind seeks completion, which is happiness, outside of itself, happiness cannot be its intrinsic quality. The mind, however, assumes itself to be incomplete and therefore seeks completion. Also, if happiness were a quality of the mind, then when the mind is resolved as in deep sleep, happiness would not be experienced. Experience shows the reverse to be the case. Deep sleep is a state that all of us desire to enter because of the sense of completion obtained there. In deep sleep, our mind completely subsides. When the mind is resolved, happiness manifests. Thus, happiness cannot be a quality residing only in the individual mind.

Now the question arises, if happiness is not a quality of an object, nor a quality of the individual mind, where does it come from? When a desired object is obtained, then the desiring mind is granted a calm moment, thus allowing us to be content with ourselves. Thus, happiness manifests as fullness (which is but the nature of the Self) when a particular desire within the mind is resolved. Therefore, happiness does not reside in objects, situations, nor in the individual mind; rather, it is a quality of fullness, the very intrinsic nature of the Self. It is for the sake of the self alone that every object is dear to us.[9] This is the psychology of happiness, the gift of discovering the peace of mind within the Self.

One cannot know peace; one can only feel it or experience it in the depth of one's being. One can only be it!

The good news is that the real peace and fulfilment that we search for outside of ourselves actually lies within all of us, and we come fully equipped to undertake this august journey and reach our true destination. Searching for peace is like searching for one's glasses everywhere when they have been perched on our nose all along. Interestingly, one even forgets that one has been searching for them while unknowingly looking through them!

The following story of the musk deer splendidly illustrates this point.

The Enchanted Deer

Once while walking in a forest, a deer became enchanted by a sweet, magical fragrance. The enchanted deer spent its entire life searching everywhere in the forest for the source of the fragrance, only to one day fall to the ground completely exhausted. Lying there curled up, with its head resting on its belly, it realized that the source of the fragrance it had been seeking its whole life was actually the scent of musk coming from within itself.[10]

Our true treasures lie within us all. We just have to look in the right place. We have drifted too far from our essence outward in search of haunts of happiness. All we need to do is to make a U-turn and return home!

The following story warns us regarding the futility of searching for peace afar, chasing shadows, and getting constantly hurt in the process.

A Bird and the Mystic Rose

A certain bulbul bird was in love with a mystic rose. Every morning, he would leave his nest in search of this rose. All day he would roam about in every direction and then return to his nest, tired and disheartened. One day the bird saw the rose inside a room made of glass. The bird could see it through the glass walls and was tempted to get it right away. Luckily, he found a side door ajar and flew in.

This was a mysterious room, full of mirrors all around. The bird could see the mystic rose reflected in every direction everywhere in the room. The bird started flying toward one of rose's images reflected in the mirror, thinking it to be the real thing. He flew into the mirror and fell on the floor. He got up again, determined to get his heart's desire. He flew toward another reflection of the mystic rose and again met the same fate.

This went on several times until the bird was wounded, his beak bleeding very badly. The bird lay exhausted on the floor in the middle of the room and soon fell asleep. When the bird woke up after resting a while, he saw the real rose hanging right above him. His gaze remained fixed on it, wondering if it was the real rose or just one of its myriad reflections, like he had experienced before. The bird gathered his courage and flew straight at the real mystic rose, finally to be united with its heart's desire once and for all![11]

Most of our struggles with becoming are of the nature of chasing shadows, not unlike the bird in the story flying at the reflections of the mystic rose. We also keep getting hurt in the process of chasing false goods, until life, in its infinite compassion, presents us with our heart's authentic desire. Practicing the seven habits of fulfillment attracts the universe's infinite generosity, guidance, and compassion to lead us to the abode of inner peace.

The Significance of Significance

The quest for significance has been one of the perennial stirrings of the human heart. Why is it that after many millennia, the search for meaning still strikes us as fresh and has to be newly won by every serious seeker? It has been observed that there are basically two types of people: those who have discovered their purpose and those who have not yet discovered their purpose. Sooner or later, we all have to ask this question of questions: What is the purpose of my life—why am I here? Until we find an answer to this most fundamental of all questions—for ourselves and by ourselves—we will remain strangers to true fulfilment, peace, and significance.

The importance of significance is so great that even animals are not untouched by this need. Search and rescue handlers and trainers learned a lot from the use of dogs in Oklahoma City bombing in 1995. The dogs worked tirelessly and found no survivors and so got little reward. At a deeper level, dogs felt lack of meaning behind their search. The dogs started getting depressed by the third day since no more survivors were to be found underneath the heaps of corpses. The rescue handlers devised a trick. They covered themselves with gowns and masks and hid themselves under the debris so that the dogs could find at least some survivors to carry on their work meaningfully. Such is the power of purposeful work. Camus put it so well: "Without work, all life goes rotten. But when work is soulless, life stifles and dies."

Implications for Leaders

It is important to note that the journey from success to significance, from happiness to harmony, is not only essential for personal mastery, it is also critical in developing and leading others. This represents the essence of leadership: devoting ourselves selflessly to a cause greater than ourselves. Put differently, serving the well-being of others and working for the benefit of many constitute the *raison d'être* of leaders: In giving of ourselves unconditionally and serving others selflessly, we truly redeem our existence and firmly plant our feet on the path that leads to peace and harmony, fulfillment, meaning, and significance.

Everyone Dies, but Few Live!

Life is short, art is long: that is the tragedy of human life. During a memorial service I attended, the minister spoke of the uncertainty and brevity of human life and the consequent need to live meaningfully all the days of our lives. He explained that on each tombstone, after the name of the deceased, the life span of a person is denoted by the year of birth and the year of death, separated by a hyphen. That's all our life is: just a little hyphen between birth and death! With certain urgency in his voice, he added, poignantly: "We, all of us, are going to be soon reduced to a hyphen—a hyphen on the tombstone. How you hyphenate your hyphen makes all the difference in what truly matters most in life." And that alone is what we all leave behind.

The following two stories convey this message. The first story is about Alexander the Great, known as the most powerful military general and conqueror of the ancient world. Before he turned 30 years old, he had conquered an empire stretching over 3,000 miles from Greece to India. The second story presents a homely conversation between a mother and a daughter and some useful hints on the art of living. The first story conveys the urgency; the second story provides some guidelines on how to address it.

Empty Hands: Death of Alexander the Great

At the time of his death, Alexander the Great offered to give half of his kingdom to anyone who could make him live long enough so he could see his mother.

All the physicians who had gathered around told him that, even if he gave his entire kingdom, they could not add one single breath to his life. Tears welled up in Alexander's eyes, his face saddened, and with a deep sigh he said, "If only I had known that a breath was so costly a thing, I would never have wasted them in useless pursuits."

Then he directed that during his funeral procession, his hands should be kept out of his coffin with palms upward so that the world might take a lesson from the Great Alexander, who had planned to conquer the world, but was leaving it with empty hands.[12]

Carrots, Eggs, and Coffee Beans

A young woman went to her mother and told her about her life and how things were so hard for her. She did not know how she was going to survive and wanted to give up. She was tired of fighting and struggling. It seemed as one problem was solved, a new one arose.

Her mother took her to the kitchen. She filled three pots with water and placed each on a high fire. Soon the pots came to boil. In the first she placed carrots, in the second she placed eggs, and in the last she placed ground coffee beans. Without saying a word, she let them sit and boil.

After twenty minutes she turned off the burners. She fished the carrots out and placed them in a bowl. She pulled the eggs out and placed them in a bowl. Then she ladled the coffee out and placed it in a bowl. Turning to her daughter, she said, "Tell me what you see." "Carrots, eggs, and coffee," the daughter replied.

Her mother brought her closer and asked her to feel the carrots. She did and noted that they were soft. The mother then asked the daughter to take an egg and break it. After pulling off the shell, she observed the hard-boiled egg.

Finally, the mother asked the daughter to sip the coffee. The daughter smiled as she tasted its rich aroma. The daughter then asked, "What does it mean, mother?"

Her mother explained that each of these objects had faced the same adversity: boiling water. Each reacted differently. The carrot went in strong, hard, and unrelenting. However, after being subjected to the boiling water, it softened and became weak. The egg had been fragile. Its thin outer shell had protected its liquid interior, but after sitting through the boiling water, its inside became hardened. The ground coffee beans were unique, however. After they were in the boiling water, they had changed the water.

"Which are you?" she asked her daughter. "When adversity knocks on your door, how do you respond? Are you a carrot, an egg, or a coffee bean?"

Think of this: Who am I? Am I the carrot that seems strong, but with pain and adversity do I wilt and become soft and lose my strength? Am I the egg that starts with a malleable heart, but changes with the heat? Did I have a fluid spirit, but after a death, a breakup, a financial hardship or some other trial, have I become hardened and stiff? Does my shell look the same, but on the inside I am bitter and tough with a stiff spirit and hardened heart?

Or am I like the coffee bean? The bean actually changes the hot water, the very circumstance that brings the pain.

(continued on next page)

(continued from previous page)

When the water gets hot, it releases the fragrance and flavor. If you are like the bean, when things are at their worst, you get better and change the situation around you. When the hour is the darkest and trials are their greatest, do you elevate yourself to another level?

How do you handle adversity? Are you a carrot, an egg, or a coffee bean?

May you have enough happiness to make you sweet, enough trials to make you strong, enough sorrow to keep you human, and enough hope to make you happy. The happiest of people don't necessarily have the best of everything; they just make the most of everything that comes along their way. The brightest future will always be based on a forgotten past; you can't go forward in life until you let go of your past failures and heartaches.

When you were born, you were crying and everyone around you was smiling. Live your life so that at the end, you're the one who is smiling and everyone around you is crying.[13]

Four Pursuits of Life: What Do We Really Want?

Consciously or unconsciously, we are all pursuing some goal. This is the most common feature of human existence. What are the possible types of goals that we all seek? Indian philosophy classifies all human pursuits into four broad categories: pleasure *(kama)*, security *(artha)*, righteousness *(dharma)*, and freedom *(moksha)*. This classification provides an ideal infrastructure for the accomplishment of all human ends, called *purusharatha* in Sanskrit. The first three pursuits are seen as the material goals while the last pursuit, *mosksa,* is considered the spiritual goal culminating in liberation through self-knowledge.

According to this philosophy, all goals of life must lead to the ultimate goal of freedom because without accomplishing spiritual freedom, human life is not deemed to be fulfilled. Without attaining this spiritual freedom, the complete sense of fulfillment cannot come; there will always be more wants and regrets at the end of one's life. In fact, spiritual freedom alone gives the joyous sense of fulfillment at the time of death. Therefore, the material accomplishments are treated as ancillary goals, while spiritual freedom is considered to be the primary goal and ultimate objective of human life. The pursuit of spiritual freedom comes last because "it becomes a direct pursuit only when one has realized the limitations inherent in the first three pursuits."[14]

The *kama* is the pursuit of all types of pleasures, such as sensual, intellectual, and aesthetic. The *artha* is the pursuit of worldly gain or wealth to seek physical, economic, emotional, social, or some other form of security. The *dharma* is the pursuit of values or righteousness. And the *moksha* is the pursuit of spiritual liberation or freedom from all limitations and dependence. It is important to note that *dharma* underpins and regulates the other three pursuits to ensure their propriety; therefore, according to Hindu scriptures, the right order of these pursuits should be *dharma*, *artha*, *kama*, and *moksha*. The ancient seers were very keen to ensure that our pursuit of pleasure and security should be guided by the spirit of righteousness and conscientiousness.[15]

Indian philosophy says that all of these are legitimate ends of life. We will consider the first three pursuits (pleasure, security, and righteousness) as one category since they share more or less the same characteristics and limitations. We will find out that they all require efforts in time and space and produce only limited results. Our touchstone will be to see how each of these measure up to our ultimate goal of seeking lasting fulfillment and/or freedom from all limitations. First and foremost, we all naturally seek pleasure. However, we all eventually come to the realization that pleasure is too trivial to satisfy our total being. Besides, as stated before, no pleasure consistently satisfies us with same level of intensity over time.

Even the most refined type of aesthetic pleasures, such as music and literature, lose their intensity over time. "There comes a time," wrote Huxley, "when one asks even of Shakespeare, even of Beethoven, is this all?"[16] Anantanand Rambachan, an *Advaita* scholar, provides a succinct analysis of the reasons why we find sense gratification to be fleeting and ultimately unsatisfying: "The sense-object is subject to time and change, the relevant sense organ is gradually worn out through indulgence, and the mind grows saturated and bored with repetitiveness."[17]

Danish philosopher Søren Kierkegaard (1813–1855) described more pointedly his disenchantment with aesthetic pleasures in his book *Sickness Unto Death*. "In the bottomless ocean of pleasure," he wrote in his journal, "I have sounded in vain for a spot to cast an anchor. I have felt the almost irresistible power with which one pleasure drags another after it, the kind of adulterated enthusiasm which it is capable of producing, the boredom, the torment which follow."[18]

Let's now look at the pursuit of security through worldly gains with its three-fold formulation of wealth, power, and fame. Although the effects of this pursuit may seem to last longer than the pursuit of pleasure, they are still not beyond the vagaries of time and limitations. Consider this poignant observation of Tolstoy, who at the height of his career—with wealth, fame and power, all accomplished—found it all sham and mockery:

> All this took place at a time when so far as all my outer circumstances went, I ought to have been completely happy. I had a good wife who loved me and whom I loved; good children and a large property which was increasing with no pains taken on my part. I was more respected by my kinsfolk and acquaintance than I had ever been; I was loaded with praise by strangers; and without exaggeration I could believe my name already famous…and yet *I could give no reasonable meaning to any actions of my life*. And I was surprised that I had not understood this from the very beginning. My state of mind was as if some wicked and stupid jest was being played upon me by someone. *One can live only so long as one is intoxicated, drunk with life; but when one grows sober one cannot fail to see that it is all a stupid cheat* [emphasis added].[19]

Of course, one can perfunctorily dismiss Tolstoy's assessment as "too pessimistic" or "too cynical," yet one cannot deny the force with which he analyzes and lays bare the terror of the human situation. If we carefully look at the pursuits of pleasure, security, and values, we realize that they are all limited and time-bound in their ultimate bidding. Even when one has had them all, one still feels, with Tolstoy, the gnawing sense of incompleteness—that something is still missing. Bhikkhu Nanamoli, a pre-eminent Buddhist scholar of *Theravada* Buddhism, concurs: "Close examination of existence finds always something of the qualities of the mirage and of the paradox behind the appearance. The ends can never be made quite to meet."[20] Eventually, it seems, every discerning human being comes to realize with Simone Weil that "there is no true good here below, that everything that appears to be good in this world is finite, limited, wears out, and once worn out, leaves necessity exposed in all its nakedness."[21]

One does not have to come to this acute perceptiveness of the terror of the human predicament to agree with Arthur Schopenhauer (1788–1860) that the "business of life does not seem to cover its expenses." Bringing out the inherent poignancy of human existence, Dogen, a thirteenth-century Zen master, said, "Flowers fall; weeds grow!" Such is life! Indian philosophy furnishes a two-fold explanation of the grim assessment of human predicament furnished by Tolstoy, Huxley, Weil, and Schopenhauer: The first reason we find the pursuit of pleasure, security, and values to be ultimately unfulfilling is that the happiness they seem to provide does not really reside in them—even if it appears to at first. If this were not the case, we should always feel an invariable intensity of gratification from our objects of desire. Our experience tells us that our perceived happiness derived from objects, people, and places changes over time. What really happens is that the acquired object of our desire temporarily relieves the agitation in our mind and heart that we felt from its lack. When we obtain the object of our desire, we feel happy for a while, until our satiety is assailed again by another desire that takes the place of the previously fulfilled desire. So the happiness we seem to experience temporarily actually comes from within due to the appeasement of the anxiety we were feeling for not having the object of our desire. This is one reason why we find the material goals ultimately unsatisfying.

The second and perhaps most important reason we are ultimately unfulfilled by the pursuit of pleasure, security, and values is that they are only incidental goals that lead to the ultimate goal of freedom *(moksha)*, and for that very reason they are inherently unsatisfactory. Their inherent limitation lies in the fact that they can only provide "finite" results and can never satisfy our total being which longs for freedom from all limitations and dependence. In fact, they are the contributing causes of our bondage according to Indian philosophy, which postulates the fourth human pursuit as freedom from the first three pursuits!

Limitations of Pleasure, Wealth, Values

At first, the foregoing conclusion may seem counterintuitive, if not blatantly unacceptable, but it isn't, really. Let's take a closer look: According to Indian philosophy, material pursuits suffer from three inherent limitations or defects *(dosha-trayam)*, as they are

+ mixed with pain *(dukha-mishritattvam)*.
+ dissatisfaction-causing *(atriptti-krattvam)*.
+ dependence-causing *(bandha-gatvam)*.[22]

To explain, the results of the pursuit of pleasure, wealth, and values are mixed with pain—pain involved in their acquisition, pain associated with their preservation, and, ultimately, pain resulting from their separation. The second limitation is that, with any amount of acquisition of these goals, there will not be total satisfaction because finite plus finite equals finite only; dissatisfaction will continue whatever the extent of the accomplishment. The third limitation is that material pursuits can cause emotional dependence.

For example, the pursuit of pleasure, security, and values can create two types of bondage: first, when the object of our desire is present, it creates stress of handling the object and strain of relating to the person; second, when the object of our desire is absent, we feel empty and lonely.

When we do not have the objects of our desire we crave them, and when we have them we crave freedom from them. So we are not very sure whether we really want them or not. Either way, there seems to be a problem, here. This, says Indian philosophy, is the ultimate tyranny of our mundane existence—*Samsara*.

In sum, the material pursuits may lead to weariness of spirit, as they, in and of themselves, are not ultimately satisfying or liberating. When the point of weariness is reached, one starts wondering if there is something beyond the finite, limited, and time-bound pursuits of pleasure, security, and values. This is the point of departure that the Buddha and all other seers and sages came to. Here is what the Buddha said regarding this seminal point:

> *There is, o monks, an unborn, unoriginated, uncreated,
> unformed. Were there not, o monks, this unborn, unoriginated,
> uncreated, unformed, there would be no escape from
> the world of the born, originated, created, formed.*
> ~UDANA 8.3[23]

This is the point of realization that every serious seeker of truth comes to, eventually, and this is exactly where the true journey of self-knowledge begins.

We All Seek Fullness of Being

It does not require superhuman intelligence to conclude that things that are inherently insecure, finite, and transient cannot give infinite happiness and security. Indian philosophy explains that these pursuits are ultimately dissatisfying because, deep down, what we really have been seeking all along is complete freedom from limitations and dependence. We all seek a fullness of being *(puranatvam)*. An important verse in Chandogya Upanishad (7.23.1) puts it well: "There is no joy in the finite. The infinite alone is joy" *(na alpey sukham asti, bhumeva sukham)*. In other words, we are all indirectly engaged in the pursuit of spiritual freedom; at this point begins the true quest for limitless being, limitless knowledge, and limitless joy. Indian philosophy calls it *Brahman*, the absolute, infinite, pure consciousness. Knowing *Brahman*, one becomes *Brahman (Brahmvit brahmaiva bhavati,* Mundaka Upanishad 3.2.9) and one transcends all sorrow *(Tarati shokam atma-vit,* Chandogya Upanishad 7.1.3). Finally, only by knowing *Brahman* can one transcend death; there is no other way to cross over *(tameva viditva ati mrityum eti; nanyah pantha vidyate 'yanaya,* Shvetashvatara Upanishad 3.8., 5.15).

With the knowledge of *Brahman/Atman* comes the freedom from all limitations, the supreme purpose of all our pursuits. This freedom does not reside solely in objects, people, or places of our desire; rather, in our final quest for fulfillment we all seek intrinsic freedom from the material pursuits.

Evaluation of Experience Regarding Four Pursuits

Indian philosophy recommends that we should carefully look at the desirability of all the pursuits and determine what one really needs to do to attain the invariable condition of fulfillment. Here is an important Vedantic verse that captures the fundamental human predicament and also suggests a way out:

> *Parīkṣya lokān karmancitān brāhmaṇo nirvedam āyān nāsty akṛtah kṛtena, tad vijñānārtham sa gurum evābhigacchet samit-pāṇih śrotriyam brahma-niṣṭham (Mundaka Up.1.2.12).*

> After having properly examined the transient nature of all things in the world that are attained through actions, a wise person should acquire a sense of dispassion: That which is not the product of any action cannot be produced by actions—*nothing that is eternal can be produced by what is not eternal.* In order to understand that Eternal, one should humbly approach a great teacher who is well-versed in the Vedas and always absorbed in Absolute.

The Bṛhadāraṇyaka (4.4.9) and Kaṭha (II.iii.14) Upaniṣads confirm:

> *Yadā sarve pramucyante, kāmā ye 'sya hṛdi śritāh;*
> *Atha martyo 'mṛto bhavaty, atra brahma samaśnute.*

When a person completely gives up all the obsessive compulsive cravings he is harboring in his heart, he moves from the mortal realm to that of the imperishable and enjoys real joy and fulfillment in the Absolute Truth.

According to *Vedanta*, all human achievements fall into two broad categories: a) attainment of not-yet-attained *(apraptasya prapati)*, and b) attainment of the already attained *(praptasya prapati)*. As stated above, *Vedanta* divides all human goals into four, called purusharthas: dharma, artha, kama, and moksha. The first three human pursuits—dharma, artha, kama: ethics, security, and pleasure—belong to the first category. They require effort in time and space and can only produce finite result(s). The fourth human goal, moksha or spiritual freedom, then perhaps belongs to the second category and is ever-attained—only hidden from the seeker by mere self-ignorance. And the quest for moksha is like the search of the proverbial possessor of glasses looking for glasses when they have been resting on his nose all along! If moksha were the product of human efforts, it will then fall in the first category and be still finite and limited.

A mature person recognizes from the close examination of his own experience that what he has been seeking all along is fullness and the threefold pursuit of ethics, security and pleasure have failed to provide him that sense of invariable limitlessness. They have only provided limited, unsustainable, and transient satisfaction. As the Mundaka Upanisad (1.2.12) states, 'nothing that is Eternal can be produced by what is not eternal.' If we have to experience fullness at all times, in all places and situations, then common sense dictates that this state cannot be the product of our limited efforts. Yet we all have occasional glimpses of this state of fullness when the world seems to fall into place without any particular effort on our part and everything is accepted as is. We experience this daily during our sleep where we have no consciousness of our possessions, power, and fame. And yet we feel so much at peace, so adequate, full and complete during deep sleep.

The state of peaceful fullness felt during sleep and other occasions without any efforts on our part must emanate from our very being. We must be "fullness" all along. It must be our natural state, which is hidden from us simply because of self-ignorance. Happiness is our natural state because we do not complain about being happy! So, what is needed is knowledge to end our ignorance. It is not a problem of *becoming*; rather, it is a question of *being*. The goal of moksha, therefore, is ever-attained, *praptasya prapati.*

True Flowering of Self-Knowledge

This is where the flowering of self-knowledge becomes truly significant—in a state of equanimity where the presence of objects and people does not create undue stress and strain in us, and their absence does not create a sense of emptiness and loneliness in us. Self-knowledge removes self-ignorance that was covering our natural state of limitlessness. This is when we can really enjoy pleasures, security, and values *(kama, artha,* and *dharma)* without anxiety or anticipation. When they are there, we are OK; when they are not there, we are OK. We are fine with objects and people and we are fine without them. Either way we are fine because we have achieved the highest goal of equanimity: We have made our peace with the universe! We have arrived! This is called freedom—*moksha* that comes from Self-Knowledge.

Rejoicing in the Self Alone!

According to the Bhagavad Gita, that person of steady wisdom, whose mind is unperturbed in sorrow, who is free from longing for delights, and who has gone beyond attachment, fear, and anger *(dukheshu anudvi-gnamanah sukheshu vigata-sprhah; veeta-raaga bhaya-karodha stihita-dhih munih ucyate,* 2.56)—that person attains *moksha*:

> One who rejoices only in the Self, who is satisfied with the Self, who is content in the Self alone—for such a person, there is nothing left to do. Such a person has nothing to gain from work done or left undone and no selfish dependence on any being for any object to serve any purpose. Therefore, remaining unattached, always perform actions which are

obligatory; by performing action without attachment, one attains the Supreme. (3.17–19)

Resting in the Absolute, with intellect steady and without delusion, the knower of Self neither rejoices in receiving what is pleasant nor grieves on receiving what is unpleasant. (5. 20)

The inner autonomy described in the above verses is the blossoming of self-knowledge that expresses itself in the threefold virtues of acceptance, courage, and discernment—captured beautifully in the "Serenity Prayer" (also cited in chapter 9):

O Lord…

Grant me the serenity to accept what I cannot change,
Grant me the courage to change what I can change; and
Grant me the wisdom to know the difference.

This equanimity of mind *(samta)* has been extolled as *yoga* in the Bhagavad Gita *(samatavvayogahauchytey,* 2.48). This is the dexterity in human action *(yogahakaramsukaushalam,* 2.50). As we reach this point, we begin to understand that all the problems of the world are not really caused by the world; rather, they are caused by our mishandling of the world due to our own self-ignorance. Self-knowledge alone accords the freedom from self-ignorance. Having attained this self-knowledge, one swiftly attains supreme peace (*jnanam labdhva param shantim acirenadhigacchati,* 4.39). And we have come full circle!

Gaining the Essential Self

In the final reckoning, self-knowledge attains our essential self. The uniqueness of this knowledge lies in the fact that, unlike all other forms of knowledge, self-knowledge does not entail any new acquisition of information. It only involves freedom from self-ignorance. The following story illustrates both the predicament of self-ignorance and a way to end it:

The Missing Tenth Man

Ten monks crossed a river, and one of them counted their number to see if everyone had safely crossed. To their dismay, one was found missing. Then everyone took their turn at counting, but the result was the same. So they began to lament, when a kind passer-by inquired what it was all about. On being told what had happened, he readily understood the situation, and asked one of them to count again. When he stopped at nine, the passer-by said to him, "You are the tenth man." This he repeated with the rest of them. Then they saw their mistake and went away happy. Everyone had left himself out in the counting![24]

Strictly speaking, we cannot know our self because we are the self. The seeker is the sought! We are the knowing self—the pure awareness—the subject; and the subject, by definition, can never become the object of knowledge. Like the tenth man in the story, gaining the essential self means realizing our mistake of self-forgetfulness or self-ignorance. The self, like the tenth man in the story, appears initially to be not known through ignorance, but subsequently becomes known through knowledge. From an absolute standpoint, again—like the tenth man in the story—the essential self was never lost to begin with and is ever-attained. Attainment of the ever-attained self, therefore, essentially means letting go of our false notion about what we take ourselves to be, that is, a limited body-mind-intellect complex subject to mortality and unhappiness. It is about chipping away, so to speak, the fabricated edifice of the false "I," the imposter self. This special understanding requires courage—the discernment and audacity to reclaim our true heritage. We just have to know ourselves as we truly are. And this requires knowledge, not action.

The underlying assumption of this book is that most psychological and emotional stress is caused by our excessive self-centeredness.

Self-centeredness is a condition borne with a deeply ingrained sense of separateness, anchored in self-ignorance. Self-knowledge is freedom from self-ignorance; when self-ignorance transforms into self-knowledge, our need to maintain our separateness is resolved into the fullness of our being. We no longer feel the gnawing sense of inadequacy, incompleteness, and insecurity. We have arrived at an unassailable stillness, blessed with the fullness of our essential nature.

The Unique Understanding of Vedanta

As may be clear from the foregoing, *Vedanta* fosters a unique understanding about our real nature. This understanding is called self-knowledge or the knowledge of our real Self. Why is it necessary to have this understanding? We have seen that behind our myriad pursuits, we all seek fullness of being *(puranattvam)*. However, through the evaluation of our experience, we realize that this fullness is not to be found in the mundane pursuits of wealth, security, pleasure or even values. We discover that the rewards that material pursuits offer are at best short-lived, finite, and subject to change. They all grant some satisfaction to a certain degree, but ultimately leave us with a gnawing sense of incompleteness. In sum, they do not lead to complete freedom or fullness of total being. And amidst all the material proliferation, life continues to seem like a meaningless, boring, and burdensome struggle.

This is precisely where *Vedanta* becomes relevant.

Vedanta says that the spiritual freedom we have been seeking all along is not a matter of "acquisition," not a result of our "doing." It is rather a matter of "understanding" and "being." It is actually our natural state. Our primal error is that we identify ourselves with our body-mind complex whose limitations we then superimpose on our real nature. In other words, we take the unreal as the real. *Vedanta* explains that you are not just the limited body-mind complex you take yourself to be. Your real essence is of the nature of pure awareness. As such, your real nature is not subject to the limitations of illness, old age, and death which are only the attributes of your body-mind complex. Of course, *Vedanta* does not free us from these limitations *per se*. It only frees us from the fear and anxiety that we experience as a result of perceiving ourselves as a limited, body-mind complex. To be firmly established in this understanding is called spiritual freedom or *mukti*. Says an important Vedantic verse: "If you detach yourself from the body and rest in Pure Awareness, you will at once be happy, peaceful, and free from bondage."[25]

What is the liberating knowledge, then, that leads to spiritual freedom? And what is the method or discipline that leads to this understanding?

Five Axioms of *Vedanta*

Vedanta encapsulates its conviction and vision into five axioms:

1. I am of the nature of eternal and all-pervading Consciousness.
2. I am the only source of permanent security, peace, and happiness.
3. By my mere presence, I give life to material body and, through body, I experience the material universe.
4. I am essentially not affected by any events that take place in my material body and the material universe.
5. By forgetting my real nature, I convert the drama of life into a struggle; by remembering my real nature, I convert life into a play, *lila*.[26]

For the harmonious integration of human personality, *Vedanta* recommends the following three-fold spiritual program of *sravanam, mananam,* and *nidhidyasanam:*

1. *Sravanam* (Listening): This means systematic study of Vedantic teachings for a length of period with a competent teacher.
2. *Mananam* (Reflection): This refers to arriving at a doubt-free knowledge through constant reflection on the teachings.

3. *Nidhidyasanam* (Contemplative Assimilation): This is the process of internalizing, imbibing or absorbing the teachings by practicing meditative contemplation on the teachings.

What should be the subject of our listening, reflection, and contemplation? *Vedanta* provides precise directions regarding this, as follows: Verily, it is the Self that should be realized—should be heard of, reflected on and meditated upon. By the realization of the Self, my dear, through hearing, reflection and meditation, all this is known (*ātmā vā are draṣṭavyaḥ śrotavyo mantavyo nididhyāsitavyaḥ: maitreyī ātmano vā are darśanenaśravaṇena matyā vijñānenedaṁ sarvaṁ viditam*-Brihadaranyaka Upanishad: IV.5). And when the Self is realized through these processes, everything else becomes known (*yasmin vijnate sarvam eva vijnatam bhavanti*[27]).

The practice of three-fold discipline is an essential requirement to imbibe the profound truths of *Vedanta*. Listening to the teachings is analogous to eating the food, reflecting on the teachings is like chewing the food, and internalizing the teaching is like digesting the food. While eating and chewing the food may happen rather quickly, digesting the food may take a very long time. Similarly, internalizing the teachings is a gradual process and not a hurried event. Therefore, utmost patience is required in approaching these three steps. Once a Seer explained to me that it is possible to practice these three steps all at once, if one is intensely focused.

The Unconditional Promise of *Vedanta*

Every challenging experience of our life can serve as an ideal opportunity for remembering that our body-mind complex is just a costume, that our real nature is that of pure awareness, that the world is a stage where the drama of our life is taking place, and that our real nature—the screen on which the drama is taking place—is not affected by the show of light and sound. The real test of this understanding is to see the drama as the divine play *(lila)*—especially when the drama is not going well. Whether the drama is a tragedy or a comedy, it is drama, nonetheless. The profound understanding that life is a Self-play, *Swalila*—and the resultant state of freedom from fear *(nirbhaya-padd)* are the twin fruits of absorbing Advaitic wisdom. This is the unconditional promise of *Vedanta: freedom from all fear and sorrow.*

Wave-Ocean-Water: Our Primal Illusion

Metaphorically speaking, all spiritual endeavors rest on the assumption of the separateness of the wave and its promptings to become one with the ocean, once and for all. And all spiritual practices and disciplines are geared toward removing this sense of separation. Actually, the very meaning of the word *yoga* presupposes this. The word *yoga* literally means "yoke," from the Sanskrit root *yuj*, meaning to join, to tie, to fasten, or to unite. Through the discipline of *Yoga*, therefore, the seeker seeks to unite with the sought. So the felt sense of separation is a precondition to every spiritual endeavor, and the complete cessation of this seeming sense of separation is generally referred to as awakening or enlightenment.

If we deeply reflect on the wave-ocean dichotomy, we realize that at no time is a wave not one with the ocean. In and throughout the wave is the water of the ocean. Wave is water, and ocean is water. The waves do not affect the ocean. The wave may change form, but the water is not affected. Wave and water are two names but one substance. Both are one, only seemingly different. After all, the wave has no existence separate from the water. The wave really does not have to do anything to become one with the ocean—it has never been separate from the ocean to begin with. Its insistence on being a wave is its only real hurdle. From the absolute point of view, both wave and ocean are just linguistic expediencies. They do not really exist as such in the actual sense. Water is the underlying reality of both the wave and the ocean—any difference between wave and ocean is only apparent to us who see a difference. Therefore, to us, the wave has only to realize its true nature as water.

The separate existence of wave and ocean is an operation of the ego, a human invention that has no absolute reality whatsoever. It is an imposter! Still, it has prompted all the troubles, conflicts, and wars in human history. Once it is seen for what it is—an illusion—it subsides and we slip into a mode of being where there is no struggle for maintaining our separateness or "one-up-ness." Freed from the servitude of ego, we enjoy our brief sojourn on this planet as a carnival, as a part of the cosmic grand play called *Lila*. Understood in this manner, all spiritual practices occur in the realm of make-believe. After all, how could an ego, itself an illusion, ever come upon what is real?!

"But what can I do?" the seeker still insists. Sri Ramana Maharshi has provided perhaps the best answer: "Be!" Just Be! Realize your essential nature. You are ocean already. Totality already! Just let go of your insistence on being a wave. That's all.

The Drop Becomes the Ocean!

The empirical self is only relatively real. It appears real due to self-ignorance. Deluded, it identifies itself with the body, mind, and the senses and assumes a separative existence like ripples floating on the surface of the ocean. Just as the bubble becomes one with the ocean when it bursts, so also the individual or the empirical self becomes one with the absolute when it frees itself from the bounds of self-ignorance. When Self-Knowledge dawns in it through the obliteration of self-ignorance, the empirical self is freed from its individuality and finitude, and its essential nature is realized. It merges itself in the ocean of blissful fullness. The stream of life seams into the ocean of existence. The drop becomes the ocean. Better yet, the drop is the ocean for it has been one with the ocean all along. That is, the ocean of *Sat-Chit-Ananda*: Existence-Consciousness-Bliss Absolute! This is the consummation of human existence.

The following story splendidly captures the message, albeit symbolically:

> ### The Salt Doll and the Ocean
>
> A salt doll journeyed for thousands of miles over the land, until it finally came to the sea. It was fascinated by this strange moving mass, quite unlike anything it had ever seen.
>
> "Who are you?" said the salt doll to the sea.
>
> The sea smilingly replied, "Come in and see."
>
> She first hesitatingly put one foot in and it dissolved. She got scared and asked the sea, "What happened?" The sea replied, "You just gave a part of you to understand my reality." So the doll waded in. The farther it walked into the sea the more it dissolved, until there was only very little of it left. Before the last bit dissolved, the doll exclaimed in wonder, "Now I know who I am! I am IT!"[28]

Concluding Remarks

We have come to the end of this presentation of the seven gifts of fulfillment. In this chapter, we also broached the subject of what really matters in life. Practicing these gifts cleanses our mind and purifies our heart. We then open ourselves to receive what matters most during our cosmic journey. The underlying assumption of this book has been that most psychological and emotional stress is caused by our excessive self-centeredness. Self-centeredness is a condition borne with a deeply ingrained sense of separateness. The seemingly felt sense of separateness is anchored in a special form of ignorance called self-ignorance. Self-knowledge is freedom from self-ignorance. The road to self-knowledge is paved by the practice of the seven gifts or habits discussed in the foregoing pages. These gifts are designed to release the stranglehold of self-centeredness and prepare the mind to receive the liberating wisdom of self-knowledge.

The most glaring fact of our life remains that it is short and the journey for self-discovery is long. There is thus an inherent urgency to redeem it through self-knowledge and fulfillment. One is reminded of

Buddha's last words to his long-time disciple, Ananda: "All composite things are subject to decay. Work out your salvation with diligence."

What kind of diligence is the Buddha talking about as he is breathing his last? It can be referred to as wisdom about the ultimate pursuit/ end of life. One Vedantic verse puts it under the guise of a seeker's prayer for spiritual freedom *(mukti mantra)* as follows:

> *asato ma sadgamaya*
> *tamaso ma jyotirgamaya*
> *mrtyorma amrtam gamaya*

> Lead me from the unreal to the real.
> Lead me from darkness to light.
> Lead me from death to immortality.
>   ~ BRHADARANYAKA UPANISHAD 1.3.28

We again turn to the metapsychologist, the Buddha, for a final word about diligence in life's means and ends:

> During one of his myriad discourses, the Buddha explains that there are four types of people in the world: those who are running from darkness toward darkness, those who are running from light toward darkness, those who are running from darkness toward light, and those who are running from light toward light. The first type of person is ignorant (surrounded by darkness) and does not possess good qualities of head and heart, such as wisdom and generosity. Every time he encounters an unfavorable situation, he becomes upset and tries to blame others for his troubles, thereby compounding his misery: he is running from darkness into more darkness!

> The second type of person has money, position, and power, but has no wisdom or generosity. Lacking wisdom, he becomes arrogant, self-centered, and egotistical, which

heralds his future downfall: He is running from light to darkness. The third type of person is in the same situation as the first one but he has wisdom to see through his situation. He works calmly to change his situation without complaining or trying to blame others for his situation: He is moving from darkness to light. The fourth type of person is similar to the second one: he has money, position, and power, but he also has the wisdom and compassion to use these gifts generously in helping and serving others. The fourth type of person is going from light to light.[29]

This analogy provides a reliable touchstone to ensure due diligence about life's means and ends and neatly sums up the gist of this book. During our earthly journey, may we all be so heedful and discerning to move from light to light! And may the two prayers quoted above, one from the Eastern wisdom *(mukti mantra)* and the other from the Western wisdom (Serenity Prayer), serve as twin lights on our pathway to the sacred sanctuary of self-knowledge. This, then, is the true fulfillment of the Delphic Oracle *(gnothi seauton): get to know yourself!*

The Chinese ideograph for "crisis" is comprised of two parts: the first part denotes "danger;" the second part signifies "opportunity." That is, we are in danger if we miss the opportunity. What is the supreme opportunity? Realization of our Self-Supreme! What is the great danger? Human status is very difficult to get and very easy to lose. *Carpe Diem*—Seize the Day!

> *Life is fleeting,*
> *Gone, gone—*
> *Awake,*
> *Awake each one!*
> *Don't waste this life!*[30]

A Final Poem: Experience the Divine
in the Silence of Your Soul!

When thoughts subside and mind is still,
Remain in this blessed state as Pure Awareness till,
One feels like just a mass of Undifferentiated Whole;
Experience the Divine in the Silence of your Soul!

Silence is Peace, Silence is Joy,
It is the master key that gods employ;
Let its benedictions keep you Whole,
Experience the Divine in the Silence of your Soul!

I have searched near and I have searched afar,
It has only left the door of my soul ajar;
Good bye now all wanderings and resting in Whole,
Experience the Divine in the Silence of your Soul!

There is no mention in this silence,
There is no tension in this silence,
There is no anxiety in this goal;
There is no more becoming in this Whole,
Experience the Divine in the Silence of your Soul!

The coming and going, the perch and the search,
All are just the weariness of the soul;
Your true Being always remains Whole,
Experience the Divine in the Silence of your Soul!

Not a whit of your effort can win this state,
At best your mongerings can lead you to the gate;
To be invited in—patiently, revel in the Whole,
Experience the Divine in the Silence of your Soul!

This silence is the source of all creation,
This silence is the goal of all creation;
Silence submerged into the Silent Sole,
Experience the Divine in the Silence of your Soul!

(continued on next page)

(continued from previous page)

Free and clear of mental chatter and clutter,
Inhere steady abidance in the Supreme Self utter;
Rejoice in the fusion of Existence-Awareness-Bliss-Whole,
Experience the Divine in the Silence of your Soul!

Relinquish all distinctions of self and not-self,
Give up all smithing about sacred and profane;
Celebrate the Blissful Dance of the Whole,
Experience the Divine in the Silence of your Soul!

See through the mirage-struggle of 'Me-My-Mine,'
A futile toil for dream-objects posing sublime;
Remain content in belonging to the Whole,
Experience the Divine in the Silence of your Soul!

Just a concept anything anyone can think or say,
A ripple in the Ocean-Endless of Existence's sway,
Firmly settled in the undifferentiated Whole,
Experience the Divine in the Silence of your Soul!

All concepts just agitations of the mind,
Figments, imaginings, ghosts of some kind;
All disappear in the Luminosity of the Whole,
Experience the Divine in the Silence of your Soul!

Amazing! The Self-same Reality sought,
Ever-shining in the gaps between thoughts;
Mind-Fasting & taking a respite from its role,
Experience the Divine in the Silence of your Soul!

Not all spiritual practices are created alike,
Most remain ploys for Ego's hike;
Take your refuge in Maha-Maunna* Sole,
Experience the Divine in the Silence of your Soul!

My friend you are complete "as is" Eternity's Grandeur,
Not a whit can be added to your Perfect Galore;
Reclaim your Majesty Be One with the Whole,
Experience the Divine in the Silence of your Soul!

The whole world is a mirage, a juggler's show!
A dream within a dream, a worm's glow!
Why do you worry? Leave it to the Whole!
Experience the Divine in the Silence of your Soul!

*The great silence or stillness

Since "All" is all that there is, there is nothing to accept or reject!
Just Be! One cannot say much more beyond this without
causing mental confusion.
The following title of a Zen book says it all:
"Open Mouth, Mistake Already!"

A true seeker's life is one continuous mistake. That is, an opportunity to learn, one mistake after another!

ART OF LEADERSHIP AND TEACHING STORIES: A BRIEF GUIDE TO RESOURCES

Teaching stories do not know the boundaries of one religion, one nation, or one mind. Being our common heritage, they are as vast as the ocean, as fresh as air, as ancient as time. In addition to the parables used by various spiritual leaders of the world, there are traditional collections such as *Aesop's Fables*, *Arabian Nights*, and *Panchatantra*. The biographies of the world's great leaders provide an endless source of fascinating legendary anecdotes, as Martin Buber called them, that have the force of character behind them. As one goes forth in life, one makes one's own anthology of best stories to savor and to share. The familiar stories assume an added significance when interpreted through the three-fold framework of entertainment value, moral value, and developmental value.

I have found the following collections of stories particularly useful due to their diversity and universality. These stories cover a very wide range of human emotions and interests and can be used by educators to illuminate moral and spiritual aspects of life and learning. These collections represent various wisdom traditions of the world, such as Zen, Taoism, Sufism, Buddhism, Hasidism, Native American, African, and

Indian mysticism. They are chosen for their ability to inspire the heart, enlighten the mind, and rekindle the spirit.

Buber, Martin. *Tales of Hasidism.* Translated by Olga Marx. New York: Schocken Books, 1947.

This treasure trove of Hasidic tales crowns Buber's lifetime of retelling Hasidic legends. In nominating Buber for the Nobel Prize in Literature in 1947, the great Swiss writer Hermann Hesse declared that with these tales Buber has enriched world literature as had no other living author.

I have used some of these stories in my leadership class to illustrate the virtue of discovering our own distinctive voice and finding a life that is truly ours. No true leader can endure by imitating others. Buber narrates a story about a young Rabbi who assumed leadership of the congregation after his father's death. The disciples found that this young man's ways were different from his father's and asked him about this. "I do just as my father did," he replied, "He did not imitate and I do not imitate" (Buber 157).

It is impossible to do justice to this deep mine of inspirational stories in a brief annotation. Every page prods the reader to do every act with *Kavana*—whole heart—and to seek fulfillment in the humdrum of daily life. These tales also have a special meaning in the context of what is now called "servant leadership."

Canfield, Jack, Mark Victor Hansen, Maida Rogerson, Martin Rutte, and Tim Clauss. *Chicken Soup for the Soul at Work: 101 Stories of Courage, Compassion & Creativity in the Workplace.* Deerfield Beach, FL: HCI, 1997.

One of the several titles published under *Chicken Soup for the Soul* series, this book is comprised of inspiring stories from the contemporary workplace. I use this book as one of the texts in my *Spirituality in the*

Workplace class. It has become a favorite of students due to its modern idiom and contemporary setting. However, I find the earlier titles in this series more pertinent.

Dosick, Wayne. *The Business Bible: Ten New Commandments for Creating an Ethical Workplace*. New York: William Morrow, 1993.

In artfully chosen passages from the scriptures, illustrated with stories, parables, and real-life business situations, this book suggests that, in the contemporary business world, it is possible to be successful while practicing a personal code of ethics. Drawing upon Hasidic heritage, the author presents concrete examples of working ethically smarter. The book contains a useful bibliography listing sources and additional books to seek in-depth discussion of specific issues presented in the book.

Fadiman, James and Robert Frager, eds. *Essential Sufism*. New York: HarperOne, 1998.

This book is an excellent resource for stories in the tradition of Sufi soul work. It presents Sufi tales on a wide variety of topics such as self-knowledge, wisdom, humor, humility, gratitude, patience, and generosity—topics that are very relevant to what has come to be characterized as "leading with soul." Each topic is accompanied by thoughtful introduction and insightful commentary.

Feldman, Christina and Jack Kornfield, eds. *Stories of the Spirit, Stories of the Heart: Parables of the Spiritual Path from Around the World*. San Francisco: HarperSanFrancisco, 1991.

This compelling collection of stories draws widely from many cultures and centuries, from Christian, Buddhist, Sufi, Zen, Hasidic, Native American, African, and other sources. I have found this collection most useful and it can be safely recommended as one of the most comprehensive anthologies on this topic currently available. The editors would have served the readers even better if only they had provided a formal bibliography at the end of the book instead of just listing acknowledgements. The book has been recently reprinted under the new title *Soul Food*. The editors have added a new index that facilities the location of subject headings.

Friedlander, Ira. *Wisdom Stories for the Planet Earth*. San Francisco: Harper and Row, 1973.

This book contains stories from the Eastern as well as Western traditions. The book, its author claims, is for all those "who are interested in tapping the higher selves within them." Some stories have a direct bearing upon what Peter Senge of MIT calls "personal mastery" and underscore the importance of self-knowledge and self-discipline as prerequisites to leadership.

Friedman, Maurice. *A Dialogue with Hasidic Tales: Hallowing the Everyday*. New York: Insight Books, 1988.

This book is a systematic presentation of representative Hasidic tales under different headings (such as Serving, Teaching, Learning Trust, Love, and Community) by one of the most important Buber scholars. The book draws very heavily upon Buber's *Tales of Hasidism,* which remains an invaluable resource for all serious students of this genre.

Leggett, Trevor. *Encounters in Yoga and Zen: Meetings of Cloth and Stone*. Tokyo: Charles E. Tuttle, 1993.

Leggett, Trevor. *Lotus Lake Dragon Pool: Musings in Yoga and Zen*. Tokyo: Charles E. Tuttle, 1994.

These two books by Trevor Leggett contain a fascinating selection of traditional Japanese and Indian stories with suggested applications for modern situations. From accounts of long-ago kings to stories of contemporary businessmen, these tales present universal precepts that speak directly to modern readers. The author, a foremost scholar and a long-time practitioner of Eastern traditions, provides pithy comments set within the stories that serve as important cues for their interpretation and application. These works are recommended for serious aspirants.

Reps, Paul, ed. *Zen Flesh, Zen Bones: A Collection of Zen and Pre-Zen Writings*. Tokyo: Charles E. Tuttle, 1964.

This book contains some of the most famous Zen stories that recount actual experience of Chinese and Zen teachers over a period of more than five centuries. I have used some stories out of this collection in my classes to celebrate the timeless qualities of kindness, compassion, and humility as hallmarks of great leadership. Actually, this book includes four books, including a little gem at the end titled *Centering* that presents 112 methods of meditation. A true desert island book!

Shah, Idries. *The Sufis*. London: Octogen Press, 1964.

Idries Shah takes a psychological approach to interpreting Sufi lore, and his remarks are always illuminating. His unique contribution to the genre of teaching stories is evident from the fact that he single-handedly published over one thousand such stories in his 25 books, whose titles also include *Sufism, Way of the Sufi, Caravan of Dreams, Tales of Dervishes, Elephant in the Dark, Learning How to Learn, Dermis Probe,* and *A Perfumed Scorpion*. Shah's work represents the finest intellectual nourishment available in endless variety under the garb of stories—a most impressive achievement by a single author.

The spiritual quest is a journey without distance.
You travel from where you are right now
To where you have always been.
From ignorance to recognition.

~ Anthony de Mello

END NOTES

Setting the Stage

[1] Author unknown.

The Journey of Self-Discovery

[1] This vignette is based on a discourse of Swami Paramarthananda.

[2] This quote is widely attributed to Sri Ramana Maharshi. I have not been able to locate its precise occurrence in Ramana literature. I have also communicated with David Godman and Michael James, two pre-eminent experts on Sri Ramana Maharshi's work. They have also not been able to trace the precise location of this quote. In an email dated December 18, 2011, Michael James wrote: "However, though the original source of this exact quotation is doubtful, and though these are probably not the exact words spoken by Bhagavan, they do express the gist of his teachings."

[3] This segment is inspired by Swami Paramarthananda's discourses on Tattva Bodha.

[4] Ramana Maharshi, *The Collected Works of Sri Ramana Maharshi* (Tiruvannamalai: Sri Ramanasramam, 2002), 36.

[5] This story was told in a commencement speech by David Foster Wallace to the 2005 graduating class at Kenyon College.

[6] *Dhondhta firtta hun ae-Iqbaal apney aapko;*
Aap hee goyaa musfir, aap hee manzill hun mein.

[7] *Miyan-e aashiko maashuk heech haayal naisstt;*
To khud hijjab-e-khuddi Hafiz, uz miyan barkheez!"

[8] *Paani Mein Meen Piyasi, Mohe suun suun aye Haansi.*

[9] A traditional tale transcribed by the author.

[10] Idries Shah, *Neglected Aspects of Sufi Study: Beginning to Begin* (London: The Octagon Press, 1977), 37.

[11] As cited in Camden Benares, *Zen without Zen Masters* (Berkeley: And/ Or Press, 1977), 13.

[12] I am indebted to Shah's psychological reading of traditional stories in numerous books, such as *Learning How to Learn*, *Elephant in the Dark*, *Perfumed Scorpion*, *Seekers after Truth*, *Tales of Dervishes*, and *Caravan of Dreams*.

[13] As cited in Arvind Sharma, ed., *Our Religions* (New York: HarperCollins, 1993), 368.

[14] Idries Shah, *The Sufis* (London: The Octagon Press, 1982), 78.

[15] Ibid., 62.

[16] Bertrand Russell, *The Conquest of Happiness* (New York: H. Liveright, 1930), 11.

CHAPTER TWO
The Pursuit of Happiness and Fulfillment

[1] As quoted in Wayne Dyer, *Your Erroneous Zones* (William Morrow Paperbacks, 1991), 68. Dyer cites C.L. James, "On Happiness," *To See a World in a Grain of Sand*, ed. Caesar Johnson (Norwalk, CT: C.R. Gibson, 1972).

[2] As cited in H. Mansfield and N. Tarcov, trans., *Discourses on Livy*, by Niccolo Machiavelli (New York: Random House, 1996), 125.

3   James Legge, trans., *Confucian Analects* (New York: Dover Publications, 1971), 173.

4   James Legge, trans., *The Works of Mencius: In the Four Books* (Shanghai: The International Publication Society, 1947), 8.

5   J.O. Urmson, *Aristotle's Ethics* (Malden, MA: Blackwell Publishers, 2001), 11, 17–18, 20.

6   Will Durant, *Heroes of History: A Brief History of Civilization from Ancient Times to the Dawn of the Modern Age* (New York: Simon and Schuster, 2001), 105.

7   Will Durant, *The Story of Philosophy: The Lives and the Opinions of the Great Philosophers* (New York: Simon and Schuster, 1962/1933), 76.

8   Mortimer Adler, *Arsitotle for Everybody: Difficult Thought Made Easy* (New York: Bantam Books, 1980).

9   Jaime L.Kurtz and Sonja Lyubomirsky, *Towards a Durable Happiness,* The Positive Psychology Perspective Series (Westport, CT : Greenwood, 2008), 21.

10   Martin Seligman, *Authentic Happiness: Using New Psychology to Realize Your Potential* (New York: Free Press, 2002), 260–262.

11   Ibid., 249.

12   Kurtz and Lyubomirsky, *Towards a Durable Happiness,* 21–23.

13   Marina Krakovsky, "The Science of Lasting Happiness," *Scientific American*, March 18, 2007, 2.

14   See, for example, Tal Ben-Shahar, *Happier: Learn the Secrets to Daily Joy and Lasting Fulfillment* (New York: McGraw Hill, 2007), 135–138.

15   Sonja Lyubomirsky, Kennon M. Sheldon, and David Schkade, "Pursuing Happiness: The Architecture of Sustainable Change," *Review of General Psychology* 9 (2005): 111–131.

16   Ibid., 118.

17   Mihaly Csikszentmihalyi, *Flow: The Psychology of Optimal Experience* (New York: Harper and Row, 1990), 2.

18   Viktor Frankl, *Man's Search for Meaning: An Introduction to Logotherapy,* 3rd ed. (New York: Touchstone Book, 1984), 12.

[19] Russell, *The Conquest of Happiness*, 43.

[20] Ibid., 88.

[21] Ibid., 123.

[22] Dan Gilbert, *Stumbling on Happines* (New York: Vintage, 2007).

[23] Dalai Lama, *Practicing Wisdom* (Boston: Wisdom, 2005).

[24] Walpola Rahula, *What the Buddha Taught*. Rev. and exp. ed. (New York: Grove Press, 1974), 17–19.

[25] Michael Carrithers, *The Buddha* (Oxford: Oxford University Press, 1988).

[26] Rahula, *What the Buddha Taught*, 25.

[27] Based on traditional Buddhist teachings, shared orally with the author.

[28] Translated by Max Muller.

[29] Stephen Batchelor, *Guide to Bodhisattva's Way of Life* (Dharmshala: LTWA, 1999), 36.

[30] Dalai Lama and H.C. Cutler, *The Art of Happiness: A Handbook for Living* (New York: Riverhead Books, 1998), 29.

[31] Thich Nhat Hanh, *The Heart of the Buddha's Teaching: Transforming Suffering into Peace, Joy & Liberation: The Four Noble Truths, the Noble Eightfold Path, & Other Basic Buddhist Teachings* (Berkeley: Parallax Press, 1998), 123–124.

[32] Ibid., 3–5.

[33] Matthiew Ricard, *Happiness: A Guide to Developing Life's Most Important Skill* (New York: Little Brown, 2007), 203.

[34] Rahula, *What the Buddha Taught*, 75.

[35] Stephen Batchelor, *Guide to Bodhisattva's Way of Life* (Dharmshala: LTWA, 1999), 126.

[36] S.N. Goenka, *The Discourse Summaries: Talks from a Ten Day Course in Vipassana Meditation*, ed. William Hart (Igatpuri: Vipassana Research Institute, 1998), 64:
Sabba-paapasa akaranam,
kusalassa upasampda,
sa-citta pariyodapanam—
etam Buddhana saasanam.

37 Frankl, *Man's Search for Meaning*, 148.

38 Ibid., 74–75

39 Idries Shah, *A Perfumed Scorpion: The Way to the Way* (San Francisco: Harper and Row, 1981), 33, 117–118.

40 Ibid., 44.

41 Based on Swami Paramarthananda's *TattvaBodha Summary* Talks, Discourse #1.

42 These encounters are pieced together from several sources, including Richard Taylor, *Ethics, Faith and Reason* (New Jersey: Prentice Hall, 1985), 47.

43 Shunryu Suzuki, *Zen Mind, Beginner's Mind* (New York: John Weatherhill, 1970), 27.

44 Jiddu Krishnamurti, *The Book of Life: Daily Meditations with Krishnamurti* (San Francisco: Harper San Francisco, 1995), ix.

45 Richard William, trans., *The Secret of Golden Flower: A Chinese Book of Life* (New York: Causeway Books, 1975), 89.

46 Cited in Sean Murphy, *One Bird, One Stone: 108 American Zen Stories* (New York: Renaissance Books, 2002), 162–163.

47 Rainer Maria Rilke, *Letters to a Young Poet*, trans. M. D. Herter Norton, rev. ed. (New York: W. W. Norton, 1954), 7.

CHAPTER THREE
The Journey From Success to Significance

1 Aldous Huxley, *Huxley and God: Essays* (New York: Harper and Row, 1992), 4.

2 Thomas Merton, *The Way of Chuang Tzu* (New York: New Directions, 1969), 114–115.

3 Bhikkhu Nanamoli, *The Life of the Buddha*: According to the Pali Canon (Seattle, BPS Pariyatti, 1992/1972), 34.

4 Hee-Jin Kim, *Eihei Dogen: Mystical Realist*. 3rd rev. ed. (Boston: Wisdom, 2000), xxiv.

[5] Norman Waddell and Abe Masao, trans., *The Heart of Shobogenzo* (New York: State University of New York Press, 2002), 41.

[6] Kim, *Eihei Dogen*, xxiv.

[7] Khalil Gibran, *The Prophet* (New York: Alfred A Knopf, 1977), 28.

CHAPTER FOUR
Living Our Highest Purpose through the Gift of Pure Motivation

[1] Author unknown.

[2] George Bernard Shaw, *Man and Superman: A Comedy and a Philosophy*, xxxi.

[3] James Fadiman and Robert Frager, eds., *Essential Sufism* (New York: HarperOne, 1998), 250.

[4] This section draws upon Abraham Maslow, *Farther Reaches of Human Nature* (New York: Harper and Row, 1971). The interested reader will be amply rewarded pursuing Maslow's wonderful masterpiece.

[5] Ibid., 35.

[6] Ibid., 36.

[7] Ibid., 43, 192.

[8] Frankl, *Man's Search for Meaning*, 90.

[9] Ibid., 12.

[10] Ibid., 75.

[11] Ibid., 75–76.

[12] Ibid., 90.

[13] Ibid., 151.

[14] Ibid., 113–114.

[15] Martin Buber, *Tales of Hasidism* (New York: Knopf Doubleday, 1987), 251.

16 Csikszentmihalyi, *Flow*. This is probably the best self-help book ever written. I had the rare opportunity to meet with Dr. Csikszentmihalyi. Undoubtedly, the great master of *Flow* personifies his teachings!

17 Mihaly Csikszentmihalyi, *Finding Flow: The Psychology of Engagement with Everyday Life*, Masterminds Series (New York: Basic Books, 1998), 29.

18 J. Geirland, "Go With The Flow," *Wired Magazine*, September 1996, 4.09.

19 Csikszentmihalyi, *Flow*, 49–70.

20 Berthold Madhukar Thompson, *The Odyssey of Enlightenment: Rare Interviews with Enlightened Teachers of Our Time* (New York: Origins Press, 2002), 282.

21 Peter D. Ouspensky, *Tertium Organum: The Third Canon of Thought, a Key to the Enigmas of the World* (New York: Cosimo Classics, 2005), 352.

22 Brian Walker, trans., *Hua Hu Ching: The Unknown Teachings of Lao Tzu* (New York: HarperOne, 1995), 52.

23 Author unknown.

24 Bhagavad Gita 2.47.

25 A traditional story transcribed by the author.

26 As cited in Wayne Dyer, *Real Magic: Creating Miracles in Everyday Life* (New York: HaperPaperbacks, 1992), 5.

27 Ira Friedlander, *Wisdom Stories for the Planet Earth* (San Francisco: Harper and Row, 1973), 69.

CHAPTER FIVE
The Gift of Gratitude

1 Nagarjuna, *Nagarjuna's Letter to a Friend,* trans. Padmakara Translation Group (Ithaca, NY: Snow Lion, 2005).

2 Yaffa Leibowitz, *Mastering the Gratitude Attitude*.

3 Stephen Mitchell, ed., *The Enlightened Mind: An Anthology of Sacred Prose* (New York: Harper Collins, 1991), 207.

[4] Robert A. Emmons and Michael E. McCullough, "Counting Blessings versus Burdens: An Experimental Investigation of Gratitude and Subjective Well-Being in Daily Life," *Journal of Personality and Social Psychology* 84 no.2 (2003): 377.

[5] Ibid., 377–389.

[6] "Want To Be Happier? Be More Grateful," *Science Daily* (2008, November 27): 2–3.

[7] Sonja Lyubomirsky, *The How of Happiness: A Scientific Approach to Getting the Life You Want* (New York: Penguin Press, 2007), 9.

[8] Ibid., 20.

[9] Ibid., 89.

[10] This parable occurs in The Majjhima Nikaya (Middle Length Discourses) under Balapandita Sutta,129.

[11] Edward O. Wilson, "Best Species: Microbes 3, Humans 2," *New York Times Magazine* (18 April, 1999), 87.

[12] Pranipata Chaitanya, trans., and Satinder Dhiman, rev. and ed., *Sri Sankara's Vivekachudamani: Devanagari Text, Transliteration, Word-for-Word Meaning, and a Lucid English Translation* (eBook, 2011), 44.

[13] Compiled from various Internet sources.

[14] Werner Gitt, "Information: The Third Fundamental Quantity," *Siemens Review* 56 no. 6 (November/December 1989).

[15] Author unknown.

[16] C. Wallis, "The New Science of Happiness," *Time Magazine* (January 9, 2005), op. cit.

[17] Ibid.

CHAPTER SIX:
The Gift of Generosity

[1] Author unknown.

[2] As cited in *New York Post* (November 28, 1972).

[3] Author unknown.

4   Compiled from personal interviews with Buddhist teacher, Ajahn Amaro (unpublished manuscript, 2009).

5   A traditional tale transcribed by the author.

6   Cited in Alexander Welsh, *What is Honor? : A Question of Moral Imperative* (New Haven, CT: Yale University Press, 2008), 179.

7   Bhikkhu Bodhi, *The Noble Eightfold Path: Way to the End of Suffering* (Seattle: BPS Pariyatti, 2000), 31.

8   As cited in J. Looper, "Be Generous, Give Freely, Be Happy: Research Shows Generosity Is a Key to Happiness," Personal Development, *@suite101*, March 21, 2008, http://jerry-lopper.suite101.com/be-generous-give-freely-be-happy-a48375.

9   Internet, author unknown.

10 Author unknown.

CHAPTER SEVEN:
The Gift of Harmlessness

1   Confucius, *Doctrine of the Mean*, 13.3.

2   Dalai Lama, address given in San Jose, Costa Rica, *Buddhist Peace Fellowship Newsletter* (Fall 1989),

3   Brhdaranyaka Upanishad, 2.4.5.

4   Samyutta Nikaya, PTS 1:75.

5   The story about the sandal is cited in Steve Hagen, *How the World Can Be the Way It Is: An Inquiry for the New Millenium into Science, Philosophy, and Perception* (Wheaton, IL: Quest Books), 300–301.

6   Albert Schweitzer, *Out of My Life and Thought* (Baltimore, MD: Johns Hopkins University Press, 1998), 236.

7   Originally written by Loren Eiseley (1907–1977), the story has appeared widely over the Web. This version was prepared by Catherine Ludgate, 21 November, 2006.

8   *"Shloka-ardhena pravakshyaami yad-uktam grantha-kotibhih; Paropakaraya punyaya, papaya para peedanam."*

(The gist of a million treatise expressed in half a verse: Highest merit is helping others; highest wrongdoing is hurting others.)

9   From a compilation of Einstein quotes published from multiple online sources and credited to Kevin Harris,1995.

10 See David Bohm, *Wholeness and the Implicate Order* (London: Routledge Classics, 2002). For general background, see also Ken Wilber, ed., *Quantum Questions: Mystical Writings of World's Great Physicists* (Boston: Shambhala, 1984).

11 *"Ahara-suddhau sattva-suddhih, Sattva-suddhau dhruva-smritih, Smritilabhe sarvagranthinam vipramokshah."*

12 This story is repeated on multiple Web and blog sites, some of which attribute it to a book called *Record of Protecting Life;* I have yet to find publication information on the book.

13 In Swami Prabhavananda, *The Sermon on the Mount According to Vedanta* (Hollywood: Vedanta Press, 1964), 59–60.

14 Reynold Nicholson, *The Mystics of Islam* (Beirut: Khayat Book, 1966), 108–109.

CHAPTER EIGHT
The Gift of Selfless Service

1   As cited in Murphy, *One Bird, One Stone*, 158.

2   Mysore Hiriyanna, *Essentials of Indian Philosophy* (London: Allen and Unwin, 1949), 120–121.

3   I am deeply indebted to Sri Ramana Maharshi, Swami Dayananda Saraswati, Swami Tejomayananda, Swami Paramarthananda, Swami Akhandananda Mahrajshri, Swami Brahmatmananda Saraswati for their profound teachings on *Advaita Vedanta*.

4   Surendranath Dasgupta, *History of Indian Philosophy, vol.1,* (Cambridge: Cambridge University Press, 1963), 71.

5   For an alternative version, see Fadiman and Frager, *Essential Sufism*, 75.

6   Sarvepalli Radhakrishnan, *Hindu View of Life,* (London: George Allen and Unwin, 1927), 75.

7 S.C. Gould, ed., *Notes and Queries and Historical Magazine* 18 (Manchester, NH: S.C. and L.M. Gould, 1900), 241.

8 Verses from the Bhagavad Gita have been translated from Sanskrit into English by Swarupananda and revised by the author in the light of other available translations.

9 Recent findings from neuroscience point out that the bacteria in our gut significantly affect our thoughts (*The Scientific American*, April 19, 2011). And the effect of our thoughts on our actions is a well-known fact. If that is the case, then we seem to have very little control over actions, let alone over their results. So, what are we really relinquishing? Perhaps, only our false sense of doership! This point becomes clearer throughout chapter eight.

10 *Guna* means "quality" or "attribute" of material nature *(Prakriti)*. According to the *Sankhya* philosophy, nature is constituted of three *gunas*: purity *(Sattva)*, activity *(Rajas)*, and inertia *(Tamas)*. *Guna* also means *rope*, or that which *binds*.

11 Swami Swarupananda, trans., *Srimad Bhagavad Gita* (1909; repr., Calcutta: Advaita Ashrama, 1996), 125.

12 Alladi M. Sastry, trans., *The Bhagavad Gita with the Commentary of Sri Sankaracharya* (1897; repr., Madras: Samta Books, 1995), 131.

13 The author is indebted to Swami Paramarthananda for his profound teachings on the Bhagavad Gita.

14 A traditional Hindu tale transcribed by the author.

15 A traditional Hindu tale transcribed by the author.

16 Compiled from personal interviews with my *Advaita* teacher, Swami Brahmatmananda Saraswati (unpublished transcripts, 2012).

CHAPTER NINE
The Gift of Total Acceptance

1 Aldous Huxley, *Island* (New York: HarperCollins, 2002), 41.

2 As cited in Murphy, *One Bird, One Stone*, 191.

3 Suzuki, *Zen Mind, Beginner's Mind*, 122.

[4] Huxley, *Huxley and God*, 4.

[5] Stephanie Rosenbloom, "But Will It Make You Happy?" *New York Times*, August 7, 2010.

[6] Lin Yutang, *The Importance of Living* (New York: Reynal and Hitchcock, 1937), 160.

[7] Eugen Herrigel, *Zen in the Art of Archery* (New York: Vintage, 1999), 31.

[8] Author unknown.

[9] Hagen, *How the World Can Be the Way It Is*, 309–310.

[10] A traditional tale transcribed by the author.

[11] A traditional tale transcribed by the author.

CHAPTER TEN
The Gift of Presence

[1] Pupul Jayankar, *Krishnamurti: A Biography* (New York: Penguin, 1996), 195–196.

[2] As cited in Murphy, *One Bird, One Stone*, 164.

[3] Thich Nhat Hanh, *The Miracle of Mindfulness: A Manual on Meditation* (Boston: Beacon Press, 1987), 20–21.

[4] Rahula, *What the Buddha Taught*, 68.

[5] As cited in Bhikkhu Khantipalo, *Practical Advice for Meditators* (Kandy, Sri Lanka: Buddhist Publication Society, 2006), 8.

[6] Peter Harvey, *An Introduction to Buddhism* (Cambridge: Cambridge University Press, 2008), 253, 255.

[7] Bodhi, *Noble Eightfold Path*, 76.

[8] Analayo, *Satipatthana: Direct Path to Realization* (Birmingham: Windhorse, 2006), 27–28.

[9] Ibid., 3–7.

[10] Buddhist psychology also identifies three unwholesome roots of mind: greed, hatred, and ignorance. If our attention emanates from any of these three unwholesome roots, then it is not appropriate and will not give us the knowledge of reality as it truly is. A sniper's concentration, for example, will not qualify as right state of mindfulness since it is does not spring from wholesome intention.

[11] Thera Nyanaponika, *The Heart of Buddhist Meditation: A Handbook of Mental Training Based on Buddha's Way of Mindfulness* (London: Ryder, 1962), 9–10.

[12] Bodhi, *Noble Eightfold Path*, 80.

[13] S.N.Tandon, *A Reappraisal of Patanjali's Yoga-Sutras In the Light of the Buddha's Teaching* (Igatpuri: Vipassana Research Institute, 2007), 76.

[14] Bodhi, *Noble Eightfold Path*, 80.

[15] Rahula, *What the Buddha Taught*, 70.

[16] As cited in Murphy, *One Bird, One Stone*, vi.

[17] Nhat Hanh, *Miracle of Mindfulness*, 16, 1.

[18] Ibid., 20–21.

[19] Analayo, *Satipatthana*, 3.

[20] I am deeply grateful to Shri S.N. Goenkaji for this gift of *Dhamma*—the *Dhamma*, which is beautiful in the beginning, beautiful in the middle, and beautiful in the end.

[21] *Vipassana Meditation: As Taught by S.N. Goenka in the Tradition of Sayagyi U Ba Khin* (North Fork, CA: California Vipassana Center, 2008), 4.

[22] *Vipassana Meditation*, 1.

[23] *Sankharas* (Sanskrit: *Sanskaras*) are accumulated mental tendencies formed over many lifetimes due to repeated patterns of reactive behavior.

[24] Nyanaponika, *Heart of Buddhist Meditation*, 22.

[25] Nhat Hanh, *Heart of the Buddha's Teaching*, 124.

[26] As cited in Wayne Dosick, *The Business Bible: Ten New Commandments for Creating an Ethical Workplace* (New York: William Morrow, 1993), 93–94.

CHAPTER ELEVEN
The Universal Quest for Significance

[1] Author unknown.

[2] As cited in Murphy, *One Bird, One Stone*, 7.

[3] Wei Wu Wei, *Ask the Awakened: The Negative Way* (Boulder, CO: Sentient, 2002), 7.

[4] Author unknown.

[5] Author unknown.

[6] The story appears on several Internet sites and books, including Gary Gemmill and George Kraus, *A View from the Cosmic Mirror: Reflections of the Self in Everyday Life* (Mindfulness Press, 2009), 3.

[7] Joshua Loth Liebman, *Peace of Mind* (New York: Simon and Schuster, 1949), 2–3.

[8] Ann Berliner, *Advaita Makaranda: Translation and Commentary* (Bombay: Asia Publishing House, 1990), 60–61.

[9] "*Atmanastu kamaya sarvam priyam bhavati,*" Brhdaranyaka Upanishad, 2.4.5.

[10] Thompson, *Odyssey of Enlightenment*, 314.

[11] A traditional folk tale transcribed by the author.

[12] Friedlander, *Wisdom Stories*, 29.

[13] Author unknown.

[14] Swami Dayananda, *Introduction to Vedanta: Understanding the Fundamental Problem* (New Delhi: Vision Books, 2009), 11.

[15] The discussion of four pursuits of life is inspired by the writings and discourses of Swami Dayananda and Swami Paramarthananda.

[16] As cited in Huston Smith, *The World's Religions: Our Great Wisdom Traditions, rev. ed.* (San Francisco: Harper San Francisco, 1991, first published 1958 as *The Religions of Man*), 19.

[17] Anantanand Rambachan, *The Advaita Worldview: God, World and Humanity* (New York: State University of New York Press, 2006), 15.

18 As cited in Huston Smith, *The World's Religions: Our Great Wisdom Traditions*, 14–15.

19 As cited in William James, *The Varieties of Religious Experience* (New York: First Modern Library Edition, 1936), 150–151.

20 Nanamoli, *Life of the Buddha*, 211.

21 As cited in Smith, *World's Religions*, 20.

22 This section is mainly based on a discourse of Swami Paramarthananda on Mundaka Upanishad.

23 Nibbana Sutta, Udana, 8.3, (Melksham, UK: Pali Text Society, 1993), 80–81.

24 Swami Madhavananda, trans., *Brhadaranyaka Upanishad: With the Commetary of Shankaracharya*, 11th imp. (Kolkata: Advaita Ashrama, 2008), 83–84.

25 Swami Nityaswarupananda, trans., *Astavakra Samhita: Text with Word-for-Word Translation, English Rendering, Comments, and Index* (Kolkata, India: Advaita Ashrama), 5. Slightly modified.

26 Based on Swami Paramarthananda's five discourses on *Tattva Bodha Summary*.

27 In the Chandogya Upanishad, Uddalaka asks his son Svetaketu if he has learnt the knowledge by which we "hear the unheard, grasp the imperceptible, and know the unknowable":"yena'shrutam shrutam bhavti, amatam matam, avijnatam vijnatam iti; kathamnu, bhagavah, saadesho bhavati iti" – Chandogya 6.1.3). Similarly in Mundaka Upanishad 1.1.3, Saunaka asks the great sage Angiras: "What is that, by knowing which, one can know everything else also?" (kasmin nu bhagavah vigyate sarvam idam vigyatam bhavati iti).

28 Author unknown.

29 Based on Goenka, *Discourse Summaries*, 44.

30 Verse inscribed on the *han* in the hallway of San Francisco Zen Center.

ABOUT THE AUTHOR

Professor Satinder Dhiman, PhD, EdD, has been preparing leaders in higher education for the last 30 years in various settings on two continents.

Born in India, Dr. Dhiman served for ten years as a Senior Lecturer in Commerce at DAV College, a premier institution of higher learning in North India. During that time, he also co-authored several textbooks in the area of managerial accounting and business management. He came to the United States in 1988 as a Rotary International Exchange Scholar.

He currently serves as a Professor of Management and as the Associate Dean, Chair, and Director of the MBA Program at Woodbury University's School of Business in Burbank, California. He holds a PhD in Social Sciences—*Management orientation*—from *Oldendorff Graduate School,* Tilburg University; an EdD in Organizational Leadership from Pepperdine University's GSEP (Graduate School of Education and Psychology); and a Master's degree in Commerce from Panjab University having earned the Gold Medal. He has also completed advanced Executive Leadership Programs at Harvard, Stanford, and Wharton.

Recipient of several teaching and professional honors, Dr. Dhiman also won ACBSP's prestigious International Teaching Excellence Award (2004), Steven Allen's Award for Educational Excellence (2006), IPCSI's Life Time Achievement Award in Management Education (2008), and Excellent Management Educator Award in 2011 and 2012, conferred by IPCSI and Punjab Government, India.

Widely published author and co-author of several management books, Dr. Dhiman is also the co-author and co-editor of five recent books entitled *From Me to We: Transforming Ourselves to Greater Awareness*

(2011); *Managing in the 21st Century: Transforming Toward Mutual Growth* (2011); *Stories to Tell Your Students: Transforming toward Organizational Growth* (2011); *The Workplace and Spirituality: New Perspectives on Research and Practice* (2009); and *Spirituality in the Workplace: What it is, Why it matters, and How to make it work for you* (2007).

Over the last 25 years, Dr. Dhiman has presented his work at various national and international conferences, and has published his research in various journals such as *Organizational Development Journal, Journal of Social Change, Journal of Human Resources and Adult Learning,* and *Journal of American Academy of Business Administration*, among others. He is the co-founder/co-director/co-editor of various journals, such as the *Business Renaissance Quarterly, Journal of Global Business Issues, Contemporary Review, and Interbeing.* He is also the co-founder and co-director of Business Renaissance Institute (BRI) and ASPEX (Academy of Spirituality and Personal/Professional Excellence), which is a multi-faceted, entrepreneurial entity that sponsors various research journals and an innovative publishing wing, called the House of Metta.

Dr. Dhiman's philosophy of life and learning is anchored in the inherent goodness of human nature and in the spiritual nature of all existence. He believes that every person brings a unique blend of gifts and circumstances. For him, the truest joy of life lies in discovering those gifts, polishing them, and giving them back to the society. Professor Dhiman's classes are structured as learning communities and are founded on the philosophy of self-growth through self-discovery.